# Elegant Glassware of the Depression Era

By Gene Florence

**COLLECTOR BOOKS**

P.O. Box 3009
Paducah, KY 42001

The current values in this book should be used only as a guide. They are not intended to set prices, which vary from one section of the country to another. Auction prices as well as dealer prices vary greatly and are affected by condition as well as demand. Neither the Author nor the Publisher assumes responsibility for any losses that might be incurred as a result of consulting this guide.

# ABOUT THE AUTHOR

Gene Florence, born in Lexington in 1944, graduated from the University of Kentucky where he held a double major in mathematics and English. He taught nine years in the Kentucky school systems at the Junior High and High School levels before his glass collecting "hobby" became his full time job.

Mr. Florence has been interested in "collecting" since childhood, beginning with baseball cards and progressing through comic books, coins, bottles and finally, glassware. He first became interested in Depression glassware after purchasing a set of Sharon Dinnerware at a garage sale for $5.00.

He has written several books on glassware: *The Collector's Encyclopedia of Depression Glass*, now in its fifth edition; *The Collector's Encyclopedia of Akro Agate; The Collector's Encyclopedia of Occupied Japan*, Volume I and II, *The Pocket Guide To Depression Glass*, now in its third edition, and *Kitchen Glassware of the Depression Years*.

Should you be in Lexington, he is often found at Grannie Bear Antique Shop located at 120 Clay Avenue. This is the shop he helped his mother set up in what was formerly her children's day care center. The shop derived its name from the term of endearment the toddlers gave her.

Should you know of any unlisted or unusual pieces of glassware IN THE PATTERNS SHOWN IN THIS BOOK, you may write him at Box 22186, Lexington, Kentucky 40522. If you expect a reply, you must enclose a self-addressed, stamped envelope and be patient. His travels and research often cause the hundreds of letters he receives weekly to backlog. He does appreciate your interest, however, and spends many hours answering your letters when time and circumstances permit.

# ACKNOWLEDGEMENTS

There are always numerous people behind the scenes of a book without whose help and encouragement the book would never be done. However, many of the people behind this book have gone above and beyond friendship, or even belief, to see that this work made it to press--- and on time! They have given unstintingly of their time, their glassware, their knowledge of their special fields of interest; they have helped pack and unpack boxes upon boxes of glass; they have sorted and arranged; they have stayed up nights after grueling show dates to discuss, sort, compile and suggest prices for various items. Much as my ego would like to swell thinking they did all this for me, I have to acknowledge that their driving inspiration was YOU, the public. They each wanted a book of this type available to you, hopefully a good book, filled with information about the better glassware. That's what we all wanted. I hereby acknowledge with much gratitude their Herculean efforts in behalf of us all! They include the following beautiful people: Dick, Pat and Yvonne Spencer; Earl and Beverly Hines; Charles, Cecelia and Raymond Larsen; Jim Cooper; Hank & Debbie Pugliese; Austin and Shirley Hartstock; Henry and Roserita Ziegler; George & Veronica Sionakides; Lucille Kennedy of Imperial Glass Company; Lynn Welker; Jim Kennon; Kelly and Priscilla McBride; Gary and Sue Clark; John and Judy Bine; Edna Kaenzig; Doris & Roy Isaacs.

For the sheer "slave" labor involved in the photography and setting up the pictures, I thank our three day assembly line personnel: Beverly Hines, Daisey Swanner, Pat Spencer, Charles Larsen, Steve Quertermous, Jane Fryberger, Bill Schroeder, and Cathy Florence.

The good photography work was done by Dana Curtis of Curtis and Mays Studios in Paducah, Kentucky.

The seemingly endless hours of typing entries and prices (and the much "cussin'" of the brand new computer she had to break in with this book and with deadline facing her) I wholly acknowledge as my wife's contribution! (In the course of the gargantuan work however, the computer went from that infernally slow, idiotic, costly pile of junk to that "lovely machine". We would still be TYPING as you read this without it!)

Family, especially, need to be acknowledged, particularly my Mom, "Grannie Bear", who spent weeks washing, packing, and listing glass in a semblance of order for the photography session; then there are Charles & Sib, "Grandpaw", and Chad and Marc who keep home operating and animals alive in our absences and who generally pitch in and do whatever needs doing.

Few people are in a position to really appreciated all the WORK that goes into writing a book; and even I underestimated this task. It was a case of thinking I knew the field until I got into it and realized how puny my knowledge was against all there was to know; even this side of the book, I acknowledge that I've only just begun!

# FOREWORD

Collecting of quality glassware of the Depression Era has been a gradual trend of several years. More and more dealers of Depression Glass per se are including better glassware in their inventories in response to collector's awakening to the desirability of the better glassware.

"Elegant" glassware, as defined in this book, refers to the mainly hand worked and etched glassware that was sold in the department stores and jewelry stores during the Depression era through the 1950's as opposed to the dime store and give away glass that is known as Depression Glass.

I would remind you that this is the first attempt ever to corral all these types of glassware into one book. There are bound to be additions and corrections to be made; but for now, I sincerely hope you will enjoy all our efforts to provide you with a book overviewing the broad spectrum of "elegant glassware" from decades past.

# PRICING

ALL PRICES IN THIS BOOK ARE RETAIL PRICES FOR MINT CONDITION GLASSWARE. This book is intended to be only A GUIDE TO PRICES. There are regional price differences which cannot be reasonably dealt with herein.

You may expect dealers to pay from thirty to fifty percent less than the prices quoted. My personal knowledge of prices come from my experience of selling glass in my Grannie Bear Antique Shop in Lexington, from my traveling to and selling at shows in various parts of the United States, and immediately prior to the pricing of this book, from attending the Fostoria, Cambridge and Heisey shows. I readily admit to soliciting price information from persons I knew to be expert in these various fields so as to provide you with the latest, most accurate pricing information possible. However, final pricing judgment was mine; so, for any errors (or praises), the buck stops here.

# MEASUREMENTS

All measurements are from factory catalogue lists. It has been my experience that the actual measurements may vary slightly from those listed, so don't be unduly concerned over slight variations.

# INDEX

About The Author . . . . . . . . . . . . . . . . 3
Foreword . . . . . . . . . . . . . . . . . . . . . . . 4
Index . . . . . . . . . . . . . . . . . . . . . . . . . . 5
American . . . . . . . . . . . . . . . . . . . . . . 6-11
Apple Blossom . . . . . . . . . . . . . . . . . . 12, 13
Baroque . . . . . . . . . . . . . . . . . . . . . . . 14-17
Cadena. . . . . . . . . . . . . . . . . . . . . . . . 18, 19
Candlewick . . . . . . . . . . . . . . . . . . . . 20-27
Candlewick First Catalogue: Reprint . . . . . 41
Caprice . . . . . . . . . . . . . . . . . . . . . . . . 42-45
Chantilly . . . . . . . . . . . . . . . . . . . . . . . 46, 47
Chintz . . . . . . . . . . . . . . . . . . . . . . . . . 48, 49
Cleo . . . . . . . . . . . . . . . . . . . . . . . . . . 50, 51
Colony . . . . . . . . . . . . . . . . . . . . . . . . 52, 53
Crystolite . . . . . . . . . . . . . . . . . . . . . . 54, 55
"Cupid" . . . . . . . . . . . . . . . . . . . . . . . 56, 57
"Dancing Girl" . . . . . . . . . . . . . . . . . . 58, 59
Decagon. . . . . . . . . . . . . . . . . . . . . . . . 60, 61
Diane . . . . . . . . . . . . . . . . . . . . . . . . . 62-65
Elaine. . . . . . . . . . . . . . . . . . . . . . . . . 66, 67
Empress . . . . . . . . . . . . . . . . . . . . . . . 68-71
Fairfax . . . . . . . . . . . . . . . . . . . . . . . . 72, 73
Gloria . . . . . . . . . . . . . . . . . . . . . . . . . 74-77
Greek Key . . . . . . . . . . . . . . . . . . . . . 78-81
Ipswich . . . . . . . . . . . . . . . . . . . . . . . . 82, 83
June . . . . . . . . . . . . . . . . . . . . . . . . . . 84, 85
Kashmir . . . . . . . . . . . . . . . . . . . . . . . 86, 87
Lariat . . . . . . . . . . . . . . . . . . . . . . . . . 88, 89
Lincoln Inn . . . . . . . . . . . . . . . . . . . . . 90, 91
Minuet . . . . . . . . . . . . . . . . . . . . . . . . 92, 93
Moondrops . . . . . . . . . . . . . . . . . . . . . 94, 95

"Nora Bird" . . . . . . . . . . . . . . . . . . . . . 96, 97
Octagon . . . . . . . . . . . . . . . . . . . . . . . 98, 99
Old Colony . . . . . . . . . . . . . . . . . . . . . 100-103
Old Sandwich . . . . . . . . . . . . . . . . . . . 104, 105
Orchid . . . . . . . . . . . . . . . . . . . . . . . . 106, 107
"Peacock Reverse" . . . . . . . . . . . . . . . 108, 109
"Peacock & Wild Rose" . . . . . . . . . . . . 108, 109
Plantation . . . . . . . . . . . . . . . . . . . . . . 110, 111
Pleat & Panel . . . . . . . . . . . . . . . . . . . 112, 113
Portia . . . . . . . . . . . . . . . . . . . . . . . . . 114-117
Provincial. . . . . . . . . . . . . . . . . . . . . . . 118, 119
Radiance . . . . . . . . . . . . . . . . . . . . . . . 120, 121
Ridgeleigh . . . . . . . . . . . . . . . . . . . . . . 122-125
Rose . . . . . . . . . . . . . . . . . . . . . . . . . . 126, 127
Rose Point . . . . . . . . . . . . . . . . . . . . . 128-131
Saturn . . . . . . . . . . . . . . . . . . . . . . . . 132, 133
Trojan . . . . . . . . . . . . . . . . . . . . . . . . 134, 135
Twist . . . . . . . . . . . . . . . . . . . . . . . . . 136, 137
Versailles . . . . . . . . . . . . . . . . . . . . . . 138, 139
Vesper . . . . . . . . . . . . . . . . . . . . . . . . 140, 141
Waverly . . . . . . . . . . . . . . . . . . . . . . . 142, 143
Wildflower . . . . . . . . . . . . . . . . . . . . . 144, 145
Yeoman . . . . . . . . . . . . . . . . . . . . . . . 146-149
Cambridge Stems . . . . . . . . . . . . . . . . 150-153
Cambridge Rarities . . . . . . . . . . . . . . . 154
Heisey Rarities. . . . . . . . . . . . . . . . . . . 155
Heisey Alexandrite. . . . . . . . . . . . . . . . 156
Heisey Cobalt & Tangerine . . . . . . . . . . 157
Heisey Dawn . . . . . . . . . . . . . . . . . . . 158
Publications & Clubs . . . . . . . . . . . . . . 159
Additional Books by Gene Florence . . . . . 160

# INDEX BY COMPANY

Cambridge Glass Company
Apple Blossom . . . . . . . . . . . . . . . . 12, 13
Caprice . . . . . . . . . . . . . . . . . . . . . 42, 45
Chantilly . . . . . . . . . . . . . . . . . . . . . 46, 47
Cleo . . . . . . . . . . . . . . . . . . . . . . . 50, 51
Decagon . . . . . . . . . . . . . . . . . . . . 60, 61
Diane . . . . . . . . . . . . . . . . . . . . . . 62-65
Elaine . . . . . . . . . . . . . . . . . . . . . . 66, 67
Gloria . . . . . . . . . . . . . . . . . . . . . . 74-77
Portia . . . . . . . . . . . . . . . . . . . . . . 114-117
Rose Point . . . . . . . . . . . . . . . . . . . 128-131
Wildflower . . . . . . . . . . . . . . . . . . . 144, 145
Cambridge Stems . . . . . . . . . . . . . . . 150-153
Fenton Glass Company
Lincoln Inn . . . . . . . . . . . . . . . . . . . 90, 91
Fostoria Glass Company
American . . . . . . . . . . . . . . . . . . . . 6-11
Baroque . . . . . . . . . . . . . . . . . . . . . 14-17
Colony . . . . . . . . . . . . . . . . . . . . . 52, 53
Fairfax . . . . . . . . . . . . . . . . . . . . . . 72, 73
June . . . . . . . . . . . . . . . . . . . . . . . 84, 85
Kashmir . . . . . . . . . . . . . . . . . . . . . 86, 87
Trojan . . . . . . . . . . . . . . . . . . . . . . 134, 135
Versailles . . . . . . . . . . . . . . . . . . . . 138, 139
Vesper . . . . . . . . . . . . . . . . . . . . . . 140, 141
Heisey Glass Company
Chintz . . . . . . . . . . . . . . . . . . . . . . 48, 49
Crystolite . . . . . . . . . . . . . . . . . . . . 54, 55
Empress . . . . . . . . . . . . . . . . . . . . . 68-71
Greek Key . . . . . . . . . . . . . . . . . . . 78-81

Ipswich . . . . . . . . . . . . . . . . . . . . . 82, 83
Lariat . . . . . . . . . . . . . . . . . . . . . . 88, 89
Minuet . . . . . . . . . . . . . . . . . . . . . . 92, 93
Octagon . . . . . . . . . . . . . . . . . . . . 98, 99
Old Colony . . . . . . . . . . . . . . . . . . . 100-103
Old Sandwich . . . . . . . . . . . . . . . . . 104, 105
Orchid . . . . . . . . . . . . . . . . . . . . . . 106, 107
Plantation . . . . . . . . . . . . . . . . . . . . 110, 111
Pleat & Panel . . . . . . . . . . . . . . . . . 112, 113
Provincial . . . . . . . . . . . . . . . . . . . . 118, 119
Ridgeleigh . . . . . . . . . . . . . . . . . . . 122, 125
Rose . . . . . . . . . . . . . . . . . . . . . . . 126, 127
Saturn . . . . . . . . . . . . . . . . . . . . . . 132, 133
Twist . . . . . . . . . . . . . . . . . . . . . . . 136, 137
Waverly . . . . . . . . . . . . . . . . . . . . . 142, 143
Yeoman . . . . . . . . . . . . . . . . . . . . . 146-149
Imperial Glass Company
Candlewick . . . . . . . . . . . . . . . . . . . 20-41
Morgantown Glass Works
"Dancing Girl" . . . . . . . . . . . . . . . . . 58, 59
New Martinsville Glass Company
Moondrops . . . . . . . . . . . . . . . . . . . 94, 59
Radiance . . . . . . . . . . . . . . . . . . . . 120, 121
Paden City Glass Company
"Cupid" . . . . . . . . . . . . . . . . . . . . . 56, 57
"Nora Bird" . . . . . . . . . . . . . . . . . . . 96, 97
"Peacock Reverse" . . . . . . . . . . . . . . 108, 109
"Peacock & Wild Rose" . . . . . . . . . . . 108, 109
Tiffin Glass Company
Cadena . . . . . . . . . . . . . . . . . . . . . . 18, 19

# AMERICAN, Line #2056, Fostoria Glass Company, 1915 - Present

Colors: Crystal; some amber, blue, green, yellow in late '20's

*The items with the asterisk by the price indicate those which are still being made by Fostoria today. The price listed is an approximate retail cost being charged. However, you should be aware that the factory outlets sell "seconds" of these same pieces at half price.

Early Fostoria advertisements stressed the prismatic effect of light diffusing through the cube designs and thereby making a "brilliant" table display of "quality" glass---for merchant and owner alike.

|  | Crystal |
|---|---|
| Ash Tray, oval | 8.50 |
| Ash tray, 2 7/8", sq. | 6.00 |
| Ash tray, 5", sq. | 7.00 |
| Ash tray, 5½", oval | 9.00 |
| Basket w/reed handle, 7" x 9" | 50.00 |
| Bell | 24.50* |
| Bottle, bitters w/tube, 5¾", 4½ oz. | 32.00 |
| Bottle, cordial w/stopper, 7¼", 9 oz. | 35.00 |
| Bottle, cologne w/stopper, 4 ½ oz. | 25.00 |
| Bottle, cologne w/stopper, 6 oz. | 30.00 |
| Bottle, cologne w/stopper, 8 oz. | 35.00 |
| Bottle, water, 44 oz., 9¼" | 45.00 |
| Bowl, banana split | 12.00 |
| Bowl, bonbon | 8.00 |
| Bowl, finger, 4½" diam., smooth edge | 7.00 |
| Bowl, bonbon, 3 ftd. | 10.00 |
| Bowl, cream soup, 2 hand. | 12.00 |
| Bowl, 3¾", almond | 8.00 |
| Bowl, 3½", rose | 10.00 |
| Bowl, 4¼", jelly, 4¼", h. | 15.00* |
| Bowl, 4½", jelly w/cover, 6¾", h. | 24.00* |
| Bowl, 4½", nappy | 15.00* |
| Bowl, 4½", oval | 7.00 |
| Bowl, 4½", 1 hand., sq. | 11.00* |
| Bowl, 4½", 1 hand. | 11.00* |
| Bowl, 4¾", fruit | 13.00* |
| Bowl, 5", 1 hand., tri-corner | 11.00* |
| Bowl, 5", nappy | 12.00* |
| Bowl, 5", rose | 14.00 |
| Bowl, 5½, lemon w/cover | 20.00 |
| Bowl, 5½", preserve, 2 hand. w/cover | 25.00 |
| Bowl, 6", nappy | 16.00* |
| Bowl, 6", olive, oblong | 9.00* |
| Bowl, 6½", wedding w/cover, sq., ped. ft., 8", h. | 35.00 |
| Bowl, 6½", wedding, sq., ped. ft., 5¼", h. | 22.50 |
| Bowl, 6¾", sauce, oval | 17.00* |
| Bowl, 7", nappy | 21.00* |
| Bowl, 7", bonbon, 3 ftd. | 14.00* |
| Bowl, 7", cupped | 17.50 |
| Bowl, 8", nappy | 22.50* |
| Bowl, 8", deep | 22.50 |
| Bowl, 8", ftd. | 25.00 |
| Bowl, 8", ftd. 2 hand. "trophy" cup | 23.50 |
| Bowl, 8", pickle, oblong | 13.00* |
| Bowl, 8", tid bit, flat, 3 ftd. | 22.50 |

7

|  | Crystal |
|---|---|
| Bowl, 8½", boat | 12.00* |
| Bowl, 8½", 2 hand. | 22.00 |
| Bowl, 9", relish, 4 pt., rect. | 23.00 |
| Bowl, 9", veg., 2 hand. | 20.00* |
| Bowl, 9", boat, 2 pt. | 18.00 |
| Bowl, 9", oval veg. | 20.00 |
| Bowl, 9½", centerpiece | 23.00* |
| Bowl, 9½", relish, 3 pt., 6", w. | 27.50 |
| Bowl, 10", oval float | 22.50 |
| Bowl, 10", float | 20.00 |
| Bowl, 10", celery, oblong | 14.00* |
| Bowl, 10", deep | 28.00* |
| Bowl, 10", oval veg., 2 pt. | 17.50 |
| Bowl, 10½", fruit, 3 ft. | 24.00* |
| Bowl, 11", centerpiece | 22.00 |
| Bowl, 11", centerpiece, tri-corner | 25.00* |
| Bowl, 11", relish/celery, 3 pt. | 27.00* |
| Bowl, 11½", float | 27.50 |
| Bowl, 11½", rolled edge | 25.00 |
| Bowl, 11½", oval float | 27.50 |
| Bowl, 11½ ", fruit, rolled edge | 25.00 |
| Bowl, 11¾", oval | 25.00* |
| Bowl, 12", fruit/sm. punch, ped. ft., flared | 37.50 |
| Bowl, 12", lily | 25.00 |
| Bowl, 12", relish "boat", 2 pt. | 15.00* |
| Bowl, 13", shallow | 27.50 |
| Bowl, 13", fruit, shallow | 27.50 |
| Bowl, 14", punch w/high ft. base (2 gal.) | 75.00* |
| Bowl, 14", punch, w/low ft. base | 65.00 |
| Bowl, 15", ctr. piece, "hat" shape | 90.00 |
| Bowl, 16", fruit, ftd. | 65.00 |
| Bowl, 16", flat fruit, ped. ft | 75.00 |
| Bowl, 18", punch w/low ft. base (3¾ gal.) | 125.00 |
| Bowl, w/cover, 5" | 15.00 |
| Box w/cover, glove, 9½" x 3½" | 25.00 |
| Box w/cover, hairpin, 3½" x 1¾" | 20.00 |
| Box w/cover, handkerchief, 5 5/8" x 4 5/8" | 24.00 |
| Box w/cover, jewel, 5¼" x 2¼" | 20.00 |
| Box w/cover, puff, 3 1/8" x 2¾" | 17.50 |
| Butter w/cover, rnd., plate 7¼" | 40.00 |
| Butter w/cover, ¼ lb. | 22.00 |
| Candle lamp, 8½", w/chimney | 35.00 |
| Candlestick, 2", chamber | 11.00* |
| Candlestick, 3", rnd. ft. | 22.00* |
| Candlestick, 4 3/8", 2-lite, rnd. ft. | 40.00* |
| Candlestick, 6", octagon ft. | 27.00* |
| Candlestick, 6½", 2-lite, bell base | 22.50 |
| Candelabrum, 6½", 2-lite, bell base w/bobeche & prisms | 35.00 |
| Candlestick, 7", sq. column | 30.00 |
| Candy box w/cover, 3 pt. | 22.50 |
| Candy w/cover, ped. ft. | 22.00* |
| Cheese (5¾", compote) & cracker (11½", plate) | 40.00 |
| Cigarette box w/cover | 17.50 |
| Coaster, 3¾" | 3.50* |
| Comport, 4½" jelly | 10.00 |
| Comport, 5", jelly, flared | 12.00 |
| Comport w/cover, 5" | 34.00* |

| | Crystal |
|---|---|
| Comport, 6¾", jelly w/cover | 30.00 |
| Cookie jar w/cover, 8 7/8", h. | 75.00 |
| Crab liner, 4 oz., blown | 5.00 |
| Creamer, tea, 3 oz., 2 3/8" (#2056½) | 7.50 |
| Creamer | 10.50* |
| Crushed fruit w/cover & spoon | 95.00 |
| Cup, ftd. sherbet, 4½ oz., 3½", h. | 7.50 |
| Cup, ftd., 7 oz. | 8.50* |
| Cup, punch, flared rim | 7.00 |
| Cup, punch, straight edge | 6.00 |
| Decanter, w/stopper, 24 oz., 9¼", h. | 87.50 |
| Dresser set: powder boxes w/covers & tray | 75.00 |
| Flower pot w/perforated cover, 9½", diam; 5½", h. | 50.00 |
| Goblet, #2056, 2½ oz., wine, hex ft., 4 3/8" h. | 13.00* |
| Goblet, #2056, 4½ oz., sherbet, flared., 4 3/8" h. | 13.00 |
| Goblet, #2056, 4½ oz., fruit, hex ft., 4¾" h. | 13.00* |
| Goblet, #2056, 4½ oz., oyster cocktail, 3½" h. | 9.00 |
| Goblet, #2056, 5 oz., low ft. sherbet, flared 3¼" h. | 13.00* |
| Goblet, #2056, 6 oz., low ft. sundae, 3 1/8" h. | 13.00* |
| Goblet, #2056, 7 oz., claret, 4 7/8" h. | 13.00* |
| Goblet, #2056, 9 oz., low ft., 4 3/8" h. | 13.00* |
| Goblet, #2056, 10 oz., hex ft. water, 6 7/8" h. | 13.00* |
| Goblet, #2056, 12 oz., low ft. tea, 5¾" h. | 13.00* |
| Goblet, #2056½, 4½ oz., sherbet, 4½" h. | 13.00* |
| Goblet, #2056½, 5 oz., low sherbet, 3½" h. | 13.00* |
| Goblet, #5056, 1 oz., cordial, 3 1/8", w/plain bowl | 15.00 |
| Goblet, #5056, 3½ oz., claret, 4 5/8", w/p. bowl | 14.00 |
| Goblet, #5056, 3½ oz., cocktail, 4", w/p. bowl | 14.00 |
| Goblet, #5056, 4 oz., oyster cocktail, 3½", w/p. bowl | 10.00 |
| Goblet, #5056, 5½ oz., sherbet, 4 1/8", w/p. bowl | 10.00 |
| Goblet, #5056, 10 oz., water, 6 1/8", w/plain bowl | 12.00 |
| Hair receiver | 35.00 |
| Hat, 2 1/8, (sm. ash tray) | 12.00 |
| Hat, 2½" | 12.00 |
| Hat, 3" | 15.00 |
| Hat, 4" | 20.00 |
| Hurricane lamp | 65.00 |
| Ice bucket w/tongs | 35.00 |
| Ice dish for 4 oz. crab or 5 oz. tomato liner | 12.00 |
| Ice tub w/liner, 5 5/8" | 25.00 |
| Ice tub w/liner, 6½" | 30.00 |
| Jam pot w/cover | 32.50 |
| Jar, pickle w/pointed cover, 6" h. | 50.00 |
| Marmalade w/cover & chrome spoon | 25.00 |
| Mayonnaise, div. w/2 ladles | 32.50 |
| Mayonnaise w/ladle, ped. ft. | 27.50 |
| Mayonnaise w/liner & ladle | 25.00 |
| Molasses can, 11 oz., 6¾" h., 1 hand. | 40.00 |
| Mug, 5½ oz., "Tom & Jerry", 3¼" h. | 15.00 |
| Mug, 12 oz., beer, 4½" h. | 22.00 |
| Mustard w/cover & spoon | 22.50 |
| Napkin ring | 3.50* |
| Oil, 5 oz. | 28.00* |
| Oil, 7 oz. | 32.00 |
| Picture frame | 9.00* |
| Pitcher, 1 pt., 5 3/8", ftd. | 27.50 |
| Pitcher, ½ gal., 8", ftd. | 47.50 |

**Crystal**

| | |
|---|---|
| Pitcher, ½ gal. w/ice lip, 8¼", flat bottom | 48.00* |
| Pitcher, 2 pt., 7¼", ftd. | 35.00 |
| Pitcher, 3 pt., 8", ftd. | 44.00* |
| Pitcher, 3 pt., w/ice lip, 6½", ftd., "fat" | 35.00 |
| Plate, cream soup/liner | 6.00 |
| Plate, 6", bread & butter | 12.00 |
| Plate, 7", salad | 14.00* |
| Plate, 7½", cresent salad | 15.00 |
| Plate, 8", sauce liner, oval | 12.50 |
| Plate, 8½", salad | 14.00* |
| Plate, 9", sandwich (sm. center) | 13.50 |
| Plate, 9½", dinner | 18.00* |
| Plate, 10", cake, 2 hand. | 21.00* |
| Plate, 10½", sandwich (sm. center) | 22.00* |
| Plate, 11½", sandwich (sm. center) | 20.00 |
| Plate, 12", cake, 3 ftd. | 27.50* |
| Plate, 13½", oval torte | 22.50* |
| Plate, 14", torte | 30.00* |
| Plate, 18", torte | 35.00 |
| Plate, 20", torte | 40.00 |
| Platter, 10½", oval | 22.50 |
| Platter, 12", oval | 25.00 |
| Salad set: 10", bowl, 14", torte wood fork & spoon | 66.00* |
| Salt, indiv. | 6.50* |
| Salver, 10", rnd., ped. ft. | 48.00* |
| Salver, 10", sq., ped. ft. | 59.00* |
| Saucer | 8.50* |
| Set: 2 jam pots w/tray | 85.00 |
| Set: appetizer, 6-3¼", indiv. inserts on rect. tray | 42.50 |
| Set: condiment 2 oils, 2 shakers, mustard w/cover & spoon w/tray | 100.00 |
| Set: decanter, 6-2 oz. whiskeys on 10½", tray | 100.00 |
| Set: toddler, w/baby tumbler & bowl | 35.00 |
| Set: youth, w/bowl, hand. mug, 6", plate | 42.00* |
| Shaker, 3½" | 7.50* |
| Shakers w/tray, indiv., 2½" | 15.00* |
| Spooner, 3¾" | 30.00 |
| Strawholder w/cover | 125.00 |
| Sugar shaker | 14.00* |
| Sugar, tea, #2056½, 2¼", h. | 7.50 |
| Sugar, handled, 3¼" h. | 11.50* |
| Sugar w/cover, 2 hand. | 21.00* |
| Sugar w/cover, no hand., 6¼" | 15.00 |
| Syrup, 6 oz., non pour screw top, 5¼"h. | 25.00 |
| Syrup, 6½ oz., #2056½, Sani-cut server | 25.00 |
| Syrup, 10 oz., w/glass cover & 6" liner plate | 35.00 |
| Syrup w/drip proof top | 20.00* |
| Tomato liner, 5 oz., blown | 4.00 |
| Toothpick | 15.00 |
| Tray, tid bit, w/question mark metal hand. | 22.50 |
| Tray, 5" x 2½", rect. | 12.50 |
| Tray, 6", oval, handled | 15.00 |
| Tray, 9½", service, 2 hand. | 18.00 |
| Tray, 10", muffin (2 upturned sides) | 15.00 |
| Tray, 10", square | 22.00 |
| Tray, 10½", cake, w/question mark metal hand. | 25.00 |
| Tray, 10½" x 5", oval, handled | 25.00 |

|  | Crystal |
|---|---|
| Tray, 10½", rectangular | 32.50 |
| Tray, 12", oval (dresser type) | 25.00 |
| Tray, 12", sand. w/ctr. handle | 30.00 |
| Tray, 13½", oval ice cream | 35.00 |
| Tray for sugar & creamer, tab hand., 6¾" | 10.00* |
| Tumbler, #2056, 2 oz., whiskey, 2½" h. | 8.50 |
| Tumbler, #2056, 3 oz., ftd. cone cocktail, 2 7/8" h. | 12.50 |
| Tumbler, #2056, 5 oz., ftd. juice, 4¾" | 13.00* |
| Tumbler, #2056, 6 oz., flat old fashioned, 3 3/8" h. | 9.00 |
| Tumbler, #2056, 8 oz., flat water, 4 1/8" h. | 13.00* |
| Tumbler, #2056, 9 oz., ftd. water, 4 3/8" h. | 12.00 |
| Tumbler, #2056, 12 oz., flat tea, flared, 5¼" h. | 13.00* |
| Tumbler, #2056½, 5 oz., straight side juice | 13.00* |
| Tumbler, #2056½, 8 oz., straight side water, 3 7/8" h. | 13.00* |
| Tumbler, #2056½, 12 oz., straight side tea, 5" h. | 13.00* |
| Tumbler, #2056, 5 oz., ftd. juice, 4 1/8" w/plain bowl | 12.00 |
| Tumbler, #2056, 12 oz., ftd. tea, 5½" w/plain bowl | 15.00 |
| Urn, 6", sq., ped. ft. | 22.50 |
| Urn, 7½", sq., ped. ft. | 27.50 |
| Vase, 4½", sweet pea | 23.00 |
| Vase, 6", bud, ftd. | 13.00* |
| Vase, 6", straight side | 16.00 |
| Vase, 6", bud, flared | 18.00 |
| Vase, 6½", flared rim | 15.00 |
| Vase, 7", flared | 17.50 |
| Vase, 8", straight side | 19.00 |
| Vase, 8", flared | 20.00 |
| Vase, 8½", bud, flared | 18.50* |
| Vase, 8½", bud, cupped | 18.50* |
| Vase, 9", w/sq. ped. ft. | 19.00 |
| Vase, 9½", flared | 20.00 |
| Vase, 10", straight side | 23.00 |
| Vase, 10", flared | 25.00 |
| Vase, 12", straight side | 35.00 |

*The items with the asterisk by the price indicate those which are still being made by Fostoria today. The price listed is an approximate retail cost being charged. However, you should be aware that the factory outlets sell these same pieces at half price.

# APPLE-BLOSSOM, Line #3400, Cambridge Glass Company, 1930's

Colors: blue, pink, green, yellow, crystal, amber

Apple-blossom pattern has a timeless, old world appeal. The design is redolent of spring orchards with bowers of fragrant blossoms and the time to walk through and enjoy them.

| | Crystal | Colors | | Crystal | Colors |
|---|---|---|---|---|---|
| Bowl, #3025, ftd. finger w/plate | 12.00 | 20.00 | Plate, sandwich, 11½", tab hand. | 12.50 | 25.00 |
| Bowl, #3130, finger w/plate . . . | 10.00 | 17.50 | Plate, sandwich, 12½", 2 hand. | 20.00 | 30.00 |
| Bowl, 5¼", 2 hand. bonbon . . . | 9.00 | 15.00 | Plate, sq. bread/butter . . . . . . . | 4.00 | 8.00 |
| Bowl, 5½", 2 hand, bonbon . . . | 9.00 | 15.00 | Plate, sq. dinner . . . . . . . . . . . . | 13.00 | 22.50 |
| Bowl, 5½", fruit "saucer" . . . . . | 6.50 | 9.00 | Plate, sq. salad . . . . . . . . . . . . . | 6.00 | 10.00 |
| Bowl, 6", 2 hand. "basket" (sides up) . . . . . . . . . . . . . . . | 10.00 | 17.50 | Plate, sq. service . . . . . . . . . . . | 10.00 | 17.50 |
| Bowl, 6", cereal . . . . . . . . . . . | 7.50 | 13.50 | Platter, 11½" . . . . . . . . . . . . . | 14.00 | 25.00 |
| Bowl, 9", pickle . . . . . . . . . . . | 10.00 | 17.50 | Platter, 13½"rect. w/tab hand. | 22.00 | 42.00 |
| Bowl, 10", 2 hand. . . . . . . . . . | 17.50 | 30.00 | Salt & pepper, pr. . . . . . . . . . . | 25.00 | 72.50 |
| Bowl, 10", baker . . . . . . . . . . . | 17.50 | 37.50 | Saucer . . . . . . . . . . . . . . . . . . . | 2.00 | 3.00 |
| Bowl, 11", fruit, tab hand. . . . . | 17.50 | 30.00 | Stem, #3025, 7 oz., low fancy ft. sherbet . . . . . . . . . . . . . . . | 8.00 | 12.00 |
| Bowl, 11", low ftd. . . . . . . . . . | 17.50 | 30.00 | Stem, #3025, 7 oz., high sherbet . . . . . . . . . . . . . . . . . | 9.00 | 13.00 |
| Bowl, 12", relish, 4 pt. . . . . . . . | 17.50 | 30.00 | Stem, #3025, 10 oz. . . . . . . . . . | 15.00 | 20.00 |
| Bowl, 12", 4 ftd. . . . . . . . . . . . | 22.50 | 37.50 | Stem, #3130, 3 oz., cocktail . . . | 12.50 | 22.50 |
| Bowl, 12", flat . . . . . . . . . . . . . | 28.00 | 32.00 | Stem, #3130, 6 oz., low sherbet | 9.00 | 17.50 |
| Bowl, 12", oval, 4 ftd. . . . . . . . | 25.00 | 47.50 | Stem, #3130, 6 oz., tall sherbet | 9.00 | 15.00 |
| Bowl, 12½", console . . . . . . . . | 17.50 | 27.50 | Stem, #3130, 8 oz., water . . . . . | 12.00 | 17.50 |
| Bowl, 13" . . . . . . . . . . . . . . . . | 17.50 | 30.00 | Stem, #3135, 3 oz., cocktail . . . | 12.50 | 22.50 |
| Bowl, cream soup w/liner plate | 12.00 | 22.00 | Stem, #3135, 6 oz., low sherbet | 9.00 | 15.00 |
| Butter w/cover, 5½" . . . . . . . . | 55.00 | 110.00 | Stem, #3135, 6 oz., tall sherbet | 9.00 | 17.50 |
| Candelabrum, 3-lite, keyhole . . | 16.50 | 25.00 | Stem, #3135, 8 oz., water . . . . . | 12.00 | 20.00 |
| Candlestick, 1-lite, keyhole . . . . | 10.00 | 17.50 | Stem, #3400, 6 oz., ftd. sherbet | 9.00 | 15.00 |
| Candlestick, 2-lite, keyhole . . . . | 14.00 | 21.00 | Stem, #3400, 9 oz., water . . . . . | 10.00 | 17.50 |
| Candy box w/cover, 4 ftd. "bowl" . . . . . . . . . . . . . . . . | 30.00 | 52.50 | Sugar, ftd. . . . . . . . . . . . . . . . . | 6.00 | 12.50 |
| Cheese (compote) & cracker (11½" plate) . . . . . . . . . . . . . | 20.00 | 35.00 | Sugar, tall ftd. . . . . . . . . . . . . . | 6.00 | 12.50 |
| Comport, 4", fruit cocktail . . . . | 11.50 | 17.50 | Tray, 11" ctr. hand. sand. . . . . | 17.50 | 27.50 |
| Comport, 7", tall . . . . . . . . . . . | 17.50 | 35.00 | Tumbler, #3025, 4 oz. . . . . . . . . | 10.00 | 15.00 |
| Creamer, ftd. . . . . . . . . . . . . . . | 7.00 | 14.00 | Tumbler, #3025, 10 oz. . . . . . . . | 12.00 | 20.00 |
| Creamer, tall ftd. . . . . . . . . . . . | 7.00 | 14.00 | Tumbler, #3025, 12 oz. . . . . . . . | 14.00 | 22.00 |
| Cup . . . . . . . . . . . . . . . . . . . . . | 8.00 | 12.00 | Tumbler, #3130, 5 oz., ftd. . . . . | 8.00 | 15.00 |
| Fruit/Oyster cocktail, #3025, 4½ oz. . . . . . . . . . . . . . . . . . . | 10.00 | 15.00 | Tumbler, #3130, 8 oz., ftd. . . . . | 10.00 | 17.50 |
| Mayonnaise w/liner & ladle, (4 ftd. bowl) . . . . . . . . . . . . . . . | 22.50 | 37.50 | Tumbler, #3130, 10 oz., ftd. . . . | 11.00 | 18.00 |
| Pitcher, 50 oz., ftd., flattened sides . . . . . . . . . . . . . . . . . . . | 50.00 | 85.00 | Tumbler, #3130, 12 oz., ftd. . . . | 12.50 | 20.00 |
| Pitcher, 64 oz., #3130 . . . . . . . | 65.00 | 100.00 | Tumbler, #3135, 5 oz., ftd. . . . . | 8.00 | 15.00 |
| Pitcher, 64 oz., #3025 . . . . . . . | 65.00 | 100.00 | Tumbler, #3135, 8 oz., ftd. . . . . | 10.00 | 17.50 |
| Pitcher, 67 oz., squeezed middle, loop handle . . . . . . . . | 70.00 | 110.00 | Tumbler, #3135, 10 oz., ftd. . . . | 11.00 | 18.00 |
| Pitcher, 76 oz. . . . . . . . . . . . . . | 67.50 | 120.00 | Tumbler, #3135, 12 oz., ftd. . . . | 12.50 | 20.00 |
| Pitcher, 80 oz., ball . . . . . . . . . | 75.00 | 125.00 | Tumbler, #3400, 2½ oz., ftd. . . | 10.00 | 17.50 |
| Pitcher w/cover, 76 oz., ftd., #3135 . . . . . . . . . . . . . . . . . . | 75.00 | 125.00 | Tumbler, #3400, 9 oz., ftd. . . . | 9.00 | 15.00 |
| Plate, 6", bread/butter . . . . . . . | 4.00 | 8.00 | Tumbler, #3400, 12 oz., ftd. . . . | 10.00 | 17.50 |
| Plate, 6", sq., 2 hand. . . . . . . . | 7.00 | 12.00 | Tumbler, 12 oz., flat (2 styles) - one mid. indent to match 67 oz. pitcher . . . . . . . . . . . . . | 15.00 | 25.00 |
| Plate, 7½", tea . . . . . . . . . . . | 6.00 | 10.00 | Tumbler, 6" . . . . . . . . . . . . . . . | 12.50 | 20.00 |
| Plate, 8½" . . . . . . . . . . . . . . . | 6.00. | 10.00 | Vase, 5" . . . . . . . . . . . . . . . . . | 17.50 | 27.50 |
| Plate, 9½", dinner . . . . . . . . . . | 13.00 | 27.50 | Vase, 6", rippled sides . . . . . . . | 18.00 | 32.50 |
| Plate, 10", grill . . . . . . . . . . . | 10.00 | 17.50 | Vase, 8", 2 styles . . . . . . . . . . | 20.00 | 37.50 |
| | | | Vase, 12", keyhole base, w/neck indent . . . . . . . . . . . . | 22.50 | 47.50 |

Note: See Pages 150-153 for stem identification.

# BAROQUE, Line #2496, Fostoria Glass Company, 1936-1966

Colors: Crystal, "Azure" blue, "Topaz" yellow

They called the pattern "Baroque", a return to the eighteenth century passion for scrolls, furls and furbelows which generally resulted in a style called rococo which is a fancy name for "too much" ornamentation. However, Fostoria applied these same ornamental scrolls sparingly to a simplistic blank and came up with a very tasteful "baroque". The pattern further lives up to its name via the rough, uneven type handles they applied to the pitcher, sugar and creamer and the odd, unlovely stems they affixed to the goblets.

| | Crystal | Blue | Yellow |
|---|---|---|---|
| Ash tray | 7.50 | 12.50 | 10.00 |
| Bowl, cream soup | 8.00 | ---- | ---- |
| Bowl, ftd. punch | 55.00 | 150.00 | 150.00 |
| Bowl, 3¾", rose | 15.00 | 25.00 | 22.50 |
| Bowl, 4", hand. (3 styles) | 8.00 | 12.00 | 10.00 |
| Bowl, 5", fruit | 8.00 | 15.00 | 12.00 |
| Bowl, 6", cereal | 9.00 | 18.00 | 15.00 |
| Bowl, 6", sq. | 7.00 | 13.00 | 11.50 |
| Bowl, 6½", 2 pt. | 8.00 | 13.00 | 11.00 |
| Bowl, 7", 3 ftd. | 9.00 | 18.00 | 16.00 |
| Bowl, 7½", jelly w/cover | 15.00 | 29.00 | 25.00 |
| Bowl, 8½", hand. | 10.00 | 20.00 | 15.00 |
| Bowl, 8", pickle | 8.00 | 15.00 | 12.50 |
| Bowl, 9½", veg., oval | 15.00 | 25.00 | 23.00 |
| Bowl, 10", hand. | 14.00 | 28.00 | 25.00 |
| Bowl, 10½", hand. | 15.00 | 28.00 | 25.00 |
| Bowl, 10" x 7½" | 18.00 | ---- | ---- |
| Bowl, 10", 3 pt. relish | 15.00 | 25.00 | 20.00 |
| Bowl, 11", celery | 10.00 | 20.00 | 16.00 |
| Bowl, 11", rolled edge | 18.00 | 32.50 | 27.50 |
| Bowl, 12", flared | 20.00 | 25.00 | 22.00 |
| Candelabrum, 8¼", 2-lite, 16 lustre | 30.00 | 27.00 | 23.00 |
| Candelabrum, 9½", 3-lite, 24 lustre | 40.00 | 37.00 | 30.00 |
| Candle, 7¾", 8 lustre | 12.50 | 20.00 | 17.50 |
| Candlestick, 4" | 8.00 | 15.00 | 12.50 |
| Candlestick, 4½", 2-lite | 11.00 | 20.00 | 17.50 |
| Candlestick, 5½" | 9.00 | 17.50 | 15.00 |
| Candlestick, 6", 3-lite | 15.00 | 23.50 | 18.50 |
| Comport, 4¾" | 6.75 | 20.00 | 16.50 |
| Comport, 6½" | 7.50 | 22.00 | 18.00 |
| Creamer, 3¼", indiv. | 6.00 | 10.00 | 10.00 |
| Creamer, 3¾", ftd. | 7.00 | 12.00 | 12.00 |

# BAROQUE, Line #2496, Fostoria Glass Company, 1936-1966 (continued)

| | Crystal | Blue | Yellow |
|---|---|---|---|
| Cup . . . . . . . . . . . . . . . . . . . . . . . . . | 6.50 | 15.00 | 11.00 |
| Cup, 6 oz. punch . . . . . . . . . . . . . . . | 6.00 | 12.00 | 10.00 |
| Ice bucket . . . . . . . . . . . . . . . . . . . . | 20.00 | 47.50 | 40.00 |
| Mayonnaise, 5½", w/liner . . . . . . . . . . . | 10.00 | 30.00 | 25.00 |
| Mustard w/cover . . . . . . . . . . . . . . . | 16.00 | 35.00 | 30.00 |
| Oil w/stopper, 5½" . . . . . . . . . . . . . | 20.00 | 75.00 | 55.00 |
| Pitcher, 6½" . . . . . . . . . . . . . . . . . | 150.00 | 450.00 | 350.00 |
| Pitcher, 7", ice lip . . . . . . . . . . . . . | 125.00 | 450.00 | 350.00 |
| Plate, 6" . . . . . . . . . . . . . . . . . . . . | 3.00 | 5.00 | 4.00 |
| Plate, 7" . . . . . . . . . . . . . . . . . . . . | 4.00 | 9.00 | 7.00 |
| Plate, 8" . . . . . . . . . . . . . . . . . . . . | 6.00 | 11.00 | 9.00 |
| Plate, 9" . . . . . . . . . . . . . . . . . . . . | 12.00 | 25.00 | 22.50 |
| Plate, 10", cake . . . . . . . . . . . . . . . . | 10.00 | 20.00 | 17.50 |
| Plate, 11", ctr. hand. sand. . . . . . . . . . | 12.50 | 37.50 | 22.50 |
| Plate, 14", torte . . . . . . . . . . . . . . . | 12.50 | 25.00 | 20.00 |
| Platter, 12", oval . . . . . . . . . . . . . . . | 12.50 | 30.00 | 27.00 |
| Salt & pepper, pr. . . . . . . . . . . . . . . . | 20.00 | 75.00 | 65.00 |
| Salt & pepper, indiv., pr. . . . . . . . . . . | 25.00 | ---- | ---- |
| Saucer . . . . . . . . . . . . . . . . . . . . . . | 2.00 | 5.00 | 4.00 |
| Sherbet, 3¾", 5 oz. . . . . . . . . . . . . . | 8.00 | 17.50 | 15.50 |
| Stem, 6¾", 9 oz., water . . . . . . . . . . . | 10.00 | 18.00 | 16.00 |
| Sugar, 3", indiv. . . . . . . . . . . . . . . . . | 5.00 | 10.00 | 10.00 |
| Sugar, 3½", ftd. . . . . . . . . . . . . . . . . | 6.00 | 11.00 | 11.00 |
| Tray, 11", oval . . . . . . . . . . . . . . . . | 10.00 | 20.00 | 17.50 |
| Tray for indiv. cream/sugar . . . . . . . . . . | 6.00 | 10.00 | 8.00 |
| Tumbler, 3½", 6½ oz., old fashioned . . . . | 9.00 | 18.00 | 16.00 |
| Tumbler, 3", 3½ oz., ftd. cocktail . . . . . . . | 8.00 | 15.00 | 12.00 |
| Tumbler, 3¾", 5 oz., juice . . . . . . . . . . . | 6.00 | 22.00 | 18.00 |
| Tumbler, 5¾", 14 oz., tea . . . . . . . . . . . | 12.00 | 25.00 | 22.00 |
| Vase, 7" . . . . . . . . . . . . . . . . . . . . . | 15.00 | 25.00 | 22.00 |

# CADENA, Tiffin Glass Company, Early 1930's

Colors: Crystal, yellow; some pink

Cadena is basically a leafy design rather than a flowered one. It's a beautiful pattern, one more people would collect were it easier to find. There is some pink to be seen, but it is very scarce.

| | Crystal | Yellow |
|---|---|---|
| Bowl, cream soup | 15.00 | 20.00 |
| Bowl, finger, ftd. | 12.00 | 15.00 |
| Bowl, grapefruit, ftd. | 17.50 | 22.50 |
| Bowl, 6", hand. | 10.00 | 13.50 |
| Bowl, 12", console | 22.50 | 32.50 |
| Candlestick | 12.50 | 17.50 |
| Creamer | 15.00 | 22.50 |
| Cup | 12.00 | 17.50 |
| Dish, 10", pickle | 12.50 | 17.50 |
| Goblet, 4¾", sherbet | 15.00 | 22.00 |
| Goblet, 5¼", cocktail | 17.50 | 25.00 |
| Goblet, 5¼", ¾ oz., cordial | 25.00 | 35.00 |
| Goblet, 6", wine | 22.00 | 30.00 |
| Goblet, 6½", champagne | 17.00 | 35.00 |
| Goblet, 7½", water | 20.00 | 27.50 |
| Mayonnaise, ftd. w/liner | 20.00 | 27.50 |
| Oyster cocktail | 15.00 | 22.00 |
| Pitcher, ftd. w/cover | 100.00 | 150.00 |
| Plate, 6" | 5.00 | 8.00 |
| Plate, 7¾" | 7.00 | 12.00 |
| Plate, 9¼" | 10.00 | 17.50 |
| Saucer | 3.00 | 4.00 |
| Sugar | 15.00 | 22.00 |
| Tumbler, 4¼", ftd. juice | 15.00 | 22.00 |
| Tumbler, 5¼", ftd. water | 17.00 | 25.00 |

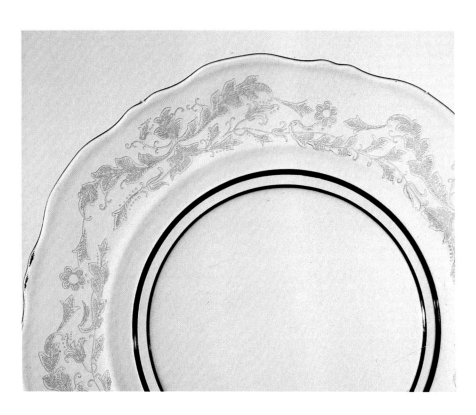

# CANDLEWICK, Line #400, Imperial Glass Company, 1936 to present

Colors: Crystal; a few items in color recently

*Those items with an asterish by the price are in Imperial's current price list at these approximate values. You should know that their outlet store sells "seconds" at half price.

An Imperial advertisement for Candlewick speaks of each serving piece being "picture framed" with beading which they describe as having been inspired by hand-tufted needlework done by pioneer women. They called it a pattern of "inimitable simplicity . . . compatible with any period of decoration".

The catalog reprint shown after the pricing is the first Candlewick catalog issued by Imperial in 1939.

| | |
|---|---|
| Ash tray, 5" | 5.00 |
| Ash tray, heart, 4½" | 4.00 |
| Ash tray, heart, 5½" | 4.50 |
| Ash tray, heart, 6½" | 5.00 |
| Ash tray, indiv. | 4.00 |
| Ash tray, oblong, 4½" | 4.50 |
| Ash tray, round, 2¾" | 3.50 |
| Ash tray, round, 4" | 4.00 |
| Ash tray, square, 3¼" | 4.00 |
| Ash tray, square, 4½" | 4.50 |
| Ash tray, square, 5¾" | 4.00 |
| Ash tray (nut dish or sugar dip), 2¾" | 3.50 |
| Ash tray (or jelly), 4" | 5.00 |
| Ash tray set, 3 pc. rnd. nest. (crys. or colors) | 10.00 |
| Ash tray set, 3 pc. sq. nesting | 10.00 |
| Ash tray, 4 pc. bridge (cig. hold at side) | 25.00 |
| Bell, 4" | 15.00 |
| Bell, 5" | 17.50 |
| Bitters bottle w/tube, 4 oz. | 32.00 |
| Bowl, bouillon, 3 hand. | 12.50 |
| Bowl, #3400, finger | 10.00 |
| Bowl, #3800, finger | 10.00 |
| Bowl, 4½", nappy, 3 ftd. | 12.50 |
| Bowl, 4¾", fruit, 2 hand. | 11.50 |
| Bowl, 4¾", round, 2 hand. | 12.00 |
| Bowl, 5", basket, 2 upturned sides | 14.00 |
| Bowl, 5", bonbon, handled | 15.00 |
| Bowl, 5", cream soup | 12.00 |
| Bowl, 5", fruit | 8.50* |
| Bowl, 5", heart | 6.00 |
| Bowl, 5", heart w/handle | 14.00 |
| Bowl, 5", square | 9.50 |
| Bowl, 5½", heart | 8.00 |
| Bowl, 5½", jelly w/cover | 15.00 |
| Bowl, 5½", sauce | 8.50 |
| Bowl, 6", baked apple, rolled edge | 12.00 |
| Bowl, 6", cottage cheese | 12.00 |
| Bowl, 6", fruit | 7.00 |
| Bowl, 6", heart w/hand. | 15.00 |
| Bowl, 6", mint | 10.00 |
| Bowl, 6", mint w/hand. | 12.00 |
| Bowl, 6", rnd. | 12.00* |
| Bowl, 6", rnd., div. | 10.00 |
| Bowl, 6", 3 ftd. | 12.00 |
| Bowl, 6", square | 10.00 |
| Bowl, 6½", basket, 1 hand. | 21.50* |
| Bowl, 6½", fruit | 12.00 |
| Bowl, 6½", relish, 2 pt. | 13.50* |
| Bowl, 6½", 2 hand. | 14.00 |
| Bowl, 7", round | 9.00 |
| Bowl, 7", round, 2 hand. | 14.75* |
| Bowl, 7", relish, sq., div. | 14.00 |
| Bowl, 7", ivy, hi. bead ft. | 20.00 |
| Bowl, 7", lily, 4 ft. | 18.00 |
| Bowl, 7", relish | 15.00 |
| Bowl, 7", sq. | 10.00 |
| Bowl, 7", sq. relish, div. | 15.00 |
| Bowl, 7¼", rose, ftd. w/crimp edge | 16.50 |
| Bowl, 7½", pickle/celery | 12.00 |

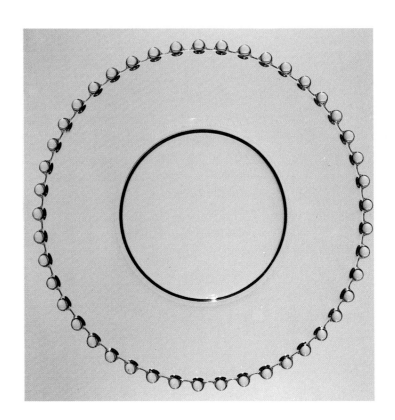

| | |
|---|---|
| Bowl, 7½", lily, bead rim, ftd. | 15.00 |
| Bowl, 7½", belled, (console base) | 15.00 |
| Bowl, 7½", pickle/celery | 13.00 |
| Bowl, 8", round | 10.00 |
| Bowl, 8", relish, 2 pt. | 11.75* |
| Bowl, 8", cov. veg. | 18.50 |
| Bowl, 8½", rnd. | 18.50* |
| Bowl, 8½", nappy, 4 ftd. | 14.00 |
| Bowl, 8½", 3 ftd. | 12.00 |
| Bowl, 8½", 2 hand. | 16.00 |
| Bowl, 8½", pickle/celery | 12.00 |
| Bowl, 8½", relish, div., 2 hand. | 14.00 |
| Bowl, 8½", relish, 4 pt. | 20.00* |
| Bowl, 9", round | 12.00 |
| Bowl, 9", crimp, ftd. | 14.00 |
| Bowl, 9", sq., fancy crimp edge, 4 ft. | 16.00 |
| Bowl, 9", fruit, low ft. | 16.00 |
| Bowl, 9", heart | 18.00 |
| Bowl, 9", heart w/hand. | 19.00 |
| Bowl, 10" | 13.00 |
| Bowl, 10", banana | 17.50 |
| Bowl, 10", belled | 15.00 |
| Bowl, 10", belled, punch base | 10.00 |
| Bowl, 10", cupped edge | 15.00 |
| Bowl, 10", deep, 2 hand. | 22.50* |
| Bowl, 10", divided, deep, 2 hand. | 18.50 |
| Bowl, 10", fruit, bead stem (like compote) | 17.50 |
| Bowl, 10", heart | 15.00 |
| Bowl, 10", heart w/hand. | 14.00 |
| Bowl, 10", relish, 3 pt. | 18.00 |
| Bowl, 10", relish, 3 pt., 3 ft. | 20.00 |
| Bowl, 10½", belled | 21.00 |
| Bowl, 10½", butter/jam, 3 pt. | 22.00 |
| Bowl, 10½", flared | 20.00 |
| Bowl, 10½", oval, flared | 22.00 |
| Bowl, 10½", salad | 20.00 |
| Bowl, 10½", 3 ft. | 22.50 |
| Bowl, 10½", relish, 3 pt. | 15.00 |
| Bowl, 11", basket, 1 hand. | 40.00 |
| Bowl, 11", celery boat, oval | 22.00 |
| Bowl, 11", center piece, flared | 19.00 |
| Bowl, 11", float, inward rim, ftd. | 12.50 |
| Bowl, 11", oval | 20.00 |
| Bowl, 11", oval w/partition | 17.50* |
| Bowl, 12", rnd. | 18.00 |
| Bowl, 12", belled | 18.00 |
| Bowl, 12", float | 17.50 |
| Bowl, 12", hand. | 15.00 |
| Bowl, 12", oval, flared | 20.00 |
| Bowl, 12", relish, oblong | 20.00 |
| Bowl, 13", center piece mushroom | 22.00 |
| Bowl, 13", float, 1½" deep | 18.00 |
| Bowl, 13½", relish, 5 pt. | 23.00 |
| Bowl, 14", belled | 25.00 |
| Bowl, 14", oval | 22.50 |
| Bowl, 14", oval, flared | 23.50 |
| Butter w/cover, rnd. 5½" | 17.50 |
| Butter w/bead top, ¼ lb. | 14.50* |
| Candleholder, signed "Candlewick" | 78.00 |
| Candleholder, 2-lite | 12.00 |
| Candleholder, 3½" | 10.50* |
| Candleholder, 3½", w/fingerhold | 28.00 |
| Candleholder, 3-lite on cir. bead ctr. | 15.00 |
| Candleholder, 5", hand. w/bowled up base | 12.00 |
| Candleholder, 5½" | 15.00 |
| Candleholder, 6½" | 17.50 |
| Candleholder, flat | 10.50 |
| Candleholder, flower, 4" | 8.00 |
| Candleholder, flower, 4½" | 9.00 |
| Candleholder, flower, 5", (epergne) | 15.00 |

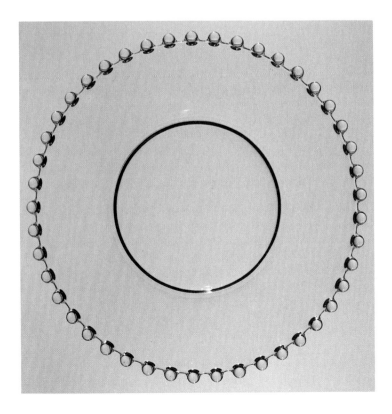

| Item | Price |
|------|------:|
| Candleholder, flower, 6" | 10.00 |
| Candleholder, flower, 6½" | 11.00 |
| Candleholder, mushroom | 8.50 |
| Candleholder, rolled edge | 10.00 |
| Candleholder, urn, 6", holders on cir. ctr. bead | 18.50 |
| Candy box, round, 5½" | 18.50 |
| Candy box, square, 6½", rnd. lid | 17.50 |
| Candy box w/cover, flared, 7" | 17.50 |
| Candy box w/cover, round, 7" | 18.00 |
| Candy jar w/cover, ftd. | 20.00 |
| Candy w/cover, partitioned | 20.00 |
| Cigarette box w/cover | 12.50 |
| Cigarette holder, 3", bead ft. | 10.00 |
| Cigarette set: 6 pc., (cig. box w/4 rect. ash trays) | 32.50 |
| Coaster, 4" | 5.00 |
| Coaster w/spoon rest | 7.50 |
| Cocktail, seafood w/bead ft. | 8.00 |
| Cocktail set: 2 pc. plate w/indent; cocktail | 14.50 |
| Compote, 4½" | 10.00 |
| Compote, 5", bulbous bead stem | 12.00 |
| Compote, 5½", bead stem, flared | 12.50 |
| Compote, 5½", low, plain stem | 12.00 |
| Compote, 5½", bead stem | 12.00 |
| Compote, 8", bead stem | 17.50 |
| Compote, 10", ftd. fruit, crimped | 22.50 |
| Compote, ft. oval | 20.00 |
| Condiment set: 4 pc., (2 squat bead ft. shakers, marmalade) | 25.00 |
| Console set, 3 pc. (14", oval bowl, 2 3-lite cand.) | 52.50 |
| Console set, 3 pc. (mushroom bowl, 2 mushroom cand.) | 39.00 |
| Console set, 4 pc. (tall, ft. mushroom bowl, 2 2-lite candles) | 45.00 |
| Creamer, 6 oz., bead candle | 6.50 |
| Creamer, indiv. bridge | 5.00 |
| Creamer, plain ft. | 6.00 |
| Cup, after dinner | 12.00 |
| Cup, coffee | 8.50* |
| Cup, punch | 4.00 |
| Cup, tea | 7.50 |
| Decanter, w/stopper | 22.50 |
| Deviled egg server, 12", ctr. hand. | 55.00 |
| Egg cup | 12.00 |
| Egg cup, bead. ft. | 15.00 |
| Hurricane lamp, 2 pc. candle base | 20.00* |
| Hurricane lamp, 3 pc. flared & crimped edge globe | 55.00 |
| Ice tub, 5½", deep, 8", diam. | 18.50 |
| Icer, 2 pc., seafood fruit cocktail | 16.00 |
| Icer, 2 pc., seafood/fruit cocktail #2800 | 17.50 |
| Jam set, 5 pc. oval tray w/2 marmalade jars w/ladles | 37.50 |
| Jar tower, 3 sect.; jar w/lid, spoon, all on tray | 27.50 |
| Knife, butter | 20.00 |
| Ladle, marmalade, 3 bead stem | 3.00 |
| Ladle, mayonnaise, 6¼" | 3.50 |
| Marmalade set, 3 pc., beaded ft. w/cover & spoon | 10.50* |
| Marmalade set, 3 pc. tall jar, bead ft. lid, & spoon | 20.00 |
| Marmalade set, 4 pc., liner saucer, jar, lid, & spoon | 28.00 |
| Mayonnaise set, 2 pc. scoop side bowl, spoon | 15.00 |
| Mayonnaise set, 3 pc. hand. tray/hand bowl/ladle | 20.00 |
| Mayonnaise set, 3 pc. plate, heart bowl, spoon | 25.00 |
| Mayonnaise set, 3 pc. scoop inside bowl, spoon, tray | 25.00 |
| Mayonnaise set, 4 pc., plate, bowl, 2 ladles | 28.00 |
| Mayonnaise w/7", liner | 17.50 |
| Mirror, 4", rnd., standing | 40.00 |
| Mustard jar w/spoon | 15.00 |
| Oil, 4 oz., bulbous bottom | 17.50 |
| Oil, 4 oz., hand. bulbous bottom | 17.50 |
| Oil, 6 oz., hand. bulbous bottom | 18.00 |
| Oil, 6 oz., bulbous bottom | 18.00 |
| Oil w/stopper, etched "Oil" | 20.00 |
| Oil w/stopper, etched "Vinegar" | 20.00 |
| Oyster cocktail, #3400, 4 oz. | 14.00 |
| Party set, 2 pc., plate w/indent for cup | 10.00 |

# CANDLEWICK, Line #400, Imperial Glass Company, 1936 to present, (continued)

| | |
|---|---|
| Pitcher, 14 oz., short rnd. | 20.00 |
| Pitcher, 16 oz., low ft. | 22.00 |
| Pitcher, 16 oz., no ice lip | 20.00 |
| Pitcher, 20 oz. | 25.00 |
| Pitcher, 40 oz., juice/cocktail | 28.00 |
| Pitcher, 64 oz. | 32.50 |
| Pitcher, 80 oz. | 35.00 |
| Pitcher, 40 oz., bead hand w/lip | 32.50 |
| Plate, birthday cake (holes for candles) | 65.00 |
| Plate, 4½" | 4.00 |
| Plate, 5½", 2 hand. | 6.00 |
| Plate, 5½", hand. | 7.50 |
| Plate, 6", bread/butter | 6.50 |
| Plate, 6", canape w/off ctr. indent | 3.50 |
| Plate, 6¾", 2 hand. crimped | 7.50 |
| Plate, 7", salad | 13.50* |
| Plate, 7½", 2 hand. | 7.50 |
| Plate, 7½", triangular | 8.50 |
| Plate, 8", oval | 9.00 |
| Plate, 8", salad | 7.00 |
| Plate, 8¼", crescent salad | 9.00 |
| Plate, 8½", 2 hand. crimped | 8.50 |
| Plate, 8½", 2 hand. | 8.50 |
| Plate, 8½", salad | 16.50* |
| Plate, 9", 2 hand. (sides upturned) | 12.00 |
| Plate, 9", luncheon | 8.50 |
| Plate, 9", oval salad | 13.00 |
| Plate, 10", 2 hand. | 15.00 |
| Plate, 10", 2 hand. crimped | 15.00 |
| Plate, 10", dinner | 12.50 |
| Plate, 10", hand. | 15.00 |
| Plate, 10", low ft. cake | 17.50 |
| Plate, 10½" | 20.50* |
| Plate, 11", tall, bead. ft. cake | 20.00 |
| Plate, 12" | 15.00 |
| Plate, 12", 2 hand. | 28.00* |
| Plate, 12", 2 hand. crimp. | 20.00 |
| Plate, 12", service | 15.00 |
| Plate, 12½", cupped edge, torte | 24.50* |
| Plate, 12½", oval | 17.50 |
| Plate, 13", cupped edge serving | 22.00 |
| Plate, 13", oval | 20.00 |
| Plate, 14", 2 hand. | 20.00 |
| Plate, 14", hand. torte | 22.00 |
| Plate, 14", service | 20.00 |
| Plate, 14", torte | 22.00 |
| Plate, 17", cupped edge | 30.00 |
| Plate, 17", reg. edge | 25.00 |
| Plate, 17", torte | 27.50 |
| Plate, w/indent, oval | 9.00 |
| Plate, w/indent, 8" | 10.00 |
| Platter, 16" | 22.50 |
| Punch ladle | 11.50* |
| Punch set, family, 8 demi cups. ladle, lid | 130.00 |
| Punch set, 15 pc. bowl on base, 12 cups, ladle | 135.00 |
| Punch set, punch bowl, 12 cups, ladle | 120.00 |
| Relish & dressing set, 4 pc. (10½", 4 pt. relish w/marmalade) | 27.50 |
| Salad fork & spoon, set | 12.00 |
| Salad set, 4 pc., buffet; lg. rnd. tray, div. bowl, 2 spoons | 30.00 |
| Salad set, 4 pc. (rnd. plate, flared bowl, fork, spoon) | 30.00 |
| Salt & pepper, bead ft., strt. side, chrome top | 9.00* |
| Salt & pepper, bead ft., bulbous, chrome top | 9.00* |
| Salt & pepper, bulbous w/bead stem, chrome top | 6.00 |
| Salt & pepper, pr., indiv. | 4.00 |
| Salt & pepper, pr. plastic top | 7.00 |
| Salt dip, 2" | 4.50 |
| Salt dip, 2¼" | 5.00 |
| Salt spoon, 3 bead hand. | 2.50 |
| Salt spoon w/ribbed bowl | 2.50 |
| Sauce boat w/plate, set | 45.00 |

| | |
|---|---|
| Saucer, after dinner | 3.00 |
| Saucer tea | 9.00* |
| Set: 2 pc. 14", CHIP plate w/div. DIP bowl | 27.50 |
| Set: 2 pc. Canape (plate w/indent; ftd. juice) | 22.50 |
| Set: 2 pc. hand. CRACKER w/CHEESE compote | 32.50 |
| Set: 2 pc. rnd. CRACKER plate w/indent; CHEESE compote | 30.00 |
| Set: 5 pc. Jam (marmalade w/lid, spoon, but. top, heart tray) | 42.50 |
| Snack jar w/cover, bead ft. | 25.00 |
| Snack jar, w/cover, ftd. | 27.50 |
| Stem, #400, 1 oz., cordial, bead ft. | 17.50 |
| Stem, #400, 3 oz., cocktail, bead ft. | 17.50 |
| Stem, #400, 4 oz., cocktail, bead ft. | 15.00* |
| Stem, #400, 5 oz., juice tumbler, bead ft. | 15.00 |
| Stem, #400, 5 oz., tall sherbet, bead ft. | 14.00 |
| Stem, #400, 5 oz., wine, bead ft. | 16.50 |
| Stem, #400, 6 oz., sherbet | 16.00* |
| Stem, #400, 10 oz., bead ft. | 15.00* |
| Stem, #400, 11 oz., goblet | 12.00 |
| Stem, #400, 12 oz., tea | 16.00* |
| Stem, #3400, low sherbet | 12.00 |
| Stem, #3400, 1 oz., cordial, grad. bead | 20.00 |
| Stem, #3400, 4 oz., cocktail | 17.50 |
| Stem, #3400, 4 oz., wine | 16.50 |
| Stem, #3400, 5 oz., claret | 17.50 |
| Stem, #3400, 5 oz., ft. juice tumbler | 17.50 |
| Stem, #3400, 6 oz., parfait | 15.00 |
| Stem, #3400, 6 oz., sherbet/saucer champagne | 16.00 |
| Stem, #3400, 9 oz., goblet | 16.00 |
| Stem, #3800, low sherbet | 12.00 |
| Stem, #3800, brandy | 17.50 |
| Stem, #3800, cocktail | 17.50 |
| Stem, #3800, 1 oz. cordial | 20.00 |
| Stem, #3800, wine | 17.50 |
| Stem, #3800, goblet | 17.50 |
| Stem, #3800, claret | 17.50 |
| Stem, #3800, champagne/sherbet | 15.00 |
| Stem, #3800, 5 oz., juice tumbler | 12.50 |
| Stem, #3800, 6 oz., parfait | 15.00 |
| Stem, #3800, 9 oz., water | 17.50 |
| Stem, #3800, 12 oz., low ft. tea tumbler | 16.00 |
| Stem, 7 oz., parfait | 13.00 |
| Strawberry set, 2 pc., (7", plate/sugar dip bowl) | 12.00 |
| Sugar, 6 oz., bead handle | 5.50 |
| Sugar, indiv. bridge | 5.00 |
| Sugar, plain ft. | 5.00 |
| Sugar/creamer w/6", tray; set | 25.00* |
| Tete-a-tete 3 pc. brandy, a.d. cup, 6½", oval tray | 25.00 |
| Tid bit server, 2 tier | 38.00 |
| Tid bit set, 3 pc. nest. heart | 20.00 |
| Toast w/cover, set | 35.00 |
| Tray, 2 hand. crimped | 27.50 |
| Tray, 5" | 12.50 |
| Tray, 5½", hand. | 12.50 |
| Tray, 5½", lemon, ctr. hand. | 13.50 |
| Tray, 5¼" x 9¼", condiment | 14.50 |
| Tray, 6", wafer, hand. bent to ctr. of dish | 16.50 |
| Tray, 6½" | 15.00 |
| Tray w/indent, 6½" | 13.50 |
| Tray, 7½", hand. | 15.00 |
| Tray, 8½", hand. | 17.50 |
| Tray, 10", hand. | 22.50 |
| Tray, 10½", ctr. hand. fruit | 25.00 |
| Tray, 11½", ctr. hand. party | 27.50 |
| Tray, 13", relish | 27.50 |
| Tray, 13½", 2 hand. celery | 25.00 |
| Tray, 14", hand. | 23.50 |
| Tumbler, #400, 5 oz., bead ft. juice | 10.00 |
| Tumbler, #400, 7 oz., old fashioned | 12.00 |
| Tumbler, #400, 10 oz. bead ft. | 12.00 |
| Tumbler, #400, 12 oz., bead ft. | 12.50 |

# CANDLEWICK, Line #400, Imperial Glass Company, 1936 to present, (continued)

| | |
|---|---:|
| Tumbler, #400, 14 oz., bead ft. tea | 14.00 |
| Tumbler, #3400, 9 oz., ft. | 14.00 |
| Tumbler, #3400, 10 oz., plain ft. | 12.00 |
| Tumbler, #3800, 9 oz. | 14.00 |
| Tumbler, #3800, 12 oz. | 15.00 |
| Vase, 3¾", ftd. ball | 17.50 |
| Vase, 4", bead ft. sm. neck ball | 12.50 |
| Vase, 5¾", bead ft. bud | 15.00 |
| Vase, 5¾", bead ft. mini bud | 15.00 |
| Vase, 6", flat, crimped edge | 15.00 |
| Vase, 6", ftd. flared rim | 15.00 |
| Vase, 6" diam. | 55.00 |
| Vase, 6½", fan | 17.00 |
| Vase, 7", rolled rim w/bead hand. | 17.50 |
| Vase, 8", fan w/bead hand. | 15.00 |
| Vase, 8", flat, crimped edge | 20.00 |
| Vase, 8", fluted rim, w/bead hand. | 22.50 |
| Vase, 8¼" | 21.50 |
| Vase, 8½", bead ft. bud | 17.50 |
| Vase, 8½", bead ft., flared rim | 16.00 |
| Vase, 8½", bead ft., inward rim | 16.00 |
| Vase, 8½", hand. (pitcher shape) | 20.00 |
| Vase, 10", bead ft., strt. side | 20.00 |

## IMPERIAL CANDLEWICK

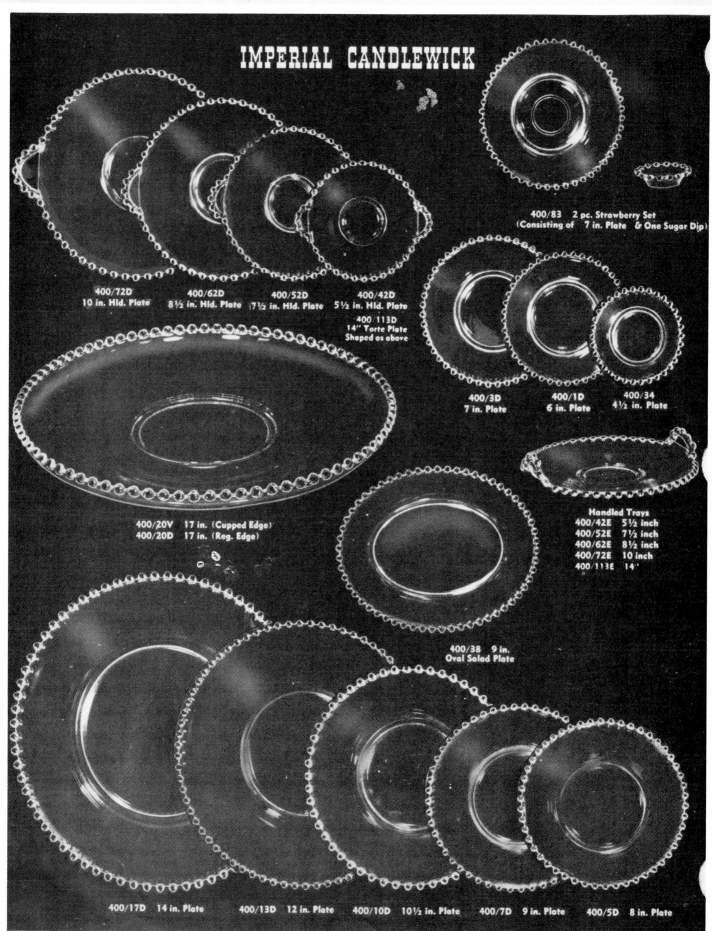

400/83    2 pc. Strawberry Set
(Consisting of    7 in. Plate    & One Sugar Dip)

400/72D
10 in. Hld. Plate

400/62D
8½ in. Hld. Plate

400/52D
7½ in. Hld. Plate

400/42D
5½ in. Hld. Plate

400/113D
14" Torte Plate
Shaped as above

400/3D
7 in. Plate

400/1D
6 in. Plate

400/34
4½ in. Plate

400/20V    17 in. (Cupped Edge)
400/20D    17 in. (Reg. Edge)

Handled Trays
400/42E    5½ inch
400/52E    7½ inch
400/62E    8½ inch
400/72E    10 inch
400/113E    14"

400/38    9 in.
Oval Salad Plate

400/17D    14 in. Plate        400/13D    12 in. Plate        400/10D    10½ in. Plate        400/7D    9 in. Plate        400/5D    8 in. Plate

## IMPERIAL CANDLEWICK

3400   Goblet

3400   Cocktail

3400   Claret

3400   Saucer Champagne
or Tall Sherbet

3400   Wine

3400   Cordial

3400   12 oz. Tumbler

3400   9 oz. Tumbler

3400   5 oz. Tumbler

3400   Low Sherbet

3400
Oyster Cocktail

400/37   Coffee Cup
& Saucer

400/77   After Dinner
Coffee Cup & Saucer

3400   2 pc. Icer
ea Food or Fruit Cocktail

400/19
Egg Cup

400/35   Tea Cup
& Saucer

3400   Finger Bowl

29

# IMPERIAL CANDLEWICK

3800 Goblet

3800 Tall Sherbet or Champagne

3800 Low Sherbet

3800 Claret

3800 Cocktail

3800 Wine

3800 Cordial

3800 12 oz. Tumbler

3800 9 oz. Tumbler

3800 5 oz. Tumbler

3800 Brandy

3800 Finger Bowl

400/19 Footed Fruit

400/19 12 oz.

400/19 10 oz.

400/19 7 oz. Old Fashioned

400/19 5 oz.

3800 2 pc. Icer Sea Food or Fruit Cocktail

## IMPERIAL CANDLEWICK

400/44  3 inch
Cigarette Holder

400/118
B'tween Place Ash Tray

400/33  4 inch
Jelly or Ash Tray

400/64  2¾ inch
Nut Dish or Ash Tray or
Sugar Dip

400/61  Salt Dip

400/109  Salt &
Pepper Set

400/29/
8-pc. Cigarette Set
Tray, Holder & Four Ash Trays

400/29  6½ inch Tray

400/89  4 pc. Marmalade Set

400/78  4½ inch Coaster

400/31  Sugar & Cream Set

400/63  Ice Tub
5½ inches Deep
8 inch Diameter

400/30
Sugar and Cream
400/122
Ind. or Bridge Size set of above

400/2930  3 pc.
Sugar & Cream Set

Cruets with Stoppers
400/71—6 oz.  400/70—4 oz.
5 Piece Condiment Set
400/701

400/24  80 oz. Pitcher

400/82  10 pc. Cordial Set
(Bottle, Stopper and 8 Cordials)

31

## IMPERIAL CANDLEWICK

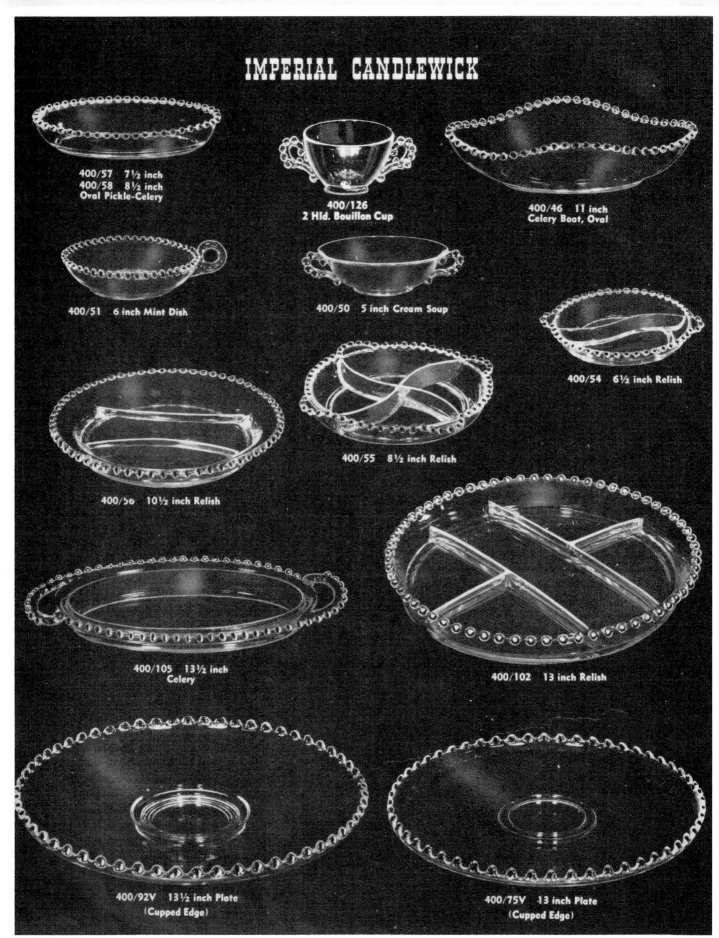

400/57   7½ inch
400/58   8½ inch
Oval Pickle-Celery

400/126
2 Hld. Bouillon Cup

400/46   11 inch
Celery Boat, Oval

400/51   6 inch Mint Dish

400/50   5 inch Cream Soup

400/54   6½ inch Relish

400/56   10½ inch Relish

400/55   8½ inch Relish

400/105   13½ inch
Celery

400/102   13 inch Relish

400/92V   13½ inch Plate
(Cupped Edge)

400/75V   13 inch Plate
(Cupped Edge)

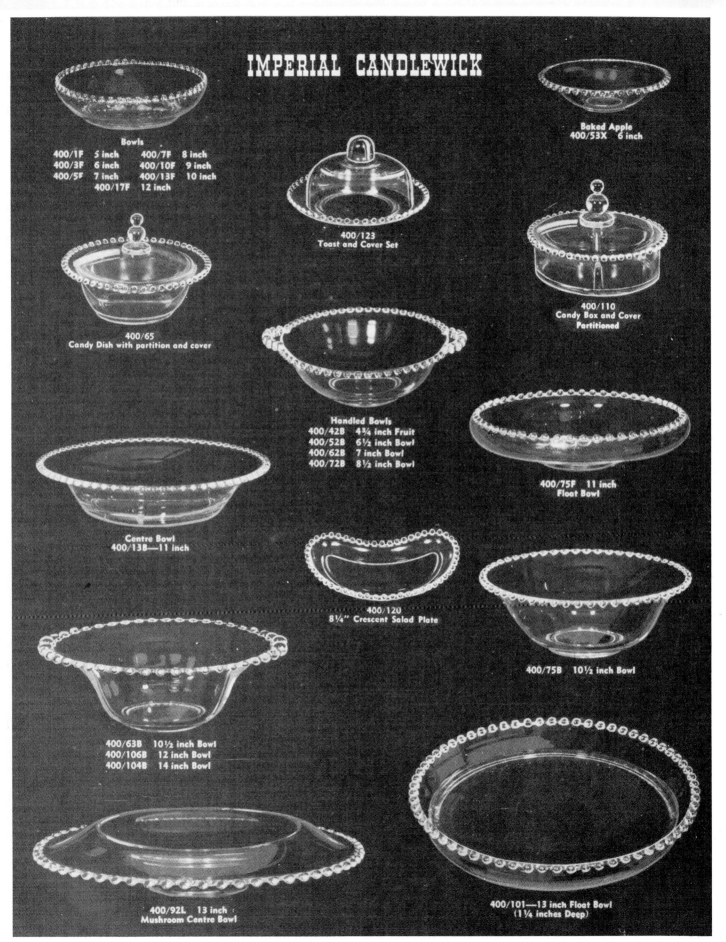

# IMPERIAL CANDLEWICK

**Bowls**

| | | | |
|---|---|---|---|
| 400/1F | 5 inch | 400/7F | 8 inch |
| 400/3F | 6 inch | 400/10F | 9 inch |
| 400/5F | 7 inch | 400/13F | 10 inch |
| | | 400/17F | 12 inch |

**Baked Apple**
400/53X   6 inch

**400/123**
Toast and Cover Set

**400/65**
Candy Dish with partition and cover

**400/110**
Candy Box and Cover
Partitioned

**Handled Bowls**

| | |
|---|---|
| 400/42B | 4¾ inch Fruit |
| 400/52B | 6½ inch Bowl |
| 400/62B | 7 inch Bowl |
| 400/72B | 8½ inch Bowl |

**400/75F   11 inch**
Float Bowl

**Centre Bowl**
400/13B—11 inch

**400/12U**
8¼" Crescent Salad Plate

**400/75B   10½ inch Bowl**

| | |
|---|---|
| 400/63B | 10½ inch Bowl |
| 400/106B | 12 inch Bowl |
| 400/104B | 14 inch Bowl |

**400/92L   13 inch**
Mushroom Centre Bowl

**400/101—13 inch Float Bowl**
(1¼ inches Deep)

33

# IMPERIAL CANDLEWICK

400/99   2 pc. Snack Set

400/98   2 pc. Party Set

400/91   Cocktail Set, 2 pcs.

400/59   5½ in.
Covered Jelly

400/36   Canape Set, 2 pcs.

400/23   3 pc. Mayonnaise Set

400/84   4 pc. Mayonnaise Set

400/65/1   8 inch
Covered Vegetable

400/40/0   6½ inch Basket

400/73H   9 inch Handled Heart

400/40/H   5 inch Handled Heart

400/73/0   11 inch Basket

400/49H   5 inch Heart

400/49H   9 inch Heart

# IMPERIAL CANDLEWICK

4000  Knife
(Gift Boxed)

400/108   Table Bell

400/75   Salad Fork & Spoon Set

400/1989
3 piece Marmalade Set

400/68D   11½ inch Pastry Tray

400/68F   10½ inch
Fruit Tray

400/66B   5½ inch
Low Compote

400/45   5½ inch Compote

400/48F   8 inch Compote

400/67D   10 inch
Low Cake Stand

400/103D   11 inch
Tall Cake Stand

400/111
Tete-A-Tete

400/103F   10 inch
Ftd. Fruit Bowl

35

# IMPERIAL GLASS CORPORATION, BELLAIRE, OHIO

## IMPERIAL CANDLEWICK

**400/79R**
Rolled Candleholder

**400/80**
3½ inch Candleholder

**400/79B**
Flat Candleholder

**400/129R**
6" Urn Candleholder

**400/86**
Mushroom Candleholder

**400/81**
3½ inch Candleholder

**400/100**
Twin Candleholder

**400/138B**
6" Footed Vase

**400/87F**
8 inch Vase

**400/87C**
8 inch Vase

**400/87R**
7 inch Vase

**400/79   2 pc.**
Hurricane Candle Lamp

**400/21**
8½ inch Vase

**400/22**
10 inch Vase

**400/27**
8½ inch Vase

**400/28**
8½ inch Vase

**400/107**
Miniature
Bud Vase
5¾ inches

**400/25**
Ball
Bud Vase
4 inch

## IMPERIAL CANDLEWICK

400/88   2 pc.
Cheese & Cracker Set

400/9266B   2 pc.
Cheese & Cracker Set

400/113A
10" 2 Hld. Deep Bowl
400/114A
10" 2 Hld. Partitioned Deep Bowl

400/52BD   3 pc.
Mayonnaise Set

400/94   4 pc.
Buffet Salad Set

400/75B   4 pc.
Salad Set

400/20   15 pc. Punch Set

400/1112
Relish and Dressing—4 piece
400/112
10½" 4 part Relish

37

# IMPERIAL CANDLEWICK

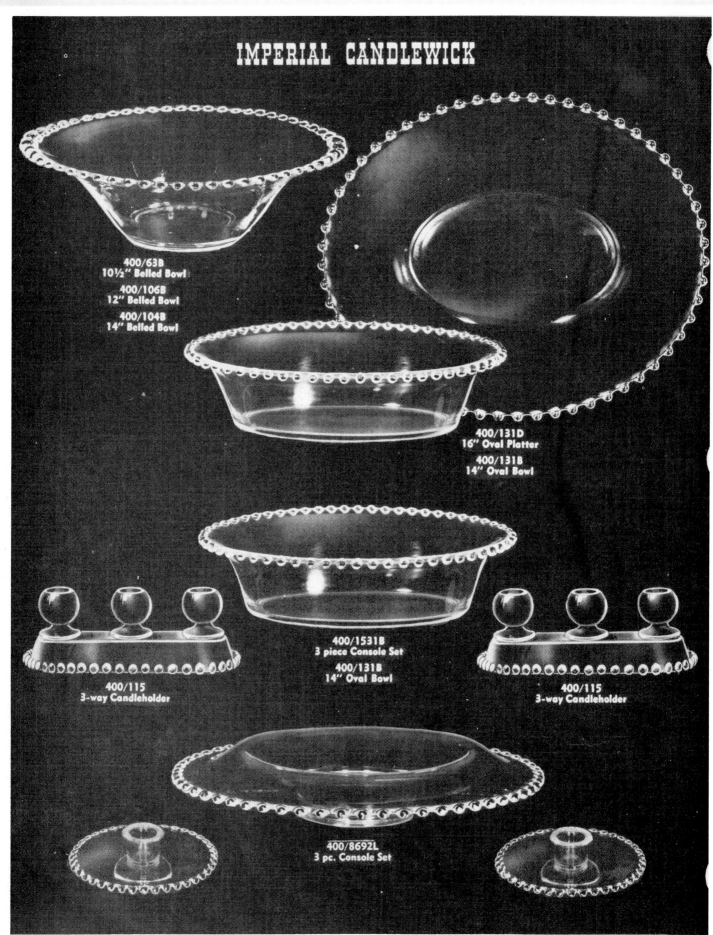

400/63B
10½" Belled Bowl

400/106B
12" Belled Bowl

400/104B
14" Belled Bowl

400/131D
16" Oval Platter

400/131B
14" Oval Bowl

400/1531B
3 piece Console Set

400/131B
14" Oval Bowl

400/115
3-way Candleholder

400/115
3-way Candleholder

400/8692L
3 pc. Console Set

# IMPERIAL CANDLEWICK

**400/127L**
4 piece Console Set

**400/8063B**
3 piece Console Set

**400/9279FR**
3 piece Console Set

# IMPERIAL CANDLEWICK

400/6300B
3 piece Console Set
(10½" Bowl)

400/1006B
3 piece Console Set
(12" Bowl)

400/1004B
3 piece Console Set
(14" Bowl)

400/136
4 piece Console Set

400/128
15 piece Punch Set
Bowl on Base
Ladle----12 Cups

400/124D
13" Oval Platter

# IMPERIAL CANDLEWICK

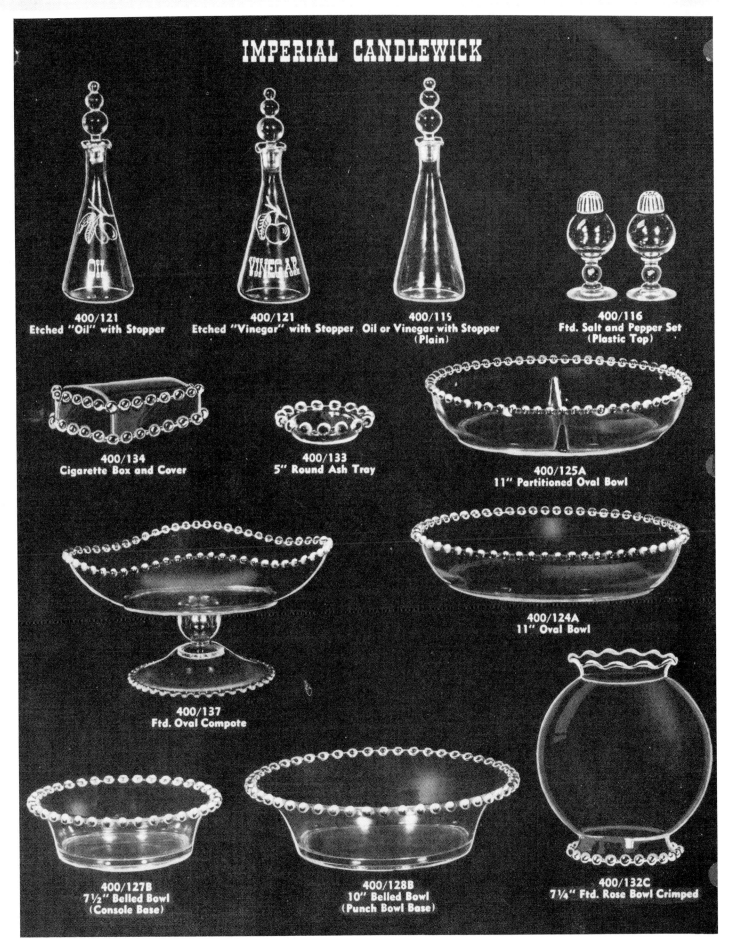

400/121
Etched "Oil" with Stopper

400/121
Etched "Vinegar" with Stopper

400/119
Oil or Vinegar with Stopper
(Plain)

400/116
Ftd. Salt and Pepper Set
(Plastic Top)

400/134
Cigarette Box and Cover

400/133
5" Round Ash Tray

400/125A
11" Partitioned Oval Bowl

400/137
Ftd. Oval Compote

400/124A
11" Oval Bowl

400/127B
7½" Belled Bowl
(Console Base)

400/128B
10" Belled Bowl
(Punch Bowl Base)

400/132C
7¼" Ftd. Rose Bowl Crimped

# CAPRICE, Cambridge Glass Company, 1940's · Early '50's, (continued)

Colors: Crystal, blue; rare in amber and amethyst

Blue Caprice is more desirable to collectors than crystal. The tall 90 oz. Daulton pitcher is collectible in any color, however, as they appear few and far between.

|  | Crystal | Blue |
|---|---|---|
| Ash tray, 2¾", 3 ftd. shell | 5.00 | 8.00 |
| Ash tray, 3" | 4.00 | 6.00 |
| Ash tray, 4" | 5.00 | 8.00 |
| Ash tray, 5" | 6.00 | 17.50 |
| Bonbon, 6", sq. 2 hand. | 7.00 | 15.00 |
| Bonbon, 6", sq., ftd. | 6.00 | 15.00 |
| Bottle, 7 oz., bitters | 25.00 | 52.50 |
| Bowl, 5", 2 hand. jelly | 6.00 | 15.00 |
| Bowl, 6½", hand., 2 pt. relish | 10.00 | 18.00 |
| Bowl, 8", 3 pt. relish | 15.00 | 25.00 |
| Bowl, 9", pickle | 10.00 | 17.50 |
| Bowl, 10½", crimped, 4 ftd. | 12.00 | 20.00 |
| Bowl, 11", 2 hand. oval, 4 ftd. | 15.00 | 25.00 |
| Bowl, 12", relish, 3 pt. | 10.00 | 20.00 |
| Bowl, 12½", belled, 4 ftd. | 16.00 | 25.00 |
| Bowl, 12½", crimped, 4 ftd. | 16.00 | 25.00 |
| Bowl, 13", crimped, 4 ftd. | 18.00 | 27.50 |
| Bowl, 13½", 4 ftd., shallow belled | 20.00 | 45.00 |
| Cake plate, 13", ftd. | 30.00 | ---- |
| Candlestick, 2½", ea. | 10.00 | 12.50 |
| Candlestick, 2-lite, keyhole | 12.00 | 27.50 |
| Candlestick, 3-lite | 20.00 | 30.00 |
| Candlestick, 5", ea. | 9.00 | 15.00 |
| Candlestick, 7", ea. w/prism | 12.00 | 22.50 |
| Candy, 6", 3 ftd. w/cover | 30.00 | 50.00 |
| Candy, 6", ftd. w/cover | 32.50 | 57.50 |
| Celery & relish, 8½", 3 pt. | 15.00 | 25.00 |
| Cigarette box w/cover, 3½" x 2¼" | 15.00 | 22.50 |
| Cigarette box w/cover, 4½" x 3½" | 15.00 | 24.00 |
| Cigarette holder, 2" x 2¼", triangular | 10.00 | 15.00 |
| Cigarette holder, 3" x 3", triangular | 12.00 | 20.00 |
| Coaster, 3½" | 7.00 | 16.00 |
| Comport, 6" | 13.50 | 22.50 |
| Comport, 7" low ftd. | 15.00 | 27.50 |
| Comport, 7" | 15.00 | 27.50 |
| Creamer, several styles | 7.00 | 12.50 |
| Creamer, indiv. | 7.00 | 10.00 |
| Cup | 9.00 | 25.00 |
| Decanter w/stopper, 36 oz. | 40.00 | 75.00 |
| Ice bucket | 35.00 | 75.00 |
| Marmalade w/cover | 30.00 | 65.00 |
| Mayonnaise, 6½", 3 pc. set | 17.50 | 30.00 |
| Mayonnaise, 8", 3 pc. set | 20.00 | 35.00 |
| Mustard w/cover | 20.00 | 35.00 |
| Oil, 3 oz., w/stopper | 12.00 | 27.50 |
| Pitcher, 32 oz., ball shape | 35.00 | 95.00 |
| Pitcher, 80 oz. ball shape | 32.50 | 85.00 |
| Pitcher, 90 oz. tall Daulton style | 175.00 | 395.00 |
| Plate, 6½", bread/butter | 4.00 | 10.00 |
| Plate, 6½", hand., lemon | 6.50 | 12.00 |
| Plate, 8½", salad | 7.00 | 16.00 |
| Plate, 9½", dinner | 20.00 | 60.00 |

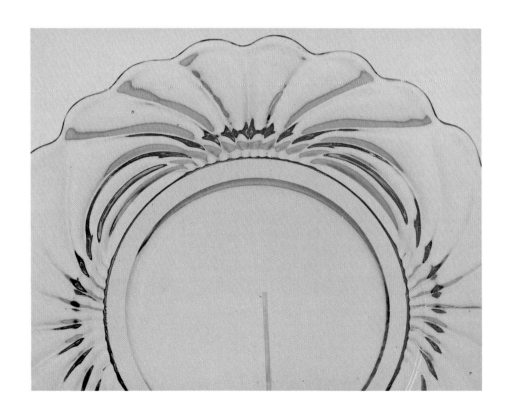

|  | Crystal | Blue |
|---|---|---|
| Plate, 11", cabaret, 4 ftd. | 15.00 | 25.00 |
| Plate, 11½", cabaret | 15.00 | 23.00 |
| Plate, 14", cabaret, 4 ftd. | 16.00 | 30.00 |
| Plate, 14" | 12.50 | 20.00 |
| Plate, 16" | 20.00 | 45.00 |
| Saucer | 2.50 | 5.00 |
| Salt & pepper, pr., egg shape | 20.00 | 40.00 |
| Salt & pepper, pr., ball | 25.00 | 35.00 |
| Salt & pepper, pr., flat | 12.00 | 20.00 |
| Salt & pepper, indiv. ball | 10.00 | 15.00 |
| Salt & pepper, indiv. flat | 5.00 | 10.00 |
| Salver, 13", 2 pc. (cake atop pedestal) | 25.00 | 60.00 |
| Stem, #300, blown, 1 oz. cordial | 25.00 | 60.00 |
| Stem, #300, blown, 2½ oz., wine | 20.00 | 37.50 |
| Stem, #300, blown, 3 oz., cocktail | 16.00 | 32.50 |
| Stem, #300, blown, 4½ oz., claret | 20.00 | 35.00 |
| Stem, #300, blown, 4½ oz., low oyster cocktail | 10.00 | 22.50 |
| Stem, #300, blown, 6 oz. low sherbet | 12.00 | 20.00 |
| Stem, #300, blown, 6 oz. sherbet | 12.00 | 20.00 |
| Stem, #300, blown, 9 oz. water | 12.00 | 20.00 |
| Stem, #301, blown, 1 oz. cordial | 25.00 | ---- |
| Stem, #301, blown, 2½ oz. wine | 20.00 | ---- |
| Stem, #301, blown, 3 oz. cocktail | 16.00 | ---- |
| Stem, #301, blown, 4½ oz. claret | 20.00 | ---- |
| Stem, #301, blown, 4½ oz. low oyster cocktail | 10.00 | ---- |
| Stem, #301, blown, 5 oz., juice | 12.00 | ---- |
| Stem, #301, blown, 6 oz., sherbet | 12.00 | ---- |
| Stem, #301, blown, 9 oz., water | 12.00 | ---- |
| Stem, #301, blown, 12 oz., tea | 15.00 | ---- |
| Stem, 3 oz., wine, molded | 18.00 | 35.00 |
| Stem, 3½ oz., cocktail, molded | 18.00 | 35.00 |
| Stem, 4½ oz., claret molded | 15.00 | 30.00 |
| Stem, 4½ oz., fruit cocktail, molded | 12.00 | 20.00 |
| Stem, 5 oz., low sherbet, molded | 12.00 | 20.00 |
| Stem, 7 oz., tall sherbet, molded | 13.00 | 27.00 |
| Stem, 10 oz., water, molded | 20.00 | 32.50 |
| Sugar, sev. styles | 7.00 | 12.50 |
| Sugar, indiv. | 7.00 | 12.00 |
| Tray, for sugar & creamer | 7.00 | 10.00 |
| Tray, 6", oval | 10.00 | 17.50 |
| Tumbler, 2 oz., flat, molded | 7.00 | 12.00 |
| Tumbler, 3 oz., ftd. molded | 10.00 | 16.00 |
| Tumbler, 5 oz., ftd., molded | 12.00 | 18.00 |
| Tumbler, 5 oz., flat, molded | 10.00 | 17.50 |
| Tumbler, #300, 5 oz., ftd. juice | 12.00 | 18.00 |
| Tumbler, 9 oz., straight side, molded | 12.00 | 18.00 |
| Tumbler, 10 oz., ftd., molded | 14.00 | 27.50 |
| Tumbler, 12 oz., ftd., molded | 15.00 | 30.00 |
| Tumbler, 12 oz., flat, molded | 12.00 | 30.00 |
| Tumbler, 12 oz., straight side, molded | 12.00 | 30.00 |
| Tumbler, #310, 12 oz., flat tea | 20.00 | 40.00 |
| Vase, 5", ivy bowl | 30.00 | 42.50 |
| Vase, 6" | 35.00 | 67.50 |
| Vase, 7½" | 25.00 | 55.00 |
| Vase, 8", ivy bowl | 40.00 | 77.50 |
| Vase, 9½" | 45.00 | 85.00 |

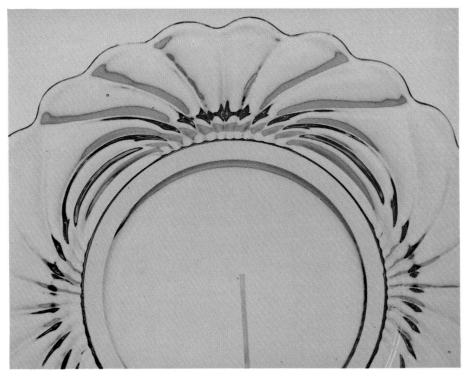

# CHANTILLY, Cambridge Glass Company, late 1940's · Early 1950's

Color: Crystal

Who was it, the 'Big Bopper', who sang of Chantilly lace and a pretty face in the rock 'n roll tune of the late 1950's?

Chantilly lace was very popular among the brides of this era; no doubt, Cambridge was cognizant of that when they produced this pattern, though strictly speaking, the exquisite lace of Chantilly, France, was black rather than white bridal lace.

Some collectors have trouble distinguishing between Chantilly and Elaine, another Cambridge pattern. (You'll notice someone suffered from that malady at the photography session as there's a Chantilly creamer and sugar in the Elaine set up.) Chantilly scrolls are horizontal, running east and west on the pieces. Elaine's scrolls droop in a catty cornered fashion.

| | Crystal | | Crystal |
|---|---|---|---|
| Bowl, 7", bonbon, 2 hand. ftd. | 15.00 | Stem, #3600, 4½ oz. low oyster cocktail . | 15.00 |
| Bowl, 7", relish/pickle, 2 pt. | 17.50 | Stem, #3600, 7 oz. tall sherbet | 17.50 |
| Bowl, 7", relish or pickle | 17.50 | Stem, #3600, 7 oz., low sherbet | 15.00 |
| Bowl, 9", celery/relish, 3 pt. | 20.00 | Stem, #3600, 10 oz., water | 19.50 |
| Bowl, 10", 4 ftd. flared | 25.00 | Stem, #3625, 1 oz., cordial | 27.50 |
| Bowl, 11", tab hand. | 22.50 | Stem, #3625, 3 oz., cocktail | 22.50 |
| Bowl, 11½", tab hand. ftd. | 27.50 | Stem, #3625, 4½ oz., claret | 22.50 |
| Bowl, 12", celery/relish, 3 pt. | 27.50 | Stem, #3625, 4½ oz., low oyster cocktail . | 15.00 |
| Bowl, 12", 4 ftd. flared | 27.50 | Stem, #3625, 7 oz., low sherbet | 15.00 |
| Bowl, 12", 4 ftd. oval | 32.50 | Stem, #3625, 7 oz., tall sherbet | 17.50 |
| Bowl, 12", celery/relish, 5 pt. | 29.50 | Stem, #3625, 10 oz., water | 22.50 |
| Butter w/cover | 125.00 | Stem, #3775, 1 oz., cordial | 27.50 |
| Candlestick, 5" | 17.50 | Stem, #3775, 2½ oz., wine | 23.50 |
| Candlestick, 6", 2-lite "fleur de lis" | 26.00 | Stem, #3775, 3 oz., cocktail | 25.00 |
| Candlestick, 6", 3-lite | 30.00 | Stem, #3775, 4½ oz., claret | 22.50 |
| Candy box, w/cover, footed | 100.00 | Stem, #3775, 4½ oz., oyster cocktail | 15.00 |
| Candy box w/cover, rnd. | 40.00 | Stem, #3775, 6 oz., low sherbet | 15.00 |
| Cocktail icer, 2 pc. | 27.50 | Stem, #3775, 6 oz., tall sherbet | 17.50 |
| Comport, 5½" | 25.00 | Stem, #3779, 1 oz., cordial | 32.50 |
| Comport, 5 3/8", blown | 32.50 | Stem, #3779, 2½ oz., wine | 25.00 |
| Creamer | 11.50 | Stem, #3779, 3 oz. cocktail | 22.50 |
| Creamer, indiv. #3900 scalloped edge | 10.00 | Stem, #3779, 4½ oz. claret | 22.50 |
| Cup | 12.50 | Stem, #3779, 4½ oz., low oyster cocktail . | 15.00 |
| Decanter, ftd. | 125.00 | Stem, #3779, 6 oz. tall sherbet | 17.50 |
| Hurricane lamp, candlestick base | 60.00 | Stem, #3779, 6 oz. low sherbet | 15.00 |
| Hurricane lamp, keyhole base w/prisms . | 75.00 | Stem, #3779, 9 oz., water | 19.50 |
| Ice bucket w/chrome handle | 52.50 | Sugar | 11.50 |
| Mayonnaise, (sherbet type bowl w/ladle) . | 22.50 | Sugar, indiv. #3900 scalloped edge | 10.00 |
| Mayonnaise div. w/liner & 2 ladles | 27.50 | Tumbler, #3600, 5 oz., ftd. juice | 13.50 |
| Mayonnaise w/liner & ladle | 25.00 | Tumbler, #3600, 12 oz., ftd. tea | 17.50 |
| Oil, 6 oz., hand. w/stopper | 37.50 | Tumbler, #3625, 5 oz., ftd. juice | 13.50 |
| Pitcher, ball | 95.00 | Tumbler, #3625, 10 oz., ftd. water | 15.00 |
| Pitcher, Daulton | 135.00 | Tumbler, #3625, 12 oz., ftd tea | 17.50 |
| Pitcher, upright | 115.00 | Tumbler, #3775, 5 oz., ftd. juice | 13.50 |
| Plate, 6½", bread/butter | 6.50 | Tumbler, #3775, 10 oz., ftd. water | 15.00 |
| Plate, 8", salad | 12.50 | Tumbler, #3775, 12 oz., ftd. tea | 17.50 |
| Plate, 8", tab hand., ftd. bonbon | 15.00 | Tumbler, #3779, 5 oz., ftd. juice | 13.50 |
| Plate, 10½", dinner | 30.00 | Tumbler, #3779, 12 oz., ftd. tea | 17.50 |
| Plate, 12", 4 ftd. service | 22.50 | Tumbler, 13 oz. | 17.50 |
| Plate, 13", 4 ftd. plate | 30.00 | Vase, 5", globe | 25.00 |
| Plate, 13½", tab hand. cake | 30.00 | Vase, 6", high ftd. flower | 17.50 |
| Plate, 14", torte | 30.00 | Vase, 8", high ftd. flower | 20.00 |
| Salt & pepper, pr. | 22.50 | Vase, 9", keyhole base | 25.00 |
| Saucer | 2.50 | Vase, 10", bud | 20.00 |
| Stem, #3600, 1 oz., cordial | 27.50 | Vase, 11", ftd. flower | 30.00 |
| Stem, #3600, 2½ oz. cocktail | 23.50 | Vase, 11", ped. ftd. flower | 35.00 |
| Stem, #3600, 2½ oz. wine | 25.00 | Vase, 12", keyhole base | 32.50 |
| Stem, #3600, 4½ oz. claret | 22.50 | Vase, 13", ftd. flower | 40.00 |

Note: See Pages 150-153 for stem identification.

# CHINTZ #1401 (Empress Blank) and CHINTZ #3389 (Duquesne Blank), A.H. Heisey Co., 1931-1938

Colors: Crystal, "Sahara" yellow, "Moongleam" green, "Flamingo" pink, and "Alexandrite" orchid.

Though this pattern also has the delicate butterflies and the tiny birds on branches that Heisey's other Chintz pattern #3389, Duquesne blank, has, they attempted to make this design more formal encompassing the floral basket with a ribbon type scroll. Thus, this Chintz etching #450½, has less freedom, but a more ordered, classic appeal.

Both patterns are pictured here so you can tell the difference.

|  | Crystal | Sahara |
|---|---|---|
| Bowl, finger #4107 | 7.00 | 12.00 |
| Bowl, 5½", ft. preserve, hand | 14.00 | 25.00 |
| Bowl, 6", ftd. mint | 17.00 | 30.00 |
| Bowl, 6", ftd., 2 hand. jelly | 15.00 | 30.00 |
| Bowl, 7½", Nasturtium | 16.00 | 29.00 |
| Bowl, 7", triplex relish | 16.00 | 28.00 |
| Bowl, 8½", ftd., 2 hand. floral | 32.00 | 60.00 |
| Bowl, 11", dolp. ft. floral | 35.00 | 70.00 |
| Bowl, 13", 2 part, pickle & olive | 15.00 | 25.00 |
| Comport, 7", oval | 35.00 | 70.00 |
| Creamer, 3 dolp. ftd. | 18.00 | 40.00 |
| Grapefruit, ftd. #3389 Duquesne | 20.00 | 35.00 |
| Mayonnaise, 5½", dolp. ft. | 35.00 | 65.00 |
| Oil, 4 oz. | 35.00 | 95.00 |
| Pitcher, 3 pint, dolp. ft. | 65.00 | 145.00 |
| Plate, 6", square bread | 6.00 | 15.00 |
| Plate, 7", square salad | 8.00 | 18.00 |
| Plate, 8", square luncheon | 10.00 | 22.00 |
| Plate, 10½", square dinner | 25.00 | 55.00 |
| Platter, 14", oval | 25.00 | 40.00 |
| Stem, #3389, Duquesne, 1 oz., cordial | 65.00 | 130.00 |
| Stem, #3389, 2½ oz., wine | 17.50 | 40.00 |
| Stem, #3389, 3 oz., cocktail | 15.00 | 32.50 |
| Stem, #3389, 4 oz., claret | 17.50 | 35.00 |
| Stem, #3389, 4 oz., oyster cocktail | 10.00 | 20.00 |
| Stem, #3389, 5 oz., parfait | 12.00 | 25.00 |
| Stem, #3389, 5 oz., saucer champagne | 11.00 | 22.50 |
| Stem, #3389, 5 oz., sherbet | 8.00 | 17.50 |
| Stem, #3389, 9 oz., water | 15.00 | 30.00 |
| Sugar, 3 dolp. ft. | 18.00 | 40.00 |
| Tray, 10", celery | 14.00 | 25.00 |
| Tray, 12", sq., ctr. hand. sandwich | 35.00 | 60.00 |
| Tray, 13", celery | 17.00 | 26.00 |
| Tumbler, #3389, 5 oz., ftd. juice | 10.00 | 20.00 |
| Tumbler, #3389, 8 oz., soda | 11.00 | 22.00 |
| Tumbler, #3389, 10 oz., ftd. water | 12.00 | 23.00 |
| Tumbler, #3389, 12 oz., iced tea | 13.00 | 25.00 |
| Vase, 9", dolp. ft. | 60.00 | 100.00 |

# CLEO, Cambridge Glass Company, introduced 1930

Colors: Pink, green, blue, amber

|  | All Colors |
|---|---|
| Basket, 7", 2 hand., (upturned sides) DECAGON | 15.00 |
| Basket, 11", 2 hand. (upturned sides) DECAGON blank | 25.00 |
| Bouillon cup w/saucer, 2 hand. DECAGON | 20.00 |
| Bowl, 2 pt. relish | 17.50 |
| Bowl, 5½", 2 hand., bonbon DECAGON | 15.00 |
| Bowl, 6", 4 ft. comport | 25.00 |
| Bowl, 6", cereal DECAGON | 12.00 |
| Bowl, 6½", 2 hand., bonbon DECAGON | 15.00 |
| Bowl, 8½" | 20.00 |
| Bowl, 8½", 2 hand. DECAGON | 22.00 |
| Bowl, 9", pickle DECAGON | 15.00 |
| Bowl, 9½", oval veg. DECAGON | 27.50 |
| Bowl, 10", 2 hand. DECAGON | 17.50 |
| Bowl, 11", oval | 24.00 |
| Bowl, 11½", oval | 25.00 |
| Bowl, cream soup w/saucer, 2 hand. DECAGON | 20.00 |
| Bowl, finger w/liner #3077 | 20.00 |
| Bowl, finger w/liner #3115 | 20.00 |
| Candlestick, 1-lite | 22.50 |
| Candlestick, 2-lite | 27.50 |
| Candy box | 39.50 |
| Comport, 7", tall #3115 | 35.00 |
| Creamer, ftd. DECAGON | 15.00 |
| Cup, DECAGON | 15.00 |
| Gravy boat w/liner plate, DECAGON | 52.50 |
| Ice pail | 57.50 |
| Mayonnaise w/liner & ladle, DECAGON | 35.00 |
| Oil, 6 oz., w/stopper, DECAGON | 50.00 |
| Pitcher w/cover, 22 oz. | 77.50 |
| Pitcher w/cover, 63 oz. #3077 | 100.00 |
| Pitcher w/cover, 68 oz. | 125.00 |
| Plate, 7" | 11.50 |
| Plate, 7", 2 hand. DECAGON | 12.50 |
| Plate, 9½", dinner, DECAGON | 22.50 |
| Plate, 11", 2 hand. DECAGON | 20.00 |
| Saucer, DECAGON | 3.00 |
| Stem, #3077, 2½ oz., cocktail | 22.00 |
| Stem, #3077, 6 oz., low sherbet | 12.00 |
| Stem, #3077, 6 oz., tall sherbet | 15.00 |
| Stem, #3077, 9 oz. | 20.00 |
| Stem, #3115, 3½ oz. | 22.00 |
| Stem, #3115, 6 oz., fruit | 10.00 |
| Stem, #3115, 6 oz., low sherbet | 12.00 |
| Stem, #3115, 6 oz., tall sherbet | 15.00 |
| Stem, #3115, 9 oz. | 20.00 |
| Sugar, ftd. DECAGON | 15.00 |
| Tray, 12", oval service DECAGON | 22.50 |
| Tumbler, #3077, 5 oz., ftd. | 15.00 |
| Tumbler, #3077, 8 oz. ftd. | 17.50 |
| Tumbler, #3077, 10 oz., ftd | 20.00 |
| Tumbler, #3077, 12 oz., ftd. | 22.00 |
| Tumbler, #3115, 5 oz., ftd. | 15.00 |
| Tumbler, #3115, 8 oz., ftd. | 17.50 |
| Tumbler, #3115, 10 oz., ftd. | 20.00 |
| Tumbler, #3115, 12 oz., ftd. | 22.00 |
| Tumbler, 12 oz. flat | 20.00 |

Note: See Pages 150-153 for stem identification.

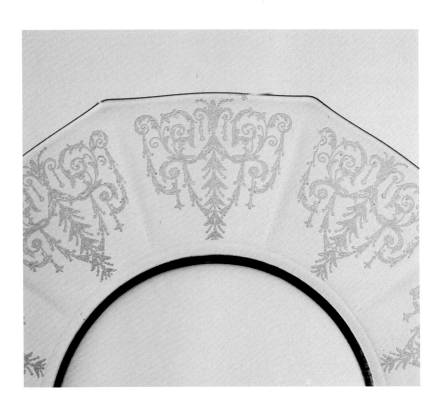

# COLONY, Line #2412, Fostoria Glass Company, Late 1920's-1970's

Colors: Crystal, some yellow, blue, green

Fostoria first introduced this line under another name in the late 1920's, making mostly huge serving pieces and console sets in colors as well as crystal. They later abandoned this idea, only to take it up again in the late 30's inder the new name Colony and making it in crystal only. This is a very graceful pattern which sets a spectacular table.

|                                           | Crystal |
|-------------------------------------------|--------:|
| Bowl, ftd. almond                         | 4.00    |
| Bowl, 4½", rnd.                           | 5.00    |
| Bowl, 4¾", finger                         | 6.50    |
| Bowl, 5", rnd.                            | 6.00    |
| Bowl, 5½", sq.                            | 5.50    |
| Bowl, 5¾", hi ft.                         | 7.50    |
| Bowl, 7", olive, oblong                   | 7.50    |
| Bowl, 8", hand.                           | 10.00   |
| Bowl, 9", low ft.                         | 15.00   |
| Bowl, 9", hi ft.                          | 15.00   |
| Bowl, 9½", pickle                         | 10.00   |
| Bowl, 10½", low ft.                       | 20.00   |
| Bowl, 10½", hi ft.                        | 22.50   |
| Bowl, 11½", celery                        | 12.00   |
| Candlestick, 3½",                         | 7.50    |
| Candlestick, 7½", w/8 prisms              | 20.00   |
| Candlestick, 9¾",                         | 12.50   |
| Candlestick, 14½", w/10 prisms            | 25.00   |
| Candy w/cover, 6½"                        | 20.00   |
| Cheese compote w/cracker plate            | 20.00   |
| Cream soup, ftd.                          | 8.00    |
| Creamer, indiv.                           | 8.00    |
| Creamer, 3¾"                              | 9.00    |
| Comport, 4"                               | 11.00   |
| Cup, ftd.                                 | 5.00    |
| Stem, 3 3/8", oyster cocktail (4 oz.)     | 8.50    |
| Stem, 3 5/8", sherbet (5 oz.)             | 9.00    |
| Stem, 4¼", wine (3¼ oz.)                  | 10.00   |
| Stem, 4", cocktail (3½ oz.)               | 9.00    |
| Stem, 5¼", (9 oz.) goblet                 | 12.00   |
| Mayonnaise w/liner                        | 12.50   |
| Oil w/stopper                             | 22.50   |
| Pitcher, 64 oz.                           | 35.00   |
| Plate, ctr. hand sand.                    | 20.00   |
| Plate, 6"                                 | 2.50    |
| Plate, 7"                                 | 3.00    |
| Plate, 8"                                 | 3.50    |
| Plate, 9"                                 | 4.50    |
| Plate, 10"                                | 7.50    |
| Plate, 12", ftd. salver                   | 15.00   |
| Plate, 13", torte                         | 13.00   |
| Salt, indiv.                              | 5.50    |
| Salt & pepper, pr.                        | 12.50   |
| Saucer                                    | 1.50    |
| Sugar, indiv.                             | 5.00    |
| Sugar, 3½"                                | 7.50    |
| Tray for indiv. sug./cream                | 7.00    |
| Tumbler, 5 oz.                            | 8.00    |
| Tumbler, 9 oz.                            | 10.00   |
| Tumbler, 4½", 5 oz., ftd.                 | 9.50    |
| Tumbler, 5¾", 12 oz., ftd.                | 11.50   |
| Tumbler, 12 oz.                           | 12.00   |
| Vase, 8"                                  | 17.50   |

# CRYSTOLITE, Blank #1503, A. H. Heisey & Co.

Colors: Crystal, Zircon/Limelight, Sahara and rare in Amber

| | Crystal |
|---|---|
| Ash tray, 3½", square | 3.00 |
| Ash tray, 4½", square | 3.50 |
| Ash tray, 5", w/book match | 25.00 |
| Ash tray (coaster), 4", rnd. | 4.00 |
| Basket, 6", hand. | 300.00 |
| Bonbon, 7", shell | 17.00 |
| Bonbon, 7½", 2 hand. | 15.00 |
| Bottle, 1 qt. rye, #107 stopper | 125.00 |
| Bottle, 4 oz. bitters w/short tube | 65.00 |
| Bottle, 4 oz. cologne w/#108 stopper | 50.00 |
| W/drip stop | 145.00 |
| Bottle, syrup w/drip & cut top | 50.00 |
| Bowl, 7½ quart punch | 75.00 |
| Bowl, 2", indiv. swan nut (or ash tray) | 25.00 |
| Bowl, 3", indiv. nut, hand. | 15.00 |
| Bowl, 4½", dessert (or nappy) | 5.00 |
| Bowl, 5", preserve | 12.00 |
| Bowl, 5", thousand island dressing, ruffled top | 15.00 |
| Bowl, 5½", dessert | 7.00 |
| Bowl, 6", oval jelly, 4 ft. | 12.00 |
| Bowl, 6", preserve, 2 hand. | 12.00 |
| Bowl, 7", shell praline | 25.00 |
| Bowl, 8", dessert (sauce) | 12.00 |
| Bowl, 8", 2 pt. conserve, hand. | 15.00 |
| Bowl, 9", leaf pickle | 15.00 |
| Bowl, 10", salad, rnd. | 22.00 |
| Bowl, 11", w/attached mayonnaise (chip 'n dip) | 45.00 |
| Bowl, 12", gardenia, shallow | 30.00 |
| Bowl, 13", oval floral, deep | 30.00 |
| Candle block, 1 lite, sq. | 12.00 |
| Candle block, 1 lite, swirl | 12.00 |
| Candlestick, 1 lite, ftd. | 12.00 |
| Candlestick, 1 lite, w/#4233, 5", vase | 22.00 |
| Candlestick, 2 lite | 20.00 |
| Candlestick, 2 lite, bobeche & 10 "D" prisms | 25.00 |
| Candlestick sans vase, 3 lite | 15.00 |
| Candlestick w/#4233, 5", vase, 3 lite | 25.00 |
| Candy, 6½", swan | 35.00 |
| Candy box w/cover, 5½" | 40.00 |
| Candy box w/cover, 7" | 50.00 |
| Cheese, 5½", ftd. | 6.00 |
| Cigarette box w/cover, 4" | 15.00 |
| Cigarette box w/cover, 4½" | 17.00 |
| Cigarette holder, ftd. | 15.00 |
| Cigarette holder, oval | 10.00 |
| Cigarette holder, rnd. | 10.00 |
| Cigarette lighter | 10.00 |
| Coaster, 4" | 6.00 |
| Cocktail shaker, 1 quart w/#1 strainer; #86 stopper | 125.00 |
| Comport, 5", ftd., deep | 20.00 |
| Creamer, indiv. | 10.00 |
| Cup | 6.00 |
| Cup, punch or custard | 10.00 |

| | Crystal |
|---|---|
| Hurricane block, 1 lite, sq. | 25.00 |
| Hurricane block w/#4061, 10", plain globe, 1 lite, sq. | 50.00 |
| Ice tub w/silver plate handle | 75.00 |
| Jam jar w/cover | 35.00 |
| Ladle, glass | 25.00 |
| Ladle, plastic | 7.50 |
| Mayonnaise, 5½", shell, 3 ft. | 30.00 |
| Mayonnaise, 6", oval, hand. | 20.00 |
| Mayonnaise ladle | 7.00 |
| Mustard & cover | 30.00 |
| Oil bottle, 3 oz. | 35.00 |
| Oil bottle w/stopper, 2 oz. | 25.00 |
| Oval creamer, sugar w/tray, set | 45.00 |
| Pitcher, ½ gallon, ice, blown | 55.00 |
| Pitcher, 2 quart swan, ice lip | 650.00 |
| Plate, 7", salad | 7.00 |
| Plate, 7", shell | 12.00 |
| Plate, 7", underline for 1000 island dressing bowl | 7.00 |
| Plate, 7½", coupe | 20.00 |
| Plate, 8", oval, mayonnaise liner | 9.00 |
| Plate, 8½", salad | 15.00 |
| Plate, 10½", service | 35.00 |
| Plate, 11", ftd. cake salver | 150.00 |
| Plate, 11", torte | 20.00 |
| Plate, 12", sand. | 20.00 |
| Plate, 14", sand. | 25.00 |
| Plate, 14", torte | 25.00 |
| Plate, 20", buffet or punch liner | 35.00 |
| Puff box w/cover, 4¾" | 45.00 |
| Salad dressing set, 3 pc. | 25.00 |
| Salt & pepper, pr. | 25.00 |
| Saucer | 5.00 |
| Stem, 1 oz., cordial, w.o., blown | 60.00 |
| Stem, 3½ oz., cocktail, w.o., blown | 20.00 |
| Stem, 3½ oz., claret, wide optic, blown | 25.00 |
| Stem, 3½ oz., oyster cocktail, w.o. blown | 20.00 |
| Stem, 6 oz., sherbet/saucer champagne | 10.00 |
| Stem, 10 oz., w. optic, blown | 15.00 |
| Sugar, indiv. | 10.00 |
| Tray, 5½", oval, liner indiv. creamer/sugar | 30.00 |
| Tray, 9", 4 pt. leaf relish | 20.00 |
| Tray, 10", 5 pt., rnd. relish | 15.00 |
| Tray, 12", 3 pt. relish | 20.00 |
| Tray, 12", rect., celery | 20.00 |
| Tray, 12", rect., celery/olive | 20.00 |
| Tumbler, 5 oz., ftd., juice, w.o., blown | 15.00 |
| Tumbler, 10 oz., pressed | 15.00 |
| Tumbler, 10 oz., iced tea, w.o. blown | 20.00 |
| Tumbler, 12 oz., ftd., iced tea, w.o., blown | 18.00 |
| Urn, 7", flower | 15.00 |
| Vase, 3", short stem | 15.00 |
| Vase, 6", ftd. | 15.00 |

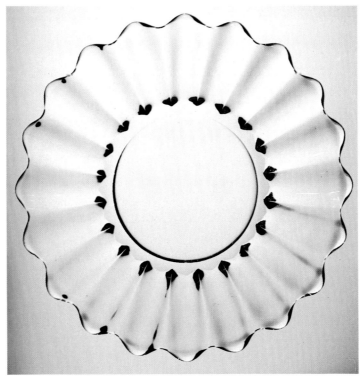

# "CUPID", Paden City Glass Company, 1930's

Colors: Pink, green, light blue

There very probably are more pieces to be found in this pattern than are listed here. Some readers have been kind enough to share the pieces they found with me so I could have this listing as complete as it is here. This past spring someone sent me a photograph of a candy dish. So, keep looking!

| | Pink, Blue, Green |
|---|---|
| Bowl, 8½", oval, ftd. | 30.00 |
| Bowl, 9¼", fruit, ftd. | 27.50 |
| Bowl, 9¼", ctr. hand. | 32.50 |
| Bowl, 11", console | 32.50 |
| Cake, 11¾", | 35.00 |
| Candlestick, 5" wide | 17.50 |
| Candy w/lid, ftd., 4¾", high | 37.50 |
| Candy w/lid, 3 pt. | 47.50 |
| Comport, 6¼" | 20.00 |
| Creamer, 4½", ftd. | 25.00 |
| Ice bucket, 6" | 47.50 |
| Ice tub, 4¾" | 38.50 |
| Mayonnaise, 6" diam./fits 8" plate | 37.50 |
| Plate, 10½" | 15.00 |
| Sugar, 4¼", ftd. | 25.00 |
| Tray, 10½", ctr. hand. | 27.50 |
| Tray, 10 7/8", oval, ftd. | 35.00 |
| Vase, 8¼", elliptical | 57.50 |

# DANCING GIRL, Morgantown Glass Works, Early 1930's

Colors: Blue, green, pink

This is a beautiful pattern; but thus far, not much of it has been seen. Hopefully, there's more out there to be found, it just hasn't been readily recognized until now.

|  | All Colors |
|---|---|
| Creamer | 25.00 |
| Sugar | 22.50 |
| Pitcher | 150.00 |
| Plate, 7½" | 12.50 |
| Stem, cocktail, (twisted or plain stem) | 25.00 |
| Tumbler, 4¾", 9 oz. | 22.50 |
| Tumbler, 5½", 12 oz. | 25.00 |
| Vase, 10", slender bud | 32.50 |

59

# DECAGON, Cambridge Glass Company, 1930's

Colors: Green, pink, red, cobalt blue, amber, Moonlight blue

| | Pastel Colors | Red, Cobalt Blue |
|---|---|---|
| Basket, 7", 2 hand. (upturned sides) | 12.00 | 20.00 |
| Bowl, bouillon w/liner | 7.50 | 12.50 |
| Bowl, cream soup w/liner | 9.00 | 15.00 |
| Bowl, 2½", indiv. almond | 10.00 | 17.50 |
| Bowl, 3¾", flat rim cranberry | 7.00 | 12.00 |
| Bowl, 3½", belled cranberry | 6.00 | 12.00 |
| Bowl, 5½", 2 hand. bonbon | 10.00 | 17.00 |
| Bowl, 5½", belled fruit | 5.50 | 10.00 |
| Bowl, 5¾", flat rim fruit | 6.00 | 11.00 |
| Bowl, 6", belled cereal | 7.00 | 12.50 |
| Bowl, 6", flat rim cereal | 6.00 | 11.00 |
| Bowl, 6", ftd. almond | 20.00 | 35.00 |
| Bowl, 6¼", 2 hand., bonbon | 10.00 | 17.00 |
| Bowl, 8½", flat rim soup "plate" | 8.00 | 15.00 |
| Bowl, 9", rnd. veg. | 12.50 | 20.00 |
| Bowl, 9", 2 pt. relish | 9.00 | 15.00 |
| Bowl, 9½", oval veg. | 12.00 | 22.00 |
| Bowl, 10", berry | 10.00 | 17.50 |
| Bowl, 10½", oval veg. | 14.00 | 25.00 |
| Bowl, 11", rnd. veg. | 14.00 | 27.00 |
| Bowl, 11", 2 pt. relish | 10.00 | 17.50 |
| Comport, 5¾" | 12.50 | 20.00 |
| Comport, 6½", low ft. | 15.00 | 25.00 |
| Comport, 7", tall | 17.50 | 27.50 |
| Creamer, ftd. | 9.00 | 20.00 |
| Creamer, scalloped edge | 8.00 | 18.00 |
| Creamer, lightning bolt handles | 6.00 | 10.00 |
| Creamer, tall, lg. ft. | 9.00 | 20.00 |
| Cup | 6.00 | 10.00 |
| French dressing bottle, "Oil/Vinegar" | 20.00 | 40.00 |
| Gravy boat w/2 hand. liner (like spouted cream soup) | 25.00 | 45.00 |
| Mayonnaise, 2 hand. w/2 hand. liner and ladle | 20.00 | 35.00 |
| Mayonnaise w/liner & ladle | 18.00 | 30.00 |
| Oil, 6 oz., tall, w/hand. & stopper | 22.50 | 37.50 |
| Plate, 6¼", bread/butter | 3.00 | 5.00 |
| Plate, 7", 2 hand. | 9.00 | 15.00 |
| Plate, 7½" | 4.00 | 10.00 |
| Plate, 8½", salad | 6.00 | 10.00 |
| Plate, 9½", dinner | 10.00 | 17.00 |
| Plate, 10", grill | 8.00 | 14.00 |
| Plate, 10", service | 8.50 | 16.00 |
| Plate, 12½", service | 9.00 | 17.50 |
| Salt dip, 1½", ftd. | 10.00 | 17.50 |
| Sauce boat & plate | 22.00 | 40.00 |
| Saucer | 1.00 | 2.50 |
| Sugar, lightning bolt handles | 5.00 | 9.00 |
| Sugar, ftd. | 8.00 | 18.00 |
| Sugar, scalloped edge | 7.00 | 17.50 |
| Sugar, tall, lg. ft. | 8.00 | 18.00 |
| Tray, 8", 2 hand., flat pickle | 10.00 | 17.00 |
| Tray, 9", pickle | 10.00 | 17.50 |
| Tray, 11", oval service | 8.00 | 15.00 |
| Tray, 11", celery | 10.00 | 20.00 |
| Tray, 12", oval service | 10.00 | 20.00 |
| Tray, 13", 2 hand. service | 20.00 | 30.00 |
| Tray, 15", oval service | 15.00 | 25.00 |

# DIANE, Cambridge Glass Company, 1934 - Early 1950's

Colors: Crystal, some pink, yellow, blue

It's a shame to do this to a beautiful pattern, but I can't resist. The way my wife remembers this pattern is by the scrolled center motif which she says reminds her of a cartoon mouse, complete with "ears" and big nose! Sorry about that Diane lovers.

A section of #3106 stems is listed but not priced. I have not seen any sold to ascertain price. The catalogue lists them as having been made. I include them here as a point of information only.

|  | Crystal |
|---|---|
| Basket, 6", 2 hand. ftd. | 16.00 |
| Bowl, #3106, finger w/liner | 20.00 |
| Bowl, #3122, finger w/liner | 20.00 |
| Bowl, #3400, cream soup w/liner | 22.00 |
| Bowl, 5", berry | 18.00 |
| Bowl, 5¼", 2 hand. bonbon | 18.00 |
| Bowl, 6", 2 hand. ftd. bonbon | 17.00 |
| Bowl, 6", 2 pt. relish | 18.00 |
| Bowl, 6", cereal | 17.50 |
| Bowl, 6½", 3 pt. relish | 18.00 |
| Bowl, 7", 2 hand. ftd. bonbon | 22.00 |
| Bowl, 7", 2 pt. relish | 20.00 |
| Bowl, 7", relish or pickle | 20.00 |
| Bowl, 9", 3 pt. celery & relish | 28.00 |
| Bowl, 9½", pickle (like corn) | 22.00 |
| Bowl, 10", 4 ft. flared | 32.00 |
| Bowl, 10", baker | 35.00 |
| Bowl, 11", 2 hand. | 35.00 |
| Bowl, 11", 4 ftd. | 38.00 |
| Bowl, 11½", tab hand., ftd. | 38.00 |
| Bowl, 12", 3 pt. celery & relish | 30.00 |
| Bowl, 12", 4 ft. | 40.00 |
| Bowl, 12", 4 ft. flared | 40.00 |
| Bowl, 12", 4 ft. oval | 42.00 |
| Bowl, 12", 4 ft. oval w/"ears" hand. | 47.00 |
| Bowl, 12", 5 pt. celery & relish | 32.50 |
| Butter, rnd. | 90.00 |
| Cabinet flask | 55.00 |
| Candelabrum, 2-lite, keyhole | 22.50 |
| Candelabrum, 3-lite, keyhole | 27.50 |
| Candlestick, 1-lite, keyhole | 17.50 |
| Candlestick, 5" | 17.50 |
| Candlestick, 6", 2-lite "fleur-de-lis" | 27.50 |
| Candlestick, 6", 3-lite | 32.50 |
| Candy box w/cover, rnd. | 50.00 |
| Cigarette urn | 30.00 |
| Cocktail shaker, glass top | 90.00 |
| Cocktail shaker, metal top | 55.00 |
| Cocktail icer, 2 pc. | 30.00 |
| Comport, 5½" | 20.00 |
| Comport, 5 3/8", blown | 32.00 |
| Creamer | 12.00 |

63

# DIANE, Cambridge Glass Company, 1934 · Early 1950's, (continued)

|  | Crystal |
|---|---|
| Creamer, indiv. #3500 (pie crust edge) | 12.00 |
| Creamer, indiv. #3900, scalloped edge | 12.00 |
| Creamer, scroll handle #3400 | 12.00 |
| Cup | 15.00 |
| Decanter, lg. ftd. | 125.00 |
| Decanter, short ft. cordial | 150.00 |
| Hurricane lamp, candlestick base | 80.00 |
| Hurricane lamp, keyhole base w/prisms | 90.00 |
| Ice bucket w/chrome hand. | 55.00 |
| Mayonnaise, div., w/liner & ladle | 27.50 |
| Mayonnaise (sherbet type w/ladle) | 25.00 |
| Mayonnaise w/liner, ladle | 25.00 |
| Oil, 6 oz. w/stopper | 35.00 |
| Pitcher, ball | 87.50 |
| Pitcher, Daulton | 140.00 |
| Pitcher, upright | 100.00 |
| Plate, 6", 2 hand. plate | 7.00 |
| Plate, 6", sq. bread/butter | 5.00 |
| Plate, 6½", bread/butter | 5.00 |
| Plate, 8", 2 hand. ftd. bonbon | 11.00 |
| Plate, 8", salad | 8.00 |
| Plate, 8½" | 8.00 |
| Plate, 10½", dinner | 40.00 |
| Plate, 12", 4 ft. service | 35.00 |
| Plate, 13", 4 ft. torte | 35.00 |
| Plate, 13½", 2 hand. | 28.00 |
| Plate, 14", torte | 38.00 |
| Platter, 13½" | 32.00 |
| Salt & pepper, ftd. w/glass tops, pr. | 30.00 |
| Salt & pepper, pr., flat | 27.00 |
| Saucer | 5.00 |
| Stem, #1066, 1 oz. cordial | 32.50 |
| Stem, #1066, 3 oz. cocktail | 16.00 |
| Stem, #1066, 3 oz., wine | 17.50 |
| Stem, #1066, 3½ oz. tall cocktail | 17.50 |
| Stem, #1066, 4½ oz., claret | 17.50 |
| Stem, #1066, 5 oz. oyster/cocktail | 12.00 |
| Stem, #1066, 7 oz. low sherbet | 11.50 |
| Stem, #1066, 7 oz. tall sherbet | 13.50 |
| Stem, #1066, 11 oz., water | 15.00 |
| Stem, #3106, ¾ oz. brandy | ---- |
| Stem, #3106, 1 oz. cordial | ---- |
| Stem, #3106, 1 oz., pousse cafe | --- |
| Stem, #3106, 2 oz., sherry | ---- |
| Stem, #3106, 2½ oz. wine | ---- |
| Stem, #3106, 2½ oz. creme de menthe | ---- |
| Stem, #3106, 3 oz. cocktail | ---- |
| Stem, #3106, 4½ oz. claret | ---- |

# DIANE, Cambridge Glass Company, 1934 - Early 1950's, (continued)

| | Crystal |
|---|---|
| Stem, #3106, 5 oz. oyster cocktail | ---- |
| Stem, #3106, 7 oz. tall sherbet | ---- |
| Stem, #3106, 7 oz. low sherbet | ---- |
| Stem, #3106, 9 oz. tall bowl goblet | ---- |
| Stem, #3106, 10 oz., low bowl goblet | ---- |
| Stem, #3122, 1 oz., cordial | 30.00 |
| Stem, #3122, 2½ oz., wine | 18.00 |
| Stem, #3122, 3 oz., cocktail | 14.00 |
| Stem, #3122, 4½ oz., claret | 19.00 |
| Stem, #3122, 4½ oz., oyster/cocktail | 15.00 |
| Stem, #3122, 7 oz., low sherbet | 11.00 |
| Stem, #3122, 7 oz., tall sherbet | 15.00 |
| Stem, #3122, 9 oz., water goblet | 18.00 |
| Sugar, indiv, #3500 (pie crust edge) | 12.00 |
| Sugar, indiv. #3900, scalloped edge | 12.00 |
| Sugar, scroll handle #3400 | 12.00 |
| Tumbler, 2½ oz. sham bottom | 22.00 |
| Tumbler, 5 oz. ft. juice | 25.00 |
| Tumbler, 5 oz. sham bottom | 25.00 |
| Tumbler, 7 oz., old fashioned w/sham bottom | 27.00 |
| Tumbler, 8 oz. ft. | 20.00 |
| Tumbler, 10 oz. sham bottom | 25.00 |
| Tumbler, 12 oz. sham bottom | 27.00 |
| Tumbler, 13 oz. | 27.00 |
| Tumbler, 14 oz. sham bottom | 30.00 |
| Tumbler, #1066, 3 oz. | 12.00 |
| Tumbler, #1066, 5 oz., juice | 10.00 |
| Tumbler, #1066, 9 oz., water | 11.00 |
| Tumbler, #1066, 12 oz., tea | 12.00 |
| Tumbler, #3106, 3 oz., ftd. | 12.50 |
| Tumbler, #3106, 5 oz., ftd., juice | 12.00 |
| Tumbler, #3106, 9 oz., ftd. water | 10.00 |
| Tumbler, #3106, 12 oz., ftd. tea | 11.00 |
| Tumbler, #3122, 2½ oz. | 13.50 |
| Tumbler, 3122, 5 oz., juice | 12.50 |
| Tumbler, #3122, 9 oz., water | 14.00 |
| Tumbler, #3122, 12 oz., tea | 16.00 |
| Tumbler, #3135, 2½ oz. ft. bar | 12.50 |
| Tumbler, #3135, 10 oz. ft. tumbler | 10.00 |
| Tumbler, #3135, 12 oz. ft. tea | 11.00 |
| Vase, 5", globe | 24.00 |
| Vase, 6", high ft. flower | 22.00 |
| Vase, 8", high ft. flower | 22.00 |
| Vase, 9", keyhole base | 35.00 |
| Vase, 10", bud | 20.00 |
| Vase, 11", flower | 32.50 |
| Vase, 11", ped. ft. flower | 38.00 |
| Vase, 12", keyhole base | 40.00 |
| Vase, 13", flower | 45.00 |

Note: See Page 150-153 for stem identification.

# ELAINE, Cambridge Glass Company, 1934 - 1950's

Color: Crystal

A late 1940's magazine advertisement describes this pattern as being "exquisite as bridal lace" and shows a bride beneath a frothy bridal veil admiring this crystal.

An entire listing of #3104 stems has not been priced because I have not seen any sell. The catalogues list them as having been made; so, I include the listing here for your information.

The creamer and sugar in the picture, although the same shape, are Chantilly pattern rather than Elaine.

| | Crystal | | Crystal |
|---|---|---|---|
| Basket, 6", 2 hand. (upturned sides) .. | 15.00 | Stem, #1402, 1 oz., cordial .......... | 27.50 |
| Bowl, #3104, finger w/liner ........ | 20.00 | Stem, #1402, 3 oz., wine............ | 22.00 |
| Bowl, 5¼", 2 hand. bonbon ........ | 12.50 | Stem, #1402, 3½ oz., cocktail ....... | 20.00 |
| Bowl, 6", 2 hand., ftd. bonbon ....... | 15.00 | Stem, #1402, 5 oz., claret .......... | 20.00 |
| Bowl, 6", 2 pt. relish............. | 15.00 | Stem, #1402, low sherbet .......... | 14.00 |
| Bowl, 6½", 3 pt. relish ........... | 14.00 | Stem, #1402, tall sherbet .......... | 15.00 |
| Bowl, 7", 2 pt. pickle or relish ....... | 15.50 | Stem, #1402, goblet .............. | 20.00 |
| Bowl, 7", ftd. tab hand. bonbon ...... | 18.00 | Stem, #3104, (very tall stems), ¾ oz., | |
| Bowl, 7", pickle or relish .......... | 17.50 | brandy ...................... | ---- |
| Bowl, 9½", pickle (like corn dish)..... | 20.00 | Stem, #3104, 1 oz., cordial .......... | ---- |
| Bowl, 9", 3 pt. celery & relish ....... | 20.00 | Stem, #3104, 1 oz., pousse-cafe ...... | ---- |
| Bowl, 10", 4 ftd. flared ........... | 25.00 | Stem, #3104, 2 oz., sherry ......... | ---- |
| Bowl, 11", tab hand................ | 22.50 | Stem, #3104, 2½ oz., creme de menthe | ---- |
| Bowl, 11½", ftd., tab handle ....... | 27.50 | Stem, #3104, 3 oz., wine........... | ---- |
| Bowl, 12", 3 pt. celery & relish ...... | 27.50 | Stem, #3104, 3½ oz., cocktail ....... | ---- |
| Bowl, 12", 4 ftd. flared ........... | 27.50 | Stem, #3104, 4½ oz., claret ........ | ---- |
| Bowl, 12", 4 ftd. oval, "ear" handles .. | 30.00 | Stem, #3104, 5 oz., roemer.......... | ---- |
| Bowl, 12", 5 pt. celery & relish ...... | 30.00 | Stem, #3104, 5 oz., tall hock ........ | ---- |
| Candlestick, 5" .............. | 17.50 | Stem, #3104, 7 oz., tall sherbet ...... | ---- |
| Candlestick, 6", 2-lite ............ | 25.00 | Stem, #3104, 9 oz., goblet ......... | ---- |
| Candlestick, 6", 3-lite ............ | 30.00 | Stem, #3121, 1 oz., cordial .......... | 32.50 |
| Candy box w/cover, rnd. .......... | 40.00 | Stem, #3121, 3 oz., cocktail ........ | 22.00 |
| Cocktail icer, 2 pc. ............ | 27.50 | Stem, #3121, 3½ oz., wine ......... | 22.00 |
| Comport, 5½" ................. | 25.00 | Stem, #3121, 4½ oz., claret ........ | 20.00 |
| Comport, 5 3/8", #3500 stem ....... | 35.00 | Stem, #3121, 4½ oz., oyster cocktail, | |
| Comport, 5 3/8", blown .......... | 32,50 | low stem .................. | 15.00 |
| Creamer..................... | 11.00 | Stem, #3121, 5 oz., parfait, low stem .. | 25.00 |
| Creamer, indiv. ................. | 10.00 | Stem, #3121, 6 oz., low sherbet ...... | 15.00 |
| Cup ..................... | 15.00 | Stem, #3121, 6 oz., tall sherbet ...... | 17.50 |
| Decanter, lg., ftd. ............ | 100.00 | Stem, #3121, 10 oz., water ......... | 20.00 |
| Hurricane lamp, candlestick base..... | 60.00 | Stem, #3500, 1 oz., cordial .......... | 30.00 |
| Hurricane lamp, keyhole ft. w/prisms . | 75.00 | Stem, #3500, 2½ oz., wine ......... | 20.00 |
| Ice bucket w/chrome handle ........ | 52.50 | Stem, #3500, 3 oz., cocktail ........ | 20.00 |
| Mayonnaise, (cupped "sherbet" | | Stem, #3500, 4½ oz., claret ........ | 20.00 |
| w/ladle) .................... | 22.00 | Stem, #3500, 4½ oz., oyster cocktail, | |
| Mayonnaise (div. bowl, liner, 2 ladles) . | 30.00 | low stem.................. | 14.00 |
| Mayonnaise w/liner & ladle ........ | 25.00 | Stem, #3500, 5 oz., parfait, low stem .. | 22.00 |
| Oil, 6 oz., hand. w/stopper ......... | 37.50 | Stem, #3500, 7 oz., low sherbet ..... | 13.00 |
| Pitcher, ball................. | 75.00 | Stem, #3500, 7 oz., tall sherbet ..... | 15.00 |
| Pitcher, Daulton ............... | 125.00 | Stem, #3500, 10 oz., water ......... | 18.00 |
| Pitcher, upright ............... | 85.00 | Sugar ..................... | 10.00 |
| Plate, 6", 2 hand. ............. | 10.00 | Sugar, indiv. ................. | 10.00 |
| Plate, 6½", bread/butter .......... | 6.50 | Tumbler, #1402, 9 oz., ftd. water ..... | 16.00 |
| Plate, 8", 2 hand., ftd. ........... | 15.00 | Tumbler, #1402, 12 oz., tea ........ | 18.00 |
| Plate, 8", salad ............... | 12.50 | Tumbler, #1402, 12 oz., tall ftd. tea ... | 18.00 |
| Plate, 8", tab hand. bonbon ....... | 15.00 | Tumbler, #3121, 5 oz., ftd. juice ..... | 18.00 |
| Plate, 10½", dinner ............. | 25.00 | Tumbler, #3121, 10 oz., ftd. water .... | 20.00 |
| Plate, 11½", 2 hand., ringed "tally ho" | | Tumbler, #3121, 12 oz., ftd. tea ...... | 22.00 |
| sand. ..................... | 20.00 | Tumbler, #3500, 5 oz., ftd. juice ..... | 16.00 |
| Plate, 12", 4 ftd. service .......... | 25.00 | Tumbler, #3500, 10 oz., ftd. water .... | 18.00 |
| Plate, 13", 4 ftd. torte ............ | 30.00 | Tumbler, #3500, 12 oz., ftd. tea ..... | 20.00 |
| Plate, 13½", tab handle cake ....... | 30.00 | Vase, 6", ftd.................. | 17.50 |
| Plate, 14", torte .............. | 30.00 | Vase, 8", ftd................... | 20.00 |
| Salt & pepper, pr. ............ | 22.50 | Vase, 9", keyhole, ftd. ............ | 25.00 |
| Saucer ................... | 3.00 | | |

Note: See Pages 150-153 for stem identification.

# EMPRESS, Blank # 1401, A. H. Heisey & Co.

Colors: Crystal, "Flamingo" pink, "Sahara" yellow, "Moongleam" green, cobalt and "Alexandrite"; some Tangerine

| | Crystal | Flam. | Sahara | Moon. | Cobalt | Alexan. |
|---|---|---|---|---|---|---|
| Ash tray | 25.00 | 40.00 | 50.00 | 60.00 | 125.00 | 200.00 |
| Bonbon, 6" | 10.00 | 15.00 | 17.00 | 20.00 | | |
| Bowl, cream soup | 10.00 | 15.00 | 18.00 | 22.00 | | |
| Bowl, cream soup w/sq. liner | 15.00 | 20.00 | 25.00 | 35.00 | | 160.00 |
| Bowl, frappe w/center | 15.00 | 25.00 | 35.00 | 45.00 | | |
| Bowl, nut, dolphin ftd., indiv. | 15.00 | 22.00 | 25.00 | 30.00 | | 75.00 |
| Bowl, 4½", nappy | 5.00 | 8.00 | 10.00 | 12.00 | | |
| Bowl, 5", preserve, 2 hand. | 10.00 | 15.00 | 20.00 | 25.00 | | |
| Bowl, 6", ftd., jelly, 2 hand. | 12.00 | 17.00 | 23.00 | 27.00 | | |
| Bowl, 6", dolp. ftd. mint | 12.00 | 17.00 | 22.00 | 27.00 | | 85.00 |
| Bowl, 6", grapefruit, sq. top, grnd. bottom | 7.00 | 10.00 | 15.00 | 20.00 | | |
| Bowl, 6½", oval lemon w/cover | 35.00 | 50.00 | 60.00 | 65.00 | | |
| Bowl, 7", 3 part relish, triplex | 12.00 | 18.00 | 22.00 | 25.00 | | |
| Bowl, 7", 3 part relish, ctr. hand. | 15.00 | 21.00 | 25.00 | 28.00 | | |
| Bowl, 7½", dolp. ftd. nappy | 22.00 | 55.00 | 60.00 | 65.00 | 250.00 | 300.00 |
| Bowl, 7½", dolp. ftd. nasturtium | 25.00 | 60.00 | 65.00 | 70.00 | 300.00 | 350.00 |
| Bowl, 8", nappy | 22.00 | 30.00 | 35.00 | 38.00 | | |
| Bowl, 8½", ftd., floral, 2 hand. | 25.00 | 40.00 | 50.00 | 60.00 | | |
| Bowl, 9", floral, rolled edge | 22.00 | 30.00 | 35.00 | 38.00 | | |
| Bowl, 9", floral, flared | 30.00 | 60.00 | 65.00 | 70.00 | | |
| Bowl, 10", 2 hand. oval dessert | 27.00 | 35.00 | 45.00 | 55.00 | | |
| Bowl, 10", lion head, floral | 200.00 | 485.00 | 400.00 | 500.00 | | |
| Bowl, 10", oval veg. | 27.00 | 35.00 | 45.00 | 55.00 | | |
| Bowl, 10", square salad, 2 hand. | 27.00 | 35.00 | 45.00 | 55.00 | | |
| Bowl, 10", triplex relish | 15.00 | 24.00 | 29.00 | 32.00 | | |
| Bowl, 11", dolphin ftd. floral | 25.00 | 60.00 | 65.00 | 70.00 | 300.00 | 350.00 |
| Bowl, 13", pickle/olive, 2 part | 10.00 | 15.00 | 18.00 | 22.00 | | |
| Bowl, 15", dolp. ftd. punch bowl | 200.00 | 450.00 | 500.00 | 550.00 | | |
| Candlestick, low, 4 ftd. w/2 hand. | 15.00 | 35.00 | 40.00 | 45.00 | | |

# EMPRESS, Blank # 1401, A. H. Heisey & Co., (continued)

| | Crystal | Flam. | Sahara | Moon. | Cobalt | Alexan. |
|---|---|---|---|---|---|---|
| Candlestick, 6", dolphin ftd. . . . . . . | 30.00 | 55.00 | 60.00 | 75.00 | 175.00 | |
| Candy w/cover, 6", dolphin ftd. . . . | 35.00 | 80.00 | 85.00 | 90.00 | | |
| Comport, 6", ftd. . . . . . . . . . . . . | 25.00 | 40.00 | 55.00 | 65.00 | | |
| Comport, 6", square . . . . . . . . . . . | 35.00 | 65.00 | 70.00 | 75.00 | | |
| Comport, 7", oval . . . . . . . . . . . . | 33.00 | 60.00 | 66.00 | 70.00 | | |
| Compotier, 6", dolphin ftd. . . . . . . | 60.00 | 100.00 | 150.00 | 165.00 | | |
| Creamer, dolphin ftd. . . . . . . . . . | 15.00 | 25.00 | 35.00 | 38.00 | | 200.00 |
| Creamer, indiv. . . . . . . . . . . . . . | 10.00 | 22.00 | 25.00 | 27.00 | | 150.00 |
| Cup . . . . . . . . . . . . . . . . . . . . | 8.00 | 25.00 | 30.00 | 35.00 | | 90.00 |
| Cup, after dinner . . . . . . . . . . . . | 10.00 | 20.00 | 30.00 | 40.00 | | |
| Cup, bouillon, 2 hand. . . . . . . . . . | 15.00 | 25.00 | 28.00 | 30.00 | | |
| Cup, 4 oz. custard or punch . . . . . . . | 10.00 | 25.00 | 28.00 | 30.00 | | |
| Cup #1401½, has rim as demi-cup . | 12.00 | 26.00 | 30.00 | 35.00 | | |
| Grapefruit w/square liner . . . . . . . . | 12.00 | 20.00 | 25.00 | 30.00 | | |
| Ice tub w/metal handles . . . . . . . . | 35.00 | 85.00 | 95.00 | 110.00 | | |
| Jug, 3 pint, ftd. . . . . . . . . . . . . . | 50.00 | 120.00 | 130.00 | 140.00 | | |
| Marmalade w/cover, dolp. ftd. . . . . . | 30.00 | 45.00 | 60.00 | 70.00 | | |
| Mayonnaise, 5½", ftd. . . . . . . . . . | 20.00 | 35.00 | 45.00 | 50.00 | | 150.00 |
| Mustard w/cover . . . . . . . . . . . . . | 20.00 | 35.00 | 45.00 | 50.00 | | |
| Oil bottle, 4 oz. . . . . . . . . . . . . . | 30.00 | 55.00 | 85.00 | 95.00 | | |
| Plate, bouillon liner . . . . . . . . . . . | 4.00 | 7.00 | 10.00 | 12.00 | | |
| Plate, cream soup liner . . . . . . . . . | 5.00 | 9.00 | 13.00 | 15.00 | | |
| Plate, 4½" . . . . . . . . . . . . . . . . . | 2.00 | 5.00 | 6.00 | 7.00 | | |
| Plate, 6" . . . . . . . . . . . . . . . . . | 5.00 | 10.00 | 13.00 | 15.00 | | 35.00 |
| Plate, 6", square . . . . . . . . . . . . . | 5.00 | 10.00 | 13.00 | 15.00 | | 35.00 |
| Plate, 7" . . . . . . . . . . . . . . . . . | 7.00 | 12.00 | 15.00 | 17.00 | | 45.00 |
| Plate, 7", square . . . . . . . . . . . . . | 7.00 | 12.00 | 15.00 | 17.00 | | 45.00 |
| Plate, 8", square . . . . . . . . . . . . . | 9.00 | 16.00 | 20.00 | 24.00 | 50.00 | 60.00 |
| Plate, 8" . . . . . . . . . . . . . . . . . | 9.00 | 16.00 | 20.00 | 24.00 | 50.00 | 60.00 |
| Plate, 9" . . . . . . . . . . . . . . . . . | 12.00 | 25.00 | 35.00 | 40.00 | | |
| Plate, 10½" . . . . . . . . . . . . . . . . | 20.00 | 40.00 | 50.00 | 55.00 | | |
| Plate, 10½", square . . . . . . . . . . . | 20.00 | 40.00 | 50.00 | 55.00 | | |

# EMPRESS, Blank # 1401, A. H. Heisey & Co., (continued)

| | Crystal | Flam. | Sahara | Moon. | Cobalt | Alexan. |
|---|---|---|---|---|---|---|
| Plate, 12" | 25.00 | 45.00 | 55.00 | 60.00 | | |
| Plate, 12", muffin, sides upturned | 30.00 | 48.00 | 58.00 | 65.00 | | |
| Plate, 13", hors d'oeuvre, 2 hand. | 26.00 | 32.00 | 38.00 | 44.00 | | |
| Plate, 13", square, 2 hand. | 26.00 | 32.00 | 38.00 | 44.00 | | |
| Platter, 14" | 22.00 | 30.00 | 35.00 | 40.00 | | |
| Salt & pepper, pr. | 40.00 | 65.00 | 85.00 | 95.00 | | 100.00 |
| Saucer, square | 3.00 | 8.00 | 14.00 | 16.00 | | 20.00 |
| Saucer, after dinner | 2.00 | 7.00 | 10.00 | 10.00 | | |
| Saucer | 3.00 | 8.00 | 14.00 | 16.00 | | |
| Stem, 2½ oz., oyster cocktail | 15.00 | 20.00 | 25.00 | 30.00 | | |
| Stem, 4 oz., saucer champagne | 20.00 | 25.00 | 30.00 | 35.00 | | |
| Stem, 4 oz., sherbet | 15.00 | 20.00 | 25.00 | 30.00 | | |
| Stem, 9 oz., Empress stemware, unusual | 25.00 | 32.00 | 42.00 | 52.00 | | |
| Sugar, indiv. | 15.00 | 25.00 | 35.00 | 38.00 | | 200.00 |
| Sugar, dolphin ftd. 3 hand. | 10.00 | 22.00 | 25.00 | 27.00 | | 150.00 |
| Tray, condiment & liner for indiv. sug/cream | 10.00 | 15.00 | 20.00 | 23.00 | | |
| Tray, 10", 3 pt. relish | 18.00 | 25.00 | 30.00 | 35.00 | | |
| Tray, 10", 7 pt. hors d'oeuvre | 25.00 | 30.00 | 35.00 | 40.00 | | |
| Tray, 10", celery | 12.00 | 16.00 | 22.00 | 26.00 | | |
| Tray, 12", ctr. hand. sand. | 30.00 | 48.00 | 57.00 | 65.00 | | |
| Tray, 12", sq. ctr. hand. sand. | 30.00 | 48.00 | 57.00 | 65.00 | | |
| Tray, 13", celery | 14.00 | 18.00 | 24.00 | 28.00 | | |
| Tray, 16", 4 pt. buffet relish | 20.00 | 25.00 | 30.00 | 35.00 | | |
| Tumbler, 8 oz., dolp. ftd., unusual | 60.00 | 85.00 | 120.00 | 125.00 | | |
| Tumbler, 8 oz., grnd. bottom | 12.00 | 17.00 | 24.00 | 27.00 | | |
| Tumbler, 12 oz., tea, grnd. bottom | 15.00 | 20.00 | 27.00 | 30.00 | | |
| Vase, 8", flared | 45.00 | 65.00 | 75.00 | 85.00 | | |
| Vase, 9", ftd. | 50.00 | 85.00 | 90.00 | 125.00 | | 400.00 |

# FAIRFAX, Fostoria Glass Company, 1927 - 1944

Colors: Blue, orchid, amber, rose, green, topaz, some ruby & black

Fairfax is actually the blank on which other Fostoria patterns (Versailles, June, Trojan) were etched. Naturally, being plain, there is not quite the demand for Fairfax as for the other patterns. On the other hand, people who prefer their dishes to form a background for food, enjoy the simplicity of Fairfax. Blue, in particular, seems to have caught the eye of the modern day collector.

As with the other patterns, pitchers, footed oils, salt & pepper shakers and the salad dressing bottles are choice pieces to own.

| | Blue, Orchid | Amber, Rose | Green, Topaz | | Blue, Orchid | Amber, Rose | Green, Topaz |
|---|---|---|---|---|---|---|---|
| Ash tray | 20.00 | 13.00 | 17.00 | Mayonnaise | 10.00 | 8.00 | 9.00 |
| Baker, 9", oval | 22.00 | 15.00 | 20.00 | Mayonnaise ladle | 5.00 | 4.00 | 4.00 |
| Baker, 10½", oval | 30.00 | 20.00 | 25.00 | Mayonnaise liner, 7" | 4.00 | 3.00 | 3.00 |
| Bonbon | 9.00 | 7.00 | 8.00 | Oil, ftd. | 75.00 | 60.00 | 70.00 |
| Bottle, salad dressing | --- | 55.00 | 65.00 | Pickle, 8½" | 10.00 | 7.00 | 9.00 |
| Bouillon, ftd. | 9.00 | 6.00 | 7.00 | Pitcher | 125.00 | 90.00 | 100.00 |
| Bowl, lemon, 2 hand. | 7.00 | 5.00 | 6.00 | Plate, canape | 5.00 | 3.00 | 4.00 |
| Bowl, whipped cream | 10.00 | 7.00 | 8.00 | Plate, 6", bread/butter | 3.00 | 2.00 | 2.50 |
| Bowl, 5", fruit | 8.00 | 5.00 | 6.00 | Plate, 7", salad | 4.00 | 3.00 | 3.50 |
| Bowl, 6", cereal | 11.00 | 7.00 | 9.00 | Plate, 7", cream soup | | | |
| Bowl, 7", soup | 13.00 | 9.00 | 10.00 | liner | 3.50 | 3.00 | 3.25 |
| Bowl, 8", rnd. nappy | 16.00 | 10.00 | 12.00 | Plate, 8", salad | 6.00 | 4.50 | 5.00 |
| Bowl, lg., hand. dessert | 12.00 | 9.00 | 11.00 | Plate, 9", luncheon | 7.50 | 5.00 | 6.00 |
| Bowl, 12" | 20.00 | 15.00 | 18.00 | Plate, 10", dinner | 15.00 | 10.00 | 12.00 |
| Bowl, 12", centerpiece | 22.00 | 17.50 | 20.00 | Plate, 10", grill | 10.00 | 7.00 | 8.00 |
| Bowl, 13", oval | | | | Plate, 10", cake | 16.00 | 12.00 | 14.00 |
| centerpiece | 25.00 | 20.00 | 22.50 | Plate, 12", bread | 12.00 | 8.00 | 10.00 |
| Bowl, 15", centerpiece | 27.50 | 20.00 | 24.00 | Plate, 14", torte | 15.00 | 13.00 | 14.00 |
| Butter dish w/cover | 125.00 | 80.00 | 90.00 | Platter, 10½", oval | 20.00 | 15.00 | 17.50 |
| Candlestick, flattened | | | | Platter, 15", oval | 27.50 | 20.00 | 25.00 |
| top | 11.00 | 9.00 | 10.00 | Relish, 8½" | 10.00 | 7.00 | 8.00 |
| Candlestick, 3" | 10.00 | 8.00 | 9.00 | Relish, 11½" | 12.00 | 9.00 | 10.00 |
| Celery, 11½" | 16.00 | 12.00 | 14.00 | Sauce boat | 30.00 | 20.00 | 25.00 |
| Cheese & cracker, set | 22.00 | 18.00 | 20.00 | Sauce boat liner | 10.00 | 7.00 | 8.00 |
| Comport, 7" | 12.00 | 7.00 | 10.00 | Saucer, after dinner | 6.00 | 4.00 | 5.00 |
| Cream soup, ftd. | 12.00 | 9.00 | 8.00 | Saucer | 4.00 | 2.50 | 3.00 |
| Creamer, flat | --- | 7.00 | 8.00 | Shaker, ftd., pr. | 45.00 | 30.00 | 35.00 |
| Creamer, ftd. | 11.00 | 7.00 | 9.00 | Shaker, indiv., ft., pr. | --- | 20.00 | 25.00 |
| Creamer, tea | 11.00 | 7.00 | 9.00 | Sugar, flat | --- | 7.00 | 8.00 |
| Cup, after dinner | 13.00 | 9.00 | 12.00 | Sugar, ftd. | 10.00 | 6.00 | 8.00 |
| Cup, flat | --- | 4.00 | 6.00 | Sugar cover | 22.00 | 18.00 | 20.00 |
| Cup, ftd. | 8.00 | 6.00 | 7.00 | Sugar, tea | 10.00 | 6.00 | 8.00 |
| Flower holder, oval | 12.00 | 8.00 | 10.00 | Sweetmeat | 11.00 | 7.00 | 9.00 |
| Ice bucket | 40.00 | 30.00 | 35.00 | Tray, 11", ctr. hand. | 15.00 | 10.00 | 12.50 |

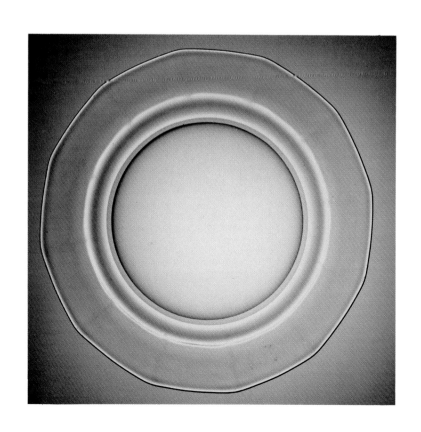

73

# GLORIA (etching 1746), Cambridge Glass 3400 Line Dinnerware Introduced 1930

Colors: Crystal, pink, yellow, green, emerald green, amber

Note: Emerald green Gloria will fetch prices about fifty percent higher than those listed for the other pastel colors.

Since Gloria and Apple Blossom were run from the same #3400 blanks, the pieces are alike save for the stemware. The Gloria etching is somewhat more flamboyant than the Apple Blossom. Gloria is slightly more desirable than Apple Blossom at present.

| | Crystal | Colors |
|---|---|---|
| Basket, 6", 2 hand. (sides up) | 12.00 | 17.50 |
| Bowl, 5", ftd., crimped edge bonbon | 14.00 | 20.00 |
| Bowl, 5", sq. fruit "saucer" | 6.00 | 12.00 |
| Bowl, 5½", bonbon, 2 hand. | 12.00 | 17.50 |
| Bowl, 5½", bonbon, ftd. | 12.00 | 17.50 |
| Bowl, 5½", flattened, ftd. bonbon | 12.00 | 17.50 |
| Bowl, 5½", fruit "saucer" | 7.50 | 12.50 |
| Bowl, 6", rnd. cereal | 7.00 | 13.00 |
| Bowl, 6", sq. cereal | 7.50 | 12.50 |
| Bowl, 8", 2 pt., 2 hand. relish | 15.00 | 22.50 |
| Bowl, 8", 3 pt., 3 hand. relish | 20.00 | 32.50 |
| Bowl, 8¾", 2 hand., figure "8" pickle | 17.50 | 25.00 |
| Bowl, 8¾", 2 pt., 2 hand. figure "8" relish | 17.50 | 27.50 |
| Bowl, 9", salad, tab hand. | 17.50 | 30.00 |
| Bowl, 9½", 2 hand., veg. | 50.00 | 75.00 |
| Bowl, 10", oblong, tab handle "baker" | 22.50 | 30.00 |
| Bowl, 10", 2 hand. | 25.00 | 40.00 |
| Bowl, 11", 2 hand. fruit | 27.00 | 40.00 |
| Bowl, 12", 4 ftd. console | 22.50 | 37.50 |
| Bowl, 12", 4 ftd. flared rim | 20.00 | 30.00 |
| Bowl, 12", 4 ftd. oval | 25.00 | 47.50 |
| Bowl, 12", 5 pt. celery & relish | 22.50 | 40.00 |
| Bowl, 13", flared rim | 17.50 | 27.50 |
| Bowl, cream soup w/rnd. liner | 12.50 | 22.50 |
| Bowl, cream soup w/sq. saucer | 12.50 | 22.50 |
| Bowl, finger, flared edge w/rnd. liner | 12.50 | 22.50 |
| Bowl, finger, ftd. | 10.00 | 17.50 |
| Bowl, finger w/rnd. plate | 12.00 | 17.50 |
| Butter w/cover, 2 hand. | 65.00 | 100.00 |
| Candlestick, 6", ea. | 15.00 | 25.00 |
| Candy box w/cover, 4 ftd. w/tab hand. | 32.50 | 57.50 |
| Cheese compote w/11½" cracker plate, tab hand. | 22.50 | 35.00 |
| Cocktail shaker, grnd. stopper, spout (like pitcher) | 60.00 | 115.00 |
| Comport, 3", indiv. nut, 4 ftd. | 15.00 | 22.50 |
| Comport, 3½", cranberry, 4 ftd. | 12.50 | 20.00 |
| Comport, 4", fruit cocktail | 9.00 | 15.00 |

(continued)

|  | Crystal | Colors |
|---|---|---|
| Comport, 5", 4 ftd. | 14.00 | 21.00 |
| Comport, 6", 4 ftd. | 15.00 | 22.50 |
| Comport, 7", low | 25.00 | 40.00 |
| Comport, 7", tall | 30.00 | 45.00 |
| Comport, 9½", tall, 2 hand., ftd bowl | 50.00 | 80.00 |
| Creamer, ftd. | 10.00 | 15.00 |
| Creamer, tall, ftd. | 10.00 | 15.00 |
| Cup, rnd. or sq. | 10.00 | 15.00 |
| Cup, 4 ftd. sq. | 15.00 | 25.00 |
| Cup, after dinner (demitasse), rnd. or sq. | 25.00 | 35.00 |
| Fruit cocktail, 6 oz., ftd., (3 styles) | 9.00 | 15.00 |
| Ice pail, metal handle w/tongs | 32.50 | 52.50 |
| Mayonnaise w/liner & ladle, (4 ftd. bowl) | 25.00 | 42.50 |
| Oil w/stopper; tall, ftd., hand. | 57.50 | 92.50 |
| Oyster cocktail, #3035, 4½ oz. | 10.00 | 15.00 |
| Oyster cocktail, 4½ oz., low stem | 10.00 | 15.00 |
| Pitcher, 67 oz., middle indent | 70.00 | 125.00 |
| Pitcher, 80 oz., ball | 65.00 | 117.50 |
| Pitcher w/cover, 64 oz. | 60.00 | 110.00 |
| Plate, 6", 2 hand. | 8.00 | 13.50 |
| Plate, 6", bread/butter | 4.00 | 7.00 |
| Plate, 7½", tea | 5.00 | 8.50 |
| Plate, 8½" | 7.00 | 12.50 |
| Plate, 9½" dinner | 15.00 | 25.00 |
| Plate, 10", tab hand. salad | 12.00 | 25.00 |
| Plate, 11", 2 hand. | 15.00 | 22.50 |
| Plate, 11", sq., ftd. cake | 35.00 | 62.50 |
| Plate, 11½", tab hand. sandwich | 17.50 | 25.00 |
| Plate, 14", chop or salad | 27.50 | 42.50 |
| Plate, sq. bread/butter | 4.50 | 7.50 |
| Plate, sq. dinner | 12.50 | 25.00 |
| Plate, sq. salad | 6.00 | 10.00 |
| Plate, sq. service | 17.50 | 30.00 |
| Platter, 11½" | 25.00 | 42.50 |
| Salt & pepper, pr., short | 25.00 | 35.00 |
| Salt & pepper, pr., w/glass top, tall | 27.50 | 50.00 |
| Salt & pepper, ftd., metal tops | 32.50 | 57.50 |
| Saucer, rnd. | 2.00 | 3.00 |
| Saucer, rnd. after dinner | 4.00 | 5.00 |
| Saucer, sq., after dinner (demitasse) | 4.00 | 5.00 |
| Saucer, sq. | 2.00 | 3.00 |
| Stem, #3035, 2½ oz., wine | 15.00 | 22.50 |
| Stem, #3035, 3 oz., cocktail | 15.00 | 22.50 |
| Stem, #3035, 4½ oz., claret | 15.00 | 21.50 |
| Stem, #3035, 9 oz., water | 12.50 | 20.00 |
| Stem, #3035, 6 oz., low sherbet | 9.00 | 13.50 |
| Stem, #3035, 6 oz., tall sherbet | 10.00 | 15.00 |

# GLORIA (etching 1746), Cambridge Glass 3400 Line Dinnerware Introduced 1930,

**(continued)**

|  | Crystal | Colors |
|---|---|---|
| Stem, #3035, 3½ oz., cocktail . . . . . . . . . . . . . . . . . . . . . | 16.00 | 22.00 |
| Stem, #3115, 9 oz. goblet. . . . . . . . . . . . . . . . . . . . . . . | 12.00 | 20.00 |
| Stem, #3120, 1 oz., cordial . . . . . . . . . . . . . . . . . . . . . . | 22.50 | 37.50 |
| Stem, #3120, 4½ oz., claret . . . . . . . . . . . . . . . . . . . . . | 15.00 | 21.50 |
| Stem, #3120, 6 oz., low sherbet . . . . . . . . . . . . . . . . . . . | 9.00 | 13.50 |
| Stem, #3120, 6 oz., tall sherbet . . . . . . . . . . . . . . . . . . . | 10.00 | 15.00 |
| Stem, #3120, 9 oz., water . . . . . . . . . . . . . . . . . . . . . . . | 12.50 | 20.00 |
| Stem, #3130, 2½" oz., wine . . . . . . . . . . . . . . . . . . . . . . | 15.00 | 22.50 |
| Stem, #3130, 6 oz., low sherbet . . . . . . . . . . . . . . . . . . . | 9.00 | 13.50 |
| Stem, #3130, 6 oz., tall sherbet . . . . . . . . . . . . . . . . . . . | 10.00 | 15.00 |
| Stem, #3130, 8 oz., water . . . . . . . . . . . . . . . . . . . . . . . | 12.50 | 20.00 |
| Stem, #3135, 1 oz., cordial . . . . . . . . . . . . . . . . . . . . . . | 22.50 | 37.50 |
| Stem, #3135, 6 oz., low sherbet . . . . . . . . . . . . . . . . . . . | 10.00 | 12.50 |
| Stem, #3135, 6 oz., tall sherbet . . . . . . . . . . . . . . . . . . . | 11.50 | 15.00 |
| Stem, #3135, 8 oz., water . . . . . . . . . . . . . . . . . . . . . . . | 12.50 | 20.00 |
| Sugar, ftd. . . . . . . . . . . . . . . . . . . . . . . . . . . . . . . . . | 10.00 | 14.00 |
| Sugar, tall, ftd. . . . . . . . . . . . . . . . . . . . . . . . . . . . . . | 10.00 | 15.00 |
| Sugar shaker w/glass top . . . . . . . . . . . . . . . . . . . . . . . | 55.00 | 95.00 |
| Syrup, tall, ftd. . . . . . . . . . . . . . . . . . . . . . . . . . . . . . | 35.00 | 57.50 |
| Tray, 11", ctr. hand. sandwich . . . . . . . . . . . . . . . . . . . . | 17.50 | 27.50 |
| Tray, 2 pt. ctr. hand. relish. . . . . . . . . . . . . . . . . . . . . . | 20.00 | 30.00 |
| Tray, 4 pt. ctr. hand. relish. . . . . . . . . . . . . . . . . . . . . . | 27.50 | 42.50 |
| Tray, 9", pickle, tab hand. . . . . . . . . . . . . . . . . . . . . . . | 12.50 | 20.00 |
| Tumbler, #3035, 5 oz., high ftd.. . . . . . . . . . . . . . . . . . . | 9.00 | 15.00 |
| Tumbler, #3035, 10 oz., high ftd.. . . . . . . . . . . . . . . . . . | 10.00 | 17.50 |
| Tumbler, #3035, 12 oz., high ftd.. . . . . . . . . . . . . . . . . . | 12.00 | 18.00 |
| Tumbler, #3115, 5 oz., ftd. juice . . . . . . . . . . . . . . . . . . | 10.00 | 15.00 |
| Tumbler, #3115, 8 oz., ftd.. . . . . . . . . . . . . . . . . . . . . . | 10.00 | 15.00 |
| Tumbler, #3115, 10 oz., ftd.. . . . . . . . . . . . . . . . . . . . . | 11.00 | 16.00 |
| Tumbler, #3115, 12 oz., ftd.. . . . . . . . . . . . . . . . . . . . . | 12.00 | 17.50 |
| Tumbler, #3120, 5 oz., ftd.. . . . . . . . . . . . . . . . . . . . . . | 10.00 | 15.00 |
| Tumbler, #3120, 10 oz., ftd.. . . . . . . . . . . . . . . . . . . . . | 10.00 | 15.00 |
| Tumbler, #3120, 12 oz., ftd.. . . . . . . . . . . . . . . . . . . . . | 12.00 | 17.50 |
| Tumbler, #3120, 2½ oz., ftd. (used w/shaker) . . . . . . . . . | 10.00 | 15.00 |
| Tumbler, #3130, 5 oz., ftd.. . . . . . . . . . . . . . . . . . . . . . | 10.00 | 15.00 |
| Tumbler, #3130, 10 oz., ftd.. . . . . . . . . . . . . . . . . . . . . | 10.00 | 15.00 |
| Tumbler, #3130, 12 oz., ftd.. . . . . . . . . . . . . . . . . . . . . | 12.00 | 17.50 |
| Tumbler, #3135, 5 oz., juice . . . . . . . . . . . . . . . . . . . . . | 10.00 | 15.00 |
| Tumbler, #3135, 10 oz., water . . . . . . . . . . . . . . . . . . . . | 10.00 | 15.00 |
| Tumbler, #3135, 12 oz., tea . . . . . . . . . . . . . . . . . . . . . | 12.00 | 17.50 |
| Tumbler, 12 oz., flat, (2 styles)-one w/indent side to match 67 oz. pitcher . . . . . . . . . . . . . . . . . . . . . . . . . . . . | 12.00 | 17.50 |
| Vase, 9", oval, 4 indent . . . . . . . . . . . . . . . . . . . . . . . . | 35.00 | 65.00 |
| Vase, 10", keyhole base . . . . . . . . . . . . . . . . . . . . . . . . | 32.50 | 52.50 |
| Vase, 10", squarish top . . . . . . . . . . . . . . . . . . . . . . . . | 30.00 | 50.00 |
| Vase, 11". . . . . . . . . . . . . . . . . . . . . . . . . . . . . . . . . . | 30.00 | 52.50 |
| Vase, 11", neck indent . . . . . . . . . . . . . . . . . . . . . . . . . | 32.50 | 55.00 |
| Vase, 12", keyhole base, flared rim . . . . . . . . . . . . . . . . | 37.50 | 60.00 |
| Vase, 12", squarish top . . . . . . . . . . . . . . . . . . . . . . . . | 35.00 | 57.50 |
| Vase, 14", keyhole base, flared rim . . . . . . . . . . . . . . . . | 42.50 | 67.50 |

Note: See Pages 150-153 for stem identification.

# GREEK KEY, A. H. Heisey & Co.

Colors: Crystal, "Flamingo" pink punch bowl and cups only

| | Crystal |
|---|---|
| Bowl, finger | 14.00 |
| Bowl, jelly w/cover, 2 hand., ftd. | 110.00 |
| Bowl, indiv. ftd. almond | 25.00 |
| Bowl, 4", nappy | 8.00 |
| Bowl, 4", shallow, low ft., jelly | 12.00 |
| Bowl, 4½", nappy | 12.00 |
| Bowl, 4½", scalloped nappy | 15.00 |
| Bowl, 4½", shallow, low ft., jelly | 12.50 |
| Bowl, 5", ftd. almond | 30.00 |
| Bowl, 5", ftd. almond w/cover | 75.00 |
| Bowl, 5", hand. jelly | 30.00 |
| Bowl, 5", low ft. jelly w/cover | 35.00 |
| Bowl, 5", nappy | 20.00 |
| Bowl, 5½", nappy | 22.50 |
| Bowl, 5½", shallow nappy, ftd. | 50.00 |
| Bowl, 6", nappy | 22.00 |
| Bowl, 6", shallow nappy | 22.50 |
| Bowl, 6½", nappy | 25.00 |
| Bowl, 7", low ft., straight side | 30.00 |
| Bowl, 7", nappy | 27.50 |
| Bowl, 8", low ft., straight side | 35.00 |
| Bowl, 8", nappy | 32.50 |
| Bowl, 8", scalloped nappy | 37.50 |
| Bowl, 8", shallow, low ft. | 40.00 |
| Bowl, 8½", shallow nappy | 40.00 |
| Bowl, 9", flat banana split | 17.00 |
| Bowl, 9", ftd. banana split | 20.00 |
| Bowl, 9", low ft., straight side | 40.00 |
| Bowl, 9", nappy | 37.50 |
| Bowl, 9", shallow, low ft. | 42.50 |
| Bowl, 9½", shallow nappy | 40.00 |
| Bowl, 10", shallow, low ft. | 42.50 |
| Bowl, 11", shallow nappy | 43.00 |
| Bowl, 12", orange bowl | 45.00 |
| Bowl, 12", punch, ftd. | 150.00 |
| (Flamingo) | 650.00 |
| Bowl, 14", orange bowl, flared rim | 60.00 |
| Bowl, 14½", orange bowl, flared rim | 55.00 |
| Bowl, 15", punch, ftd. | 105.00 |
| Bowl, 18", punch, shallow | 110.00 |
| Butter, indiv. (plate) | 13.00 |
| Butter/Jelly, 2 hand. w/cover | 160.00 |
| Candy w/cover, ½ lb. | 100.00 |

# GREEK KEY, A. H. Heisey & Co. (continued)

|  | Crystal |
|---|---|
| Candy w/cover, 1 lb. | 110.00 |
| Candy w/cover, 2 lb. | 140.00 |
| Cheese & cracker set, 10" | 50.00 |
| Compote, 5" | 50.00 |
| Compote, 5", w/cover | 55.00 |
| Creamer | 25.00 |
| Creamer, oval, hotel | 27.00 |
| Creamer, rnd., hotel | 25.00 |
| Cup, 4½ oz., punch | 18.00 |
| (Flamingo) | 30.00 |
| Egg cup, 5 oz. | 45.00 |
| Hair receiver | 52.00 |
| Ice tub, lg., tab hand. | 60.00 |
| Ice tub, sm., tab hand. | 45.00 |
| Ice tub w/cover, hotel | 75.00 |
| Ice tub w/cover, 5", individual w/5", plate | 60.00 |
| Jar, 1 qt., crushed fruit w/cover | 150.00 |
| Jar, 2 qt., crushed fruit w/cover | 200.00 |
| Jar, lg. cover horseradish | 65.00 |
| Jar, sm. cover horseradish | 55.00 |
| Jar, tall celery | 62.00 |
| Jar w/knob cover, pickle | 80.00 |
| Pitcher, 1 pint | 50.00 |
| Pitcher, 1 quart | 56.00 |
| Pitcher, 3 pint | 70.00 |
| Pitcher, ½ gal. | 80.00 |
| Oil bottle, 2 oz., squat w/#8 stopper | 55.00 |
| Oil bottle, 2 oz., w/#6 stopper | 60.00 |
| Oil bottle, 4 oz., squat w/#8 stopper | 65.00 |
| Oil bottle, 4 oz., w/#6 stopper | 70.00 |
| Oil bottle, 6 oz., w/#6 stopper | 80.00 |
| Oil bottle, 6 oz., squat w/#8 stopper | 75.00 |
| Plate, 4½" | 10.00 |
| Plate, 5" | 11.00 |
| Plate, 5½" | 11.00 |
| Plate, 6" | 12.00 |
| Plate, 6½" | 12.00 |
| Plate, 7" | 13.00 |
| Plate, 8" | 15.00 |
| Plate, 9" | 20.00 |
| Plate, 10" | 45.00 |
| Plate, 16", orange bowl liner | 50.00 |
| Puff box, #1 w/cover | 50.00 |
| Puff box, #3 w/cover | 65.00 |
| Salt & pepper, pr. | 50.00 |
| Sherbet, 4½ oz., ftd., straight rim | 10.00 |

# GREEK KEY, A. H. Heisey & Co. (continued)

|  | Crystal |
|---|---|
| Sherbet, 4½ oz., ftd., flared rim | 10.00 |
| Sherbet, 4½ oz., hi. ft., shallow | 10.00 |
| Sherbet, 4½ oz., ftd., shallow | 10.00 |
| Sherbet, 4½ oz., ftd., cupped rim | 10.00 |
| Sherbet, 6 oz., low ft. | 11.00 |
| Spooner, lg. | 60.00 |
| Spooner, 4½", (or straw jar) | 55.00 |
| Stem, ¾ oz., cordial | 135.00 |
| Stem, 2 oz., wine | 120.00 |
| Stem, 2 oz., sherry | 115.00 |
| Stem, 3 oz., cocktail | 17.00 |
| Stem, 3½ oz., burgundy | 85.00 |
| Stem, 4½ oz., saucer champagne | 16.00 |
| Stem, 4½ oz., claret | 80.00 |
| Stem, 7 oz. | 50.00 |
| Stem, 9 oz. | 60.00 |
| Stem, 9 oz., low ft. | 58.00 |
| Straw jar w/cover | 200.00 |
| Sugar | 25.00 |
| Sugar, oval, hotel | 27.00 |
| Sugar, rnd., hotel | 25.00 |
| Sugar & creamer, oval, individual | 60.00 |
| Tankard, 1 pint | 50.00 |
| Tankard, 3 pint | 70.00 |
| Tankard, quart | 55.00 |
| Tankard, ½ gallon | 90.00 |
| Tray, 9", oval celery | 15.00 |
| Tray, 12", oval celery | 18.00 |
| Tray, 12½", French roll | 50.00 |
| Tray, 13", oblong | 55.00 |
| Tray, 15", oblong | 58.00 |
| Tumbler, 2½ oz., (or toothpick) | 200.00 |
| Tumbler, 5 oz., flared rim | 15.00 |
| Tumbler, 5 oz., straight side | 15.00 |
| Tumbler, 5½ oz., water | 16.00 |
| Tumbler, 7 oz., flared rim | 20.00 |
| Tumbler, 7 oz., straight side | 22.00 |
| Tumbler, 8 oz., w/straight, flared, cupped, shallow | 25.00 |
| Tumbler, 10 oz., flared rim | 27.00 |
| Tumbler, 10 oz., straight side | 27.00 |
| Tumbler, 12 oz., flared rim | 28.00 |
| Tumbler, 12 oz., straight side | 28.00 |
| Tumbler, 13 oz., straight side | 29.00 |
| Tumbler, 13 oz., flared rim | 30.00 |
| Water bottle w/center compote attached | 65.00 |

# IPSWICH, Blank #1405, A. H. Heisey & Co.

Colors: Crystal, "Flamingo" pink, "Sahara" yellow, "Moongleam" green, cobalt, and "Alexandrite"

| | Crystal | Pink | Sahara | Green | Cobalt | Alexan. |
|---|---|---|---|---|---|---|
| Bowl, finger w/underplate . . . . . . . . | 15.00 | 25.00 | 35.00 | 40.00 | | |
| Bowl, 11", ft. floral . . . . . . . . . . . . | 30.00 | | | | 275.00 | |
| Candlestick, 6", 1-lite . . . . . . . . . . | 75.00 | 110.00 | 135.00 | 150.00 | 300.00 | |
| Candlestick center piece, ft., vase, "A" prisms . . . . . . . . . . . . . . . . . | 110.00 | 185.00 | 200.00 | 275.00 | 425.00 | |
| Candy jar, ½ lb., w/cover . . . . . . . . | 40.00 | 150.00 | 200.00 | 250.00 | | |
| Cocktail shaker, 1 quart, strainer #86 stopper . . . . . . . . . . . . . . . . | 150.00 | 250.00 | 350.00 | 450.00 | | |
| Creamer . . . . . . . . . . . . . . . . . . . | 15.00 | 25.00 | 30.00 | 35.00 | | |
| Stem, 4 oz., oyster cocktail . . . . . . . | 7.00 | | | | | |
| Stem, 5 oz., saucer champagne . . . . | 10.00 | | | | | |
| Stem, 10 oz., goblet . . . . . . . . . . . | 15.00 | | | | | |
| Stem, 12 oz., schoppen . . . . . . . . . | 25.00 | | | | | |
| Pitcher, ½ gal. . . . . . . . . . . . . . . . | 100.00 | 150.00 | 200.00 | 400.00 | 300.00 | |
| Oil bottle, 2 oz., ft. #86 stopper . . . . | 50.00 | 70.00 | 80.00 | 90.00 | | |
| Plate, 7", square . . . . . . . . . . . . . . | 15.00 | 20.00 | 22.00 | 25.00 | | |
| Plate, 8", square . . . . . . . . . . . . . . | 16.00 | 22.00 | 24.00 | 27.00 | | |
| Sherbet, 4 oz. . . . . . . . . . . . . . . . | 7.00 | 15.00 | 20.00 | 25.00 | | |
| Sugar . . . . . . . . . . . . . . . . . . . . . | 15.00 | 25.00 | 30.00 | 35.00 | | |
| Tumbler, 5 oz., ft. . . . . . . . . . . . . . | 8.00 | 15.00 | 20.00 | 25.00 | | |
| Tumbler, 8 oz., ft. . . . . . . . . . . . . . | 9.00 | 16.00 | 22.00 | 27.00 | | |
| Tumbler, 10 oz., cupped rim . . . . . . | 10.00 | 25.00 | 28.00 | 30.00 | | |
| Tumbler, 10 oz., straight rim . . . . . . | 10.00 | 25.00 | 28.00 | 30.00 | | 390.00 |
| Tumbler, 12 oz., ft. . . . . . . . . . . . . | 12.00 | 30.00 | 35.00 | 40.00 | | |

# JUNE, Fostoria Glass Company, 1928 - 1944

Colors: Crystal, "Azure" blue, "Topaz" yellow, "Rose" pink

This is one of the most highly collected of the Fostoria patterns. Choice pieces to own include the pitcher, footed oils, shakers with those glass lids, cordials, 2½ oz. tumblers and the grapefruits with liners. Blue, again, seems the color most eagerly sought by collectors today.

| | Crystal | Blue | Rose, Topaz | | Crystal | Blue | Rose, Topaz |
|---|---|---|---|---|---|---|---|
| Ash tray . . . . . . . . . . . . | 20.00 | 30.00 | 30.00 | Grapefruit liner . . . . . . . . | 20.00 | 50.00 | 40.50 |
| Bottle, salad dressing, | | | | Ice bucket . . . . . . . . . . . | 45.00 | 85.00 | 75.00 |
| sterling top . . . . . . . . . | 125.00 | 225.00 | 200.00 | Ice dish . . . . . . . . . . . . | 20.00 | 40.00 | 35.00 |
| Bowl, baker, 9", oval . . . . | 30.00 | 50.00 | 45.00 | Ice dish liner (tomato, | | | |
| Bowl, bonbon . . . . . . . . . | 12.00 | 19.00 | 17.00 | crab, fruit) . . . . . . . . . . | 5.00 | 10.00 | 7.50 |
| Bowl, bouillon, ftd. . . . . . . | 12.00 | 23.00 | 20.00 | Mayonnaise w/liner . . . . . | 20.00 | 40.00 | 35.00 |
| Bowl, finger w/liner . . . . . | 30.00 | 30.00 | 40.00 | Oil, ftd. . . . . . . . . . . . . . | 150.00 | 300.00 | 250.00 |
| Bowl, lemon . . . . . . . . . . | 14.00 | 22.00 | 18.00 | Oyster cocktail, 5½ oz. . . | 16.00 | 28.00 | 22.00 |
| Bowl, mint . . . . . . . . . . . | 10.00 | 18.00 | 14.00 | Parfait, 5¼" . . . . . . . . . | 20.00 | 40.00 | 32.50 |
| Bowl, 5", fruit . . . . . . . . | 10.00 | 20.00 | 16.50 | Pitcher . . . . . . . . . . . . . | 200.00 | 395.00 | 325.00 |
| Bowl, 6", cereal . . . . . . . | 15.00 | 25.00 | 22.00 | Plate, canape . . . . . . . . . | 10.00 | 18.00 | 15.00 |
| Bowl, 6", nappy, ftd. . . . . | 10.00 | 22.00 | 17.50 | Plate, 6", bread/butter . . | 4.50 | 6.00 | 5.00 |
| Bowl, 7", nappy . . . . . . . | 15.00 | 22.50 | 20.00 | Plate, 6", finger bowl | | | |
| Bowl, 7", soup . . . . . . . . | 16.50 | 30.00 | 25.00 | liner . . . . . . . . . . . . . . | 4.50 | 6.00 | 5.00 |
| Bowl, lg., dessert, hand. . | 16.00 | 32.00 | 24.00 | Plate, 7½", salad . . . . . . | 5.00 | 10.00 | 8.00 |
| Bowl, 10" . . . . . . . . . . . | 20.00 | 45.00 | 35.00 | Plate, 7½", cream soup . . | 4.00 | 9.00 | 7.50 |
| Bowl, 10", Grecian . . . . . . | 30.00 | 55.00 | 50.00 | Plate, 8¾", luncheon . . . . | 6.00 | 11.00 | 9.00 |
| Bowl, 11", centerpiece . . . | 20.00 | 40.00 | 30.00 | Plate, 9½", sm. dinner . . | 8.00 | 16.00 | 14.00 |
| Bowl, 12", ctr. piece, sev. | | | | Plate, 10", grill . . . . . . . . | 16.00 | 30.00 | 25.00 |
| type . . . . . . . . . . . . . . | 25.00 | 50.00 | 40.00 | Plate, 10", cake, handled | 20.00 | 45.00 | 35.00 |
| Bowl, 13", oval | | | | Plate, 10¼", dinner . . . . . | 20.00 | 40.00 | 32.50 |
| centerpiece . . . . . . . . . | 30.00 | 60.00 | 45.00 | Plate, 13", chop . . . . . . . | 20.00 | 40.00 | 35.00 |
| Candlestick, 2" . . . . . . . | 10.00 | 17.50 | 15.00 | Platter, 12", . . . . . . . . . | 20.00 | 40.00 | 35.00 |
| Candlestick, 3" . . . . . . . | 12.00 | 19.00 | 16.50 | Platter, 15" . . . . . . . . . | 25.00 | 60.00 | 45.00 |
| Candlestick, 3", Grecian . | 15.00 | 20.00 | 17.50 | Relish, 8½" . . . . . . . . . . | 14.00 | 20.00 | 18.00 |
| Candlestick, 5" . . . . . . . | 12.50 | 20.00 | 17.50 | Sauce boat . . . . . . . . . . | 30.00 | 65.00 | 50.00 |
| Candy w/cover, 3 pt. . . . . | 40.00 | 85.00 | 70.00 | Sauce boat liner . . . . . . . | 5.00 | 15.00 | 10.00 |
| Candy w/cover, ½ lb. . . . | 45.00 | 100.00 | 75.00 | Saucer, after dinner . . . . . | 6.00 | 10.00 | 8.00 |
| Celery, 11½" . . . . . . . . . . | 25.00 | 40.00 | 35.00 | Saucer . . . . . . . . . . . . . | 4.00 | 7.50 | 5.00 |
| Cheese & cracker, set . . . | 25.00 | 45.00 | 35.50 | Shaker, ftd. pr. . . . . . . . . | 60.00 | 125.00 | 90.00 |
| Comport, 5" . . . . . . . . . . | 18.00 | 30.00 | 25.00 | Sherbet, high, 6", 6 oz. . . | 17.50 | 27.50 | 24.00 |
| Comport, 6" . . . . . . . . . . | 18.00 | 30.00 | 25.00 | Sherbet, low, 4¼", 6 oz. . | 15.00 | 24.00 | 19.00 |
| Comport, 7" . . . . . . . . . . | 22.00 | 30.50 | 27.50 | Sugar, ftd. . . . . . . . . . . . | 12.00 | 35.00 | 30.00 |
| Comport, 8" . . . . . . . . . . | 24.00 | 40.00 | 35.00 | Sugar cover . . . . . . . . . . | 35.00 | 80.00 | 60.00 |
| Cream soup, ftd. . . . . . . . | 12.00 | 35.00 | 30.00 | Sugar pail . . . . . . . . . . . | 50.00 | 90.00 | 80.00 |
| Creamer, ftd. . . . . . . . . . | 12.00 | 20.00 | 16.00 | Sugar, tea . . . . . . . . . . . | 15.00 | 24.00 | 20.00 |
| Creamer, tea . . . . . . . . . | 15.00 | 35.00 | 30.00 | Tray, 11", ctr. hand. . . . . | 20.00 | 40.00 | 30.00 |
| Cup, after dinner . . . . . . . | 20.00 | 40.00 | 30.00 | Tumbler, 2½ oz. . . . . . . . . | 20.00 | 35.00 | 30.00 |
| Cup, ftd. . . . . . . . . . . . . | 15.00 | 25.00 | 20.00 | Tumbler, 5 oz., 4½" . . . . | 15.00 | 25.00 | 20.00 |
| Decanter . . . . . . . . . . . . | 100.00 | 225.00 | 200.00 | Tumbler, 9 oz., 5¼" . . . . | 12.50 | 25.00 | 18.00 |
| Goblet, claret, 6" . . . . . . | 30.00 | 50.00 | 50.00 | Tumbler, 12 oz., 6" . . . . . | 15.00 | 28.00 | 22.00 |
| Goblet, cocktail, 5¼" . . . | 20.00 | 30.00 | 28.00 | Vase, 8" . . . . . . . . . . . . | 45.00 | 120.00 | 100.00 |
| Goblet, cordial, 4" . . . . . . | 30.00 | 75.00 | 45.00 | Vase, 8½", fan ftd. . . . . . | 50.00 | 100.00 | 85.00 |
| Goblet, water, 8¼" . . . . . | 20.00 | 32.00 | 27.50 | Whipped cream bowl . . . . | 10.00 | 12.00 | 15.00 |
| Goblet, wine, 5½" . . . . . . | 20.00 | 50.00 | 42.50 | Whipped cream pail . . . . . | 50.00 | 90.00 | 80.00 |
| Grapefruit . . . . . . . . . . . | 25.00 | 60.00 | 50.00 | | | | |

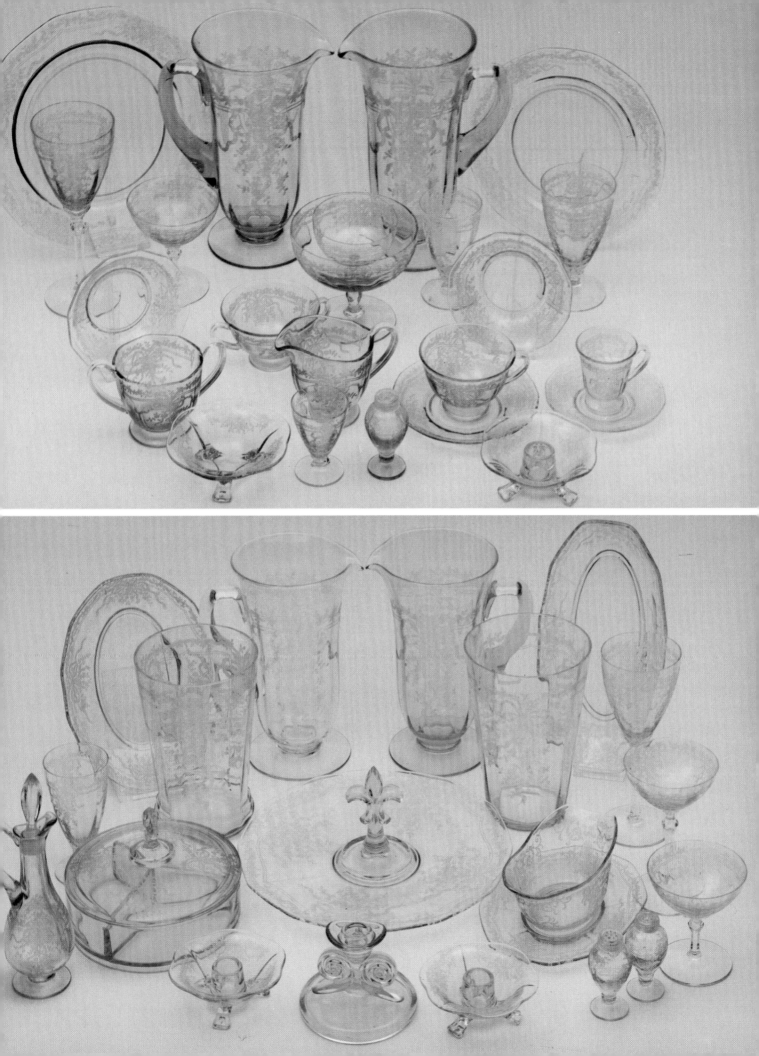

# KASHMIR, Fostoria Glass Company, 1930 - 1934

Colors: "Topaz" yellow, green; some blue

The few blue pieces being shown for sale are somewhat higher than the yellow or green; however, because of its scarcity, there are very few collectors for the blue, so whether the pieces actually bring higher prices is speculative at this point.

There are some blank spaces in the price column due to none of these having been sold to my knowledge. The items are in the original catalogue listings as having been manufactured.

|  | Yellow, Green |
|---|---|
| Ash tray | 25.00 |
| Bowl, cream soup | 18.00 |
| Bowl, finger | 14.00 |
| Bowl, 5", fruit | 12.00 |
| Bowl, 6", cereal | 16.00 |
| Bowl, 7", soup | 25.00 |
| Bowl, 8½", pickle | 16.00 |
| Bowl, 9", baker | 32.00 |
| Bowl, 10" | 40.00 |
| Bowl, 12", centerpiece | 38.00 |
| Candlestick, 2" | 14.00 |
| Candlestick, 3" | 17.50 |
| Candlestick, 5" | 17.50 |
| Candlestick, 9½" | 35.00 |
| Candy w/cover | 40.00 |
| Cheese and cracker set | 42.00 |
| Comport, 6" | 30.00 |
| Creamer, ftd. | 15.00 |
| Cup | 15.00 |
| Cup, after dinner, flat | 18.00 |
| Cup, after dinner, ftd. | 18.00 |
| Grapefruit | 35.00 |
| Grapefruit liner | 22.00 |
| Ice bucket | 60.00 |
| Oil, ftd. | 125.00 |
| Pitcher, ftd. | 350.00 |
| Plate, 6", bread and butter | 5.00 |
| Plate, 7", salad, rnd. | 6.00 |
| Plate, 7", salad, sq. | 6.00 |
| Plate, 8", salad | 8.00 |
| Plate, 9", luncheon | 9.00 |
| Plate, 10", dinner | 28.00 |
| Plate, 10", grill | 22.00 |
| Plate, cake, 10" | ---- |
| Salt and pepper | 65.00 |
| Sandwich, center hand. | 35.00 |
| Sauce boat w/liner | 60.00 |
| Saucer, rnd. | 5.00 |
| Saucer, sq. | 5.00 |
| Saucer, after dinner, rnd. | 6.00 |
| Stem, ¾ oz., cordial | 40.00 |
| Stem, 2½ oz., ftd. | 18.00 |
| Stem, 2 oz., ftd. whiskey | 22.00 |
| Stem, 2½ oz., wine | 28.00 |
| Stem, 3 oz., cocktail | 22.00 |
| Stem, 3½ oz., ftd. cocktail | 22.00 |
| Stem, 4 oz., claret | 28.00 |
| Stem, 4½ oz., oyster cocktail | 16.00 |
| Stem, 5½ oz. parfait | ---- |
| Stem, 5 oz., ftd. juice | 14.00 |
| Stem, 5 oz., low sherbet | 12.00 |
| Stem, 6 oz., high sherbet | 16.00 |
| Stem, 9 oz., water | ---- |
| Stem, 10 oz., ftd. water | ---- |
| Stem, 11 oz. | ---- |
| Stem, 12 oz., ftd. | ---- |
| Stem, 13 oz., ftd. tea | ---- |
| Stem, 16 oz., ftd. tea | ---- |
| Sugar, ftd. | 13.00 |
| Vase, 8" | 65.00 |

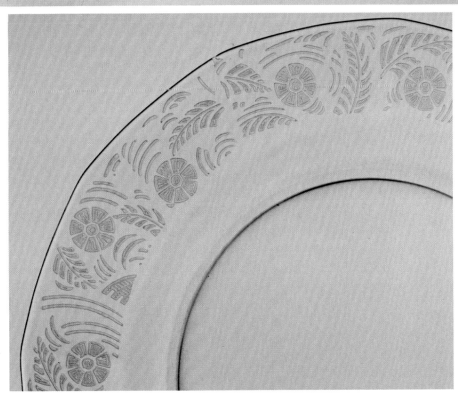

# LARIAT, Blank #1540, A. H. Heisey & Co.

Color: Crystal, rare in black

|  | Crystal |  | Crystal |
|---|---|---|---|
| Ash tray, 4" | 6.00 | Oil bottle, 4 oz., hand. w/#133 stopper | 50.00 |
| Basket, 7½", bonbon | 60.00 | Oil bottle, 6 oz., oval | 45.00 |
| Basket, 8½", ftd. | 100.00 | Plate, 6", fingerbowl liner | 5.00 |
| Basket, 10", ftd. | 125.00 | Plate, 7", salad | 7.00 |
| Bowl, 7 quart punch | 60.00 | Plate, 8", salad | 9.00 |
| Bowl, 4", nut | 12.00 | Plate, 11", cookie | 17.00 |
| Bowl, 7", 2 part relish | 15.00 | Plate, 12", demi-torte, rolled edge | 20.00 |
| Bowl, 7", nappy | 12.50 | Plate, 13", deviled egg | 115.00 |
| Bowl, 8", flat nougat | 12.50 | Plate, 14", 2 hand. sandwich | 30.00 |
| Bowl, 9½", camellia | 15.00 | Plate, 21", buffet | 35.00 |
| Bowl, 10", hand. celery | 25.00 | Platter, 15", oval | 25.00 |
| Bowl, 10½", 2 hand. salad | 25.00 | Salt & pepper, pr. | 150.00 |
| Bowl, 10½", salad | 25.00 | Saucer | 4.00 |
| Bowl, 11", 2 hand., oblong relish | 17.00 | Stem, 1 oz., cordial, double loop | 130.00 |
| Bowl, 12", floral or fruit | 15.00 | Stem, 1 oz., cordial blown | 90.00 |
| Bowl, 13", celery | 18.00 | Stem, 2½ oz., wine, blown | 17.00 |
| Bowl, 13", gardenia | 20.00 | Stem, 3½ oz., cocktail, pressed | 6.00 |
| Bowl, 13", oval floral | 25.00 | Stem, 3½ oz., cocktail, blown | 7.00 |
| Candlestick, 1-lite | 7.00 | Stem, 3½ oz., wine, pressed | 7.00 |
| Candlestick, 2-lite | 12.50 | Stem, 4 oz., claret, blown | 10.00 |
| Candlestick, 3-lite | 20.00 | Stem, 4¼ oz., oyster cocktail or fruit | 6.00 |
| Candy box w/cover | 28.00 | Stem, 4½ oz., oyster cocktail, blown | 7.00 |
| Candy w/cover, 7" | 30.00 | Stem, 5½ oz., sherbet/saucer champagne, blown | 9.00 |
| Cheese, 5", ftd. w/cover | 25.00 | Stem, 6 oz., low sherbet | 5.00 |
| Cheese dish w/cover, 8" | 35.00 | Stem, 6 oz., sherbet/saucer champagne, pressed | 7.00 |
| Cigarette box | 20.00 | Stem, 9 oz., pressed | 11.00 |
| Coaster, 4" | 6.00 | Stem, 10 oz., blown | 12.50 |
| Compote, 10", w/cover | 50.00 | Sugar | 10.00 |
| Creamer | 10.00 | Tray for sugar & creamer | 12.00 |
| Creamer & sugar w/tray, individual | 30.00 | Tumbler, 5 oz., ftd, juice | 6.00 |
| Cup | 10.00 | Tumbler, 5 oz., ftd., juice, blown | 7.00 |
| Cup, punch | 4.00 | Tumbler, 12 oz., ftd. iced tea | 12.00 |
| Ice tub | 50.00 | Tumbler, 12 oz., ftd. iced tea, blown | 13.00 |
| Jar w/cover, 12", urn | 95.00 | Vase, 7", ftd. fan | 25.00 |
| Lamp & globe, 7", black-out | 45.00 | | |
| Lamp & globe, 8", candle | 40.00 | | |
| Mayonnaise, 5", bowl, 7", plate | 30.00 | | |

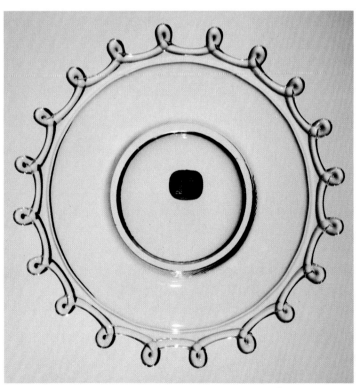

# LINCOLN INN, Fenton Glass Company, late 1920's

Colors: Amethyst, cobalt, black, red, green, pink, crystal, jade (opaque), green, light blue

   Choice pieces to own in this pattern include the pitcher and the salt & pepper shakers. Oddly enough, the stemware is easier to come by than basic serving pieces. Some of the red, particularly in the stems, show an amberina (yellow/red) cast.

| | Cobalt Blue, Red | All Other Colors |
|---|---|---|
| Ash tray | 10.00 | 5.00 |
| Bonbon, hand., sq. | 10.50 | 6.50 |
| Bonbon, hand., oval | 10.50 | 6.50 |
| Bowl, 5", fruit | 5.50 | 4.50 |
| Bowl, 6", cereal | 7.50 | 5.00 |
| Bowl, 6", crimped | 8.50 | 5.50 |
| Bowl, hand., olive | 8.50 | 5.50 |
| Bowl, finger | 7.50 | 6.00 |
| Bowl, 9", shallow | 17.50 | 13.00 |
| Bowl, 9¼", ftd. | 14.00 | 11.00 |
| Bowl, 10½", ftd. | 18.50 | 13.50 |
| Bowl, nut dish, ftd. | 11.50 | 6.50 |
| Candy dish, ftd. oval | 10.50 | 6.50 |
| Comport | 8.50 | 5.50 |
| Creamer | 16.50 | 11.50 |
| Cup | 9.50 | 6.50 |
| Pitcher, 7¼", 46 oz. | --- | 350.00 |
| Plate, 6" | 5.00 | 3.50 |
| Plate, 8" | 7.00 | 5.00 |
| Plate, 9¼" | 9.00 | 7.00 |
| Plate, 12" | 14.00 | 9.50 |
| Salt/pepper, pr. | 127.50 | 77.50 |
| Saucer | 3.50 | 2.00 |
| Sherbet, 4½", cone shape | --- | 7.50 |
| Sherbet, 4¾" | 12.50 | 7.50 |
| Stem, water | 16.50 | 11.00 |
| Stem, wine | 12.50 | 8.50 |
| Sugar | 15.00 | 11.50 |
| Tumbler, 4 oz., flat juice | 11.50 | 6.50 |
| Tumbler, 5 oz., ftd. | 11.50 | 7.50 |
| Tumbler, 7 oz., ftd. | 12.50 | 8.00 |
| Tumbler, 9 oz., ftd. | 13.50 | 8.50 |
| Tumbler, 12 oz., ftd. | 16.50 | 11.00 |
| Vase, 12", ftd. | 57.50 | 37.50 |

91

# MINUET, Etch 1503, QUEEN ANN Blank, #1509; TOUJOURS Blank, #1511; SYMPHONE Blank, #5010, et. al.; 1939 - 1950's

Color: Crystal

Here is a pattern for music lovers! This design has musicians and dancers within the cameo frames of a single piece. The dancers appear to be appropriately dressed for the minuet.

| | Crystal | | Crystal |
|---|---|---|---|
| Bell, dinner | 30.00 | Plate, 7", salad #1511 TOUJOURS | 12.00 |
| Bowl, finger #3309 | 12.00 | Plate, 8", luncheon | 15.00 |
| Bowl, 6", ftd. mint | 10.00 | Plate, 8", luncheon #1511 | |
| Bowl, 6", ftd., 2 hand. jelly | 15.00 | TOUJOURS | 17.00 |
| Bowl, 6½", salad dressings | 20.00 | Plate, 10½", service | 35.00 |
| Bowl, 7", salad dressings | 25.00 | Plate, 12", rnd., 2 hand. sandwich | 42.00 |
| Bowl, 7", triplex relish | 20.00 | Plate, 13", floral salver #1511 | |
| Bowl, 7½", sauce, ftd. | 20.00 | TOUJOURS | 35.00 |
| Bowl, 9½", 3 pt., "5 o'clock" relish | 30.00 | Plate, 14", torte, #1511 TOUJOURS | 35.00 |
| Bowl, 10", salad, #1511, | | Plate, 15", sand., #1511 TOUJOURS | 37.00 |
| TOUJOURS | 30.00 | Plate, 16", snack rack w/1447 | |
| Bowl, 11", ftd., floral | 40.00 | 2-lite candle | 60.00 |
| Bowl, 11", 3 pt., "5 o'clock" relish | 45.00 | Salt & pepper, pr. (#10) | 40.00 |
| Bowl, 12", oval floral, #1511 | | Saucer | 5.00 |
| TOUJOURS | 45.00 | Stem, #5010, SYMPHONE, 1 oz., | |
| Bowl, 12", oval #1514 | 40.00 | cordial | 75.00 |
| Bowl, 13", floral, #1511 TOUJOURS | 39.00 | Stem, #5010, 2½ oz., wine | 50.00 |
| Bowl, 13", pickle & olive | 20.00 | Stem, #5010, 3½ oz., cocktail | 30.00 |
| Bowl, 13½", shallow salad | 28.00 | Stem, #5010, 4 oz., claret | 30.00 |
| Candelbrum, 1-lite w/prisms | 110.00 | Stem, #5010, 4½ oz., oyster | |
| Candelabrum, 2-lite, bobeche & | | cocktail | 20.00 |
| prisms | 100.00 | Stem, #5010, 6 oz., saucer | |
| Candlestick, 1-lite, #112 | 17.50 | champagne | 25.00 |
| Candlestick, 3-lite, #142 CASCADE | 50.00 | Stem, #5010, 6 oz., sherbet | 15.00 |
| Candlestick, 5", 2-lite, #134 | | Stem, #5010, 9 oz., water | 25.00 |
| TRIDENT | 42.50 | Sugar, indiv. #1511 TOUJOURS | 20.00 |
| Centerpiece vase & prisms #1511 | | Sugar, indiv. #1509 QUEEN ANN | 20.00 |
| TOUJOURS | 150.00 | Sugar, dolp. ft., #1509 QUEEN ANN | 30.00 |
| Cocktail icer w/liner #3304 | | Sugar, #1511 TOUJOURS | 25.00 |
| UNIVERSAL | 27.00 | Tray, 12", celery #1511 TOUJOURS | 27.00 |
| Comport, 5½", #5010 | 30.00 | Tray, 15", social hour | 37.00 |
| Comport, 7½", #1511 TOUJOURS | 65.00 | Tray for indiv. sugar/creamer | 10.00 |
| Creamer, #1511 | 25.00 | Tumbler, #5010, 5 oz., fruit juice | 20.00 |
| Creamer, dolp. ft. | 30.00 | Tumbler, #5010, 9 oz., low ft water | 24.00 |
| Creamer, indiv. #1509 | 20.00 | Tumbler, #5010, 12 oz., tea | 30.00 |
| Creamer, indiv. #1511 | 25.00 | Tumbler, #2351, 12 oz., tea | 15.00 |
| Cup | 20.00 | Vase, 5", #5013 | 15.00 |
| Ice bucket, dolp. ft. | 95.00 | Vase, 5½", ftd. #1511 TOUJOURS | 37.50 |
| Marmalade w/cover, #1511 | | Vase, 6", urn #5012 | 25.00 |
| TOUJOURS (apple shape) | 50.00 | Vase, 7½", urn #5012 | 35.00 |
| Mayonnaise, 5½", dolp. ft. | 28.00 | Vase, 8", #4196 | 37.50 |
| Mayonnaise, ftd. #1511 TOUJOURS | 30.00 | Vase, 9", urn #5012 | 45.00 |
| Pitcher, 73 oz., #4164 | 100.00 | Vase, 10", #4192 | 50.00 |
| Plate, 7", mayonnaise liner | 10.00 | Vase, 10", #4192, SATURN optic | 52.50 |
| Plate, 7", salad | 10.00 | | |

93

# MOONDROPS, New Martinsville Glass Co., 1932 - 1940

Colors: Amber, pink, green, cobalt, ice blue, red, amethyst, crystal, dark green, light green, jadite, smoke, black

Flat pieces in Moondrops are more elusive than any other. Collectors tend to favor the "rocket" and "winged" styles over the "bee hive". Crystal only has merit with collectors as far as the butter dish.

| | Blue, Red | All Other Colors | | Blue, Red | All Other Colors |
|---|---|---|---|---|---|
| Ash tray . . . . . . . . . . . . . . . | 25.00 | 8.50 | Goblet, 6¼", 9 oz. water . . . . | 17.50 | 13.50 |
| Bowl, 5¼", berry . . . . . . . . . | 6.00 | 4.00 | Mug, 5 1/8", 12 oz. . . . . . . . . | 25.00 | 15.00 |
| Bowl, 6¾", soup . . . . . . . . . . | 10.00 | 8.00 | Perfume bottle, "Rocket" . . . . | 45.00 | 25.00 |
| Bowl, 7½", pickle . . . . . . . . . | 12.00 | 9.50 | Pitcher, 6 7/8", 22 oz., sm. | 125.00 .. | 70.00 |
| Bowl, 8 3/8", ftd., concave | | | Pitcher, 8 1/8", 32 oz., med. | 135.00 .. | 95.00 |
| top . . . . . . . . . . . . . . . . . | 13.00 | 12.00 | Pitcher, 8", 50 oz., lg. w/lip | 145.00 | 105.00 |
| Bowl, 8½", relish, div., 3 ft. . . . | 12.00 | 9.50 | Pitcher, 8 1/8", 53 oz., lg., no | | |
| Bowl, 9½", crimped, 3 ft. . . . | 17.50 | 12.50 | lip | 145.00 | 110.00 |
| Bowl, 9¾", veg., oval . . . . . . . | 22.50 | 17.50 | Plate, 5 7/8", bread & butter | 3.00 .. | 2.50 |
| Bowl, 9¾", casserole w/cover | 67.50 | 45.00 | Plate, 6", rnd., off-ctr. sherbet | | |
| Bowl, 9¾", oval, 2 hand. . . . . | 30.00 | 25.00 | indent . . . . . . . . . . . . . . . | 5.00 .. | 4.00 |
| Bowl, 11½", celery boat . . . . . | 20.00 | 17.50 | Plate, 6 1/8", sherbet . . . . . | 4.00 .. | 2.50 |
| Bowl, 12", console, 3 ft., rnd. | 30.00 | 22.50 | Plate, 7 1/8", salad . . . . . . . . | 6.00 .. | 5.00 |
| Bowl, 13", console w/"wings" | 57.00 | 27.50 | Plate, 8½", luncheon . . . . . . . | 10.00 | 5.00 |
| Butter dish w/cover | 350.00 | 225.00 | Plate, 9½", dinner . . . . . . . . . | 13.00 | 9.00 |
| Candlestick, 2", ruffled . . . . . | 12.00 | 9.00 | Plate, 15", sandwich, rnd. . . . | 22.50 | 13.00 |
| Candlestick, 4½", sherbet | | | Plate, 15", sandwich, 2 hand. | 27.50 | 20.00 |
| style. . . . . . . . . . . . . . . . . | 10.00 | 8.00 | Platter, 12", oval . . . . . . . . . | 17.50 | 12.00 |
| Candlestick, 5", "wings" . . . . | 25.00 | 17.00 | Powder jar w/cover . . . . . . . | 45.00 | 35.00 |
| Candlestick, 5¼", 3-lite . . . . . | 32.50 | 17.50 | Saucer. . . . . . . . . . . . . . . . . | 3.50 | 3.00 |
| Candlestick, 8½", metal stem | 13.00 | 10.00 | Sherbet, 2 5/8" . . . . . . . . . . | 10.00 | 6.50 |
| Candy dish, 8", ruffled. . . . . . | 15.00 | 12.50 | Sherbet, 4½" . . . . . . . . . . . . | 15.00 | 8.50 |
| Cocktail shaker w/or sans | | | Sugar, 2¾" . . . . . . . . . . . . . | 13.00 | 8.00 |
| hand. ftd., metal top . . . . . . | 25.00 | 17.00 | Sugar, 4" . . . . . . . . . . . . . . | 11.00 | 6.50 |
| Comport, 4" . . . . . . . . . . . . . | 12.50 | 7.50 | Tumbler, 2¾", 2 oz., shot . . . | 10.00 | 6.50 |
| Comport, 11½" . . . . . . . . . . | 27.50 | 17.50 | Tumbler, 2¾", 2 oz., hand. | | |
| Creamer, 2¾", indiv. . . . . . . . | 14.00 | 9.00 | shot . . . . . . . . . . . . . . . . . | 12.00 | 7.50 |
| Creamer, 3¾", reg. . . . . . . . . | 12.00 | 7.50 | Tumbler, 3¼", 3 oz., juice, | | |
| Cup . . . . . . . . . . . . . . . . . . | 9.00 | 7.50 | ftd. . . . . . . . . . . . . . . . . . | 11.00 | 7.50 |
| Decanter, 7¾", sm. . . . . . . . | 50.00 | 30.00 | Tumbler, 3 5/8", 5 oz. . . . . . . | 10.00 | 6.00 |
| Decanter, 8½", med. . . . . . . . | 55.00 | 32.50 | Tumbler, 4 3/8", 7 oz. . . . . . . | 11.00 | 7.50 |
| Decanter, 11¼", lg. . . . . . . . . | 65.00 | 37.50 | Tumbler, 4 3/8", 8 oz. . . . . . . | 12.00 | 8.50 |
| Decanter, 10¼", "rocket" . . . | 75.00 | 47.50 | Tumbler, 4 7/8", 9 oz., hand. | 13.50 | 9.50 |
| Goblet, 2 7/8", ¾ oz., liqueur | 17.50 | 12.50 | Tumbler, 4 7/8", 9 oz. . . . . . . | 12.50 | 10.00 |
| Goblet, 4", 4 oz. wine . . . . . . | 15.00 | 9.00 | Tumbler, 5 1/8", 12 oz. . . . . . . | 17.50 | 10.50 |
| Goblet, 4¾", "Rocket" wine. . | 25.00 | 17.50 | Tray, 7½", for indiv. | | |
| Goblet, 4¾", 5 oz. . . . . . . . . | 12.50 | 8.00 | sugar/creamer . . . . . . . . . . | 20.00 | 14.00 |
| Goblet, 5 1/8", metal stem | | | Vase, 7¾", flat, crimped top . | 40.00 | 32.50 |
| wine. . . . . . . . . . . . . . . . . | 12.00 | 8.00 | Vase, 9¼", "Rocket" style . . . | 75.00 | 55.00 |
| Goblet, 5½", metal stem wine | 13.50 | 8.50 | | | |

# "NORA BIRD", Paden City Glass Company, Line #300, 1929 - 30's

Colors: Pink, green

Collectors have "named" this pattern. To Paden City it was a certain numbered etching on their popular #300 line blank. I've found it in pink and green; possibly it exists in their other colors of yellow and blue. This etching is distinguished by the bird being poised ready for flight. On the cup, saucer and candleholders however, the bird is already in flight.

| | Pink, Green |
|---|---|
| Candlestick, pr. . . . . . . . . . . . . . . . . . . . . . . . . . . . . . | 35.00 |
| Candy w/lid, ftd., 4¾", high . . . . . . . . . . . . . . . . . . . . . . . | 37.50 |
| Candy dish w/cover, 6½", 3 pt. . . . . . . . . . . . . . . . . . . . . . | 37.50 |
| Creamer, rnd. hand. . . . . . . . . . . . . . . . . . . . . . . . . . . . . | 20.00 |
| Creamer, pointed hand. . . . . . . . . . . . . . . . . . . . . . . . . . . | 18.50 |
| Cup . . . . . . . . . . . . . . . . . . . . . . . . . . . . . . . . . . . . . . . . | 35.00 |
| Ice tub, 6" . . . . . . . . . . . . . . . . . . . . . . . . . . . . . . . . . . | 42.50 |
| Mayonnaise and liner . . . . . . . . . . . . . . . . . . . . . . . . . . . | 35.00 |
| Plate, 8" . . . . . . . . . . . . . . . . . . . . . . . . . . . . . . . . . . . . | 15.00 |
| Saucer . . . . . . . . . . . . . . . . . . . . . . . . . . . . . . . . . . . . . | 10.00 |
| Sugar, rnd. hand. . . . . . . . . . . . . . . . . . . . . . . . . . . . . . | 20.00 |
| Sugar, pointed hand. . . . . . . . . . . . . . . . . . . . . . . . . . . . | 18.50 |
| Tumbler, 3" . . . . . . . . . . . . . . . . . . . . . . . . . . . . . . . . . . | 20.00 |
| Tumbler, 4" . . . . . . . . . . . . . . . . . . . . . . . . . . . . . . . . . . | 25.00 |
| Tumbler, 4¾", ftd. . . . . . . . . . . . . . . . . . . . . . . . . . . . . . | 30.00 |

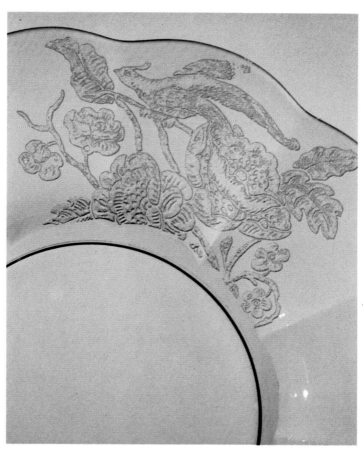

# OCTAGON, Blank #1231 - Ribbed; also Blank 500 and Blank 1229, A. H. Heisey & Co.

Colors: Crystal, "Flamingo" pink, "Sahara" yellow, "Moongleam" green, "Hawthorne" orchid; "Marigold", a deep, amber/yellow, and "Dawn"

| | Crystal | Flam. | Sahara | Moon. | Hawth. | Marigold |
|---|---|---|---|---|---|---|
| Basket, 5", #500 . . . . . . . . . . . . . . | 50.00 | 70.00 | 85.00 | 80.00 | 110.00 | |
| Bonbon, 6", sides up, #1229 . . . . . . | 5.00 | 8.00 | 10.00 | 12.00 | 15.00 | |
| Bowl, cream soup, 2 hand. . . . . . . . | 10.00 | 15.00 | 20.00 | 25.00 | 30.00 | |
| Bowl, 5½", jelly, #1229 . . . . . . . . . | 5.00 | 8.00 | 10.00 | 12.00 | 15.00 | |
| Bowl, 6", mint, #1229 . . . . . . . . . . | 5.00 | 8.00 | 10.00 | 12.00 | 15.00 | |
| Bowl, 6", #500 . . . . . . . . . . . . . . | 12.00 | 17.00 | 19.00 | 20.00 | 25.00 | |
| Bowl, 6½", grapefruit . . . . . . . . . . | 9.00 | 14.00 | 16.00 | 15.00 | 20.00 | |
| Bowl, 8", ftd., #1229 . . . . . . . . . | 12.00 | 17.00 | 20.00 | 24.00 | 28.00 | |
| Bowl, 9", vegetable . . . . . . . . . . . . | 10.00 | 15.00 | 18.00 | 23.00 | 35.00 | |
| Bowl, 12½", salad . . . . . . . . . . . . | 12.00 | 18.00 | 22.00 | 27.00 | 40.00 | |
| Candlestick, 3", 1-lite . . . . . . . . . . | 7.00 | 15.00 | 20.00 | 25.00 | 35.00 | |
| Cheese dish, 6", 2 hand. #1229 . . . . | 5.00 | 8.00 | 10.00 | 12.00 | 15.00 | |
| Creamer #500 . . . . . . . . . . . . . . | 5.00 | 12.00 | 16.00 | 17.00 | 22.00 | |
| Creamer, hotel . . . . . . . . . . . . . . | 7.00 | 12.00 | 15.00 | 18.00 | 25.00 | |
| Cup, after dinner . . . . . . . . . . . . | 5.00 | 10.00 | 15.00 | 20.00 | 25.00 | |
| Dish, frozen dessert #500 . . . . . . . . | 7.00 | 10.00 | 14.00 | 12.00 | 22.00 | 32.00 |
| Ice tub, #500 . . . . . . . . . . . . . | 20.00 | 40.00 | 55.00 | 60.00 | 75.00 | 80.00 |
| Mayonnaise, 5½", ftd. #1229 . . . . . . | 10.00 | 14.00 | 16.00 | 18.00 | 22.00 | |
| Plate, cream soup liner . . . . . . . . . | 3.00 | 5.00 | 7.00 | 9.00 | 12.00 | |
| Plate, 6" . . . . . . . . . . . . . . . . . | 4.00 | 6.00 | 8.00 | 10.00 | 12.00 | |
| Plate, 7", bread . . . . . . . . . . . . . | 5.00 | 7.00 | 9.00 | 11.00 | 13.00 | |
| Plate, 8", luncheon . . . . . . . . . . . | 6.00 | 8.00 | 10.00 | 12.00 | 14.00 | |
| Plate, 9", soup . . . . . . . . . . . . . | 10.00 | 14.00 | 18.00 | 22.00 | 26.00 | |
| Plate, 10", sand., #1229 . . . . . . . . | 13.00 | 18.00 | 22.00 | 25.00 | 30.00 | |
| Plate, 10", muffin, #1229 . . . . . . . . | 15.00 | 20.00 | 24.00 | 27.00 | 32.00 | |
| Plate, 10½" . . . . . . . . . . . . . . . | 15.00 | 20.00 | 27.00 | 29.00 | 32.00 | |
| Plate, 10½", ctr. hand. sandwich . . . | 20.00 | 27.00 | 32.00 | 35.00 | 45.00 | |
| Plate, 12", muffin, #1229 . . . . . . . . | 17.00 | 23.00 | 28.00 | 30.00 | 35.00 | |
| Plate, 13", hors d'oeuvre #1229 . . . . | 15.00 | 20.00 | 25.00 | 30.00 | 35.00 | |
| Plate, 14" . . . . . . . . . . . . . . . . | 17.00 | 22.00 | 25.00 | 28.00 | 32.00 | |
| Platter, 12¾" . . . . . . . . . . . . . . | 20.00 | 27.00 | 32.00 | 35.00 | 45.00 | |
| Saucer, after dinner . . . . . . . . . . . | 2.00 | 5.00 | 6.00 | 6.00 | 12.00 | |
| Sugar #500 . . . . . . . . . . . . . . . | 5.00 | 12.00 | 16.00 | 17.00 | 22.00 | |
| Sugar, hotel . . . . . . . . . . . . . . . | 7.00 | 12.00 | 15.00 | 18.00 | 25.00 | |
| Tray, 6", oblong, #500 . . . . . . . . . | 5.00 | 12.00 | 16.00 | 17.00 | 22.00 | |
| Tray, 9", celery . . . . . . . . . . . . . | 7.00 | 15.00 | 18.00 | 20.00 | 25.00 | |
| Tray, 12", celery . . . . . . . . . . . . | 10.00 | 20.00 | 25.00 | 27.00 | 32.00 | (Dawn) |
| Tray, 12", 4 pt., #500 . . . . . . . . . . | 20.00 | 45.00 | 55.00 | 65.00 | 75.00 | 150.00 |

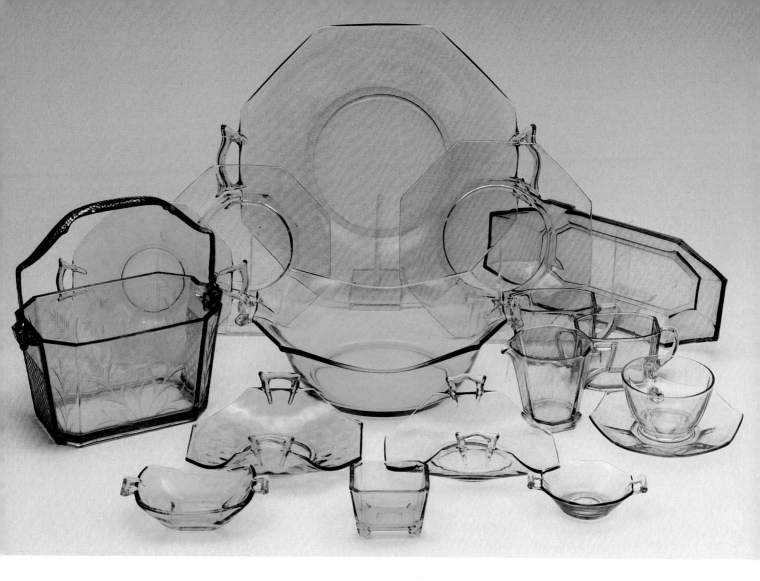

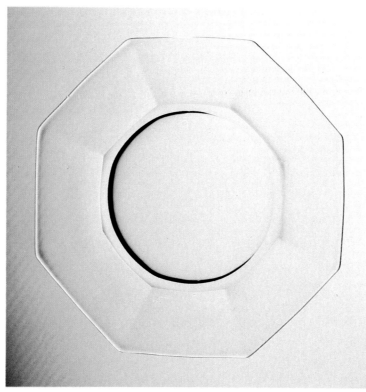

# OLD COLONY, Empress Blank #1401; Carcassone Blank #3390; and Old Dominion

## Blank #3380, A. H. Heisey & Co., 1930 - 1939

Colors: Crystal, "Sahara" yellow, "Moongleam" green, "Flamingo" pink, "Marigold" (a deep, amber/yellow), cobalt

| | Crystal | Flam. | Sahara | Moon. | Mari. |
|---|---|---|---|---|---|
| Bar glass, #3390, 2 oz., ftd. | 7.00 | 15.00 | 20.00 | 25.00 | |
| Bouillon cup, 2 hand., ftd. | 12.00 | 17.00 | 19.00 | 22.00 | |
| Bowl, finger, #4075 | 5.00 | 9.00 | 10.00 | 13.00 | 15.00 |
| Bowl, ftd. finger #3390 | 5.00 | 15.00 | 20.00 | 25.00 | |
| Bowl, 4½", nappy | 7.00 | 10.00 | 12.00 | 14.00 | |
| Bowl, 5", ftd., 2 hand. | 12.00 | 17.00 | 22.00 | 27.00 | |
| Bowl, 6", ftd., 2 hand. jelly | 14.00 | 19.00 | 24.00 | 30.00 | |
| Bowl, 6", dolp. ftd. mint | 14.00 | 19.00 | 24.00 | 30.00 | |
| Bowl, 7", triplex relish | 14.00 | 20.00 | 24.00 | 27.00 | |
| Bowl, 7½", dolp. ftd. nappy | 20.00 | 55.00 | 60.00 | 65.00 | |
| Bowl, 8", nappy | 24.00 | 33.00 | 38.00 | 40.00 | |
| Bowl, 8½", ftd. floral, 2 hand. | 30.00 | 45.00 | 55.00 | 65.00 | |
| Bowl, 9", 3 hand. | 33.00 | 65.00 | 75.00 | 80.00 | |
| Bowl, 10", rnd., 2 hand. salad | 30.00 | 40.00 | 50.00 | 60.00 | |
| Bowl, 10", sq. salad, 2 hand. | 30.00 | 40.00 | 50.00 | 60.00 | |
| Bowl, 10", oval dessert, 2 hand. | 30.00 | 40.00 | 48.00 | 58.00 | |
| Bowl, 10", oval veg. | 30.00 | 34.00 | 42.00 | 50.00 | |
| Bowl, 11", floral, dolp. ft. | 30.00 | 65.00 | 70.00 | 75.00 | |
| Bowl, 13", ftd. flared | 28.00 | 34.00 | 38.00 | 42.00 | |
| Bowl, 13", 2 pt. pickle & olive | 12.00 | 18.00 | 20.00 | 25.00 | |
| Cigarette holder #3390, (Cobalt $75.00) | 12.00 | 40.00 | 35.00 | 45.00 | |
| Comport, 7", oval, ftd. | 35.00 | 65.00 | 70.00 | 75.00 | |
| Comport, 7", ftd. #3368 | 30.00 | 50.00 | 55.00 | 75.00 | 60.00 |
| Cream soup, 2 hand. | 12.00 | 18.00 | 20.00 | 25.00 | |
| Creamer, dolp. ft. | 16.00 | 29.00 | 40.00 | 44.00 | |
| Creamer, indiv. | 12.00 | 24.00 | 27.00 | 30.00 | |
| Cup, after dinner | 12.00 | 22.00 | 33.00 | 45.00 | |
| Cup | 10.00 | 26.00 | 32.00 | 38.00 | |
| Decanter, 1 pt. | 110.00 | 230.00 | 200.00 | 400.00 | |
| Flagon, 12 oz., #3390 | 20.00 | 40.00 | 40.00 | 65.00 | |

## OLD COLONY, Empress Blank #1401; Carcassone Blank #3390; and Old Dominion Blank #3380, A. H. Heisey & Co., 1930 - 1939 (continued)

| | Crystal | Flam. | Sahara | Moon. | Mari. |
|---|---|---|---|---|---|
| Grapefruit, 6" | 15.00 | 23.00 | 30.00 | 35.00 | |
| Grapefruit, ftd. #3380 | 9.00 | 15.00 | 16.00 | 18.00 | 20.00 |
| Ice tub, dolp. ft. | 40.00 | 90.00 | 100.00 | 120.00 | |
| Mayonnaise, 5½", dolp. ft. | 35.00 | 50.00 | 65.00 | 75.00 | |
| Oil, 4 oz., ftd. | 35.00 | 60.00 | 90.00 | 100.00 | |
| Pitcher, 3 pt., #3390 | 65.00 | 200.00 | 150.00 | 300.00 | |
| Pitcher, 3 pt., dolp. ft. | 60.00 | 130.00 | 140.00 | 150.00 | |
| Plate, bouillon | 5.00 | 8.00 | 12.00 | 15.00 | |
| Plate, cream soup | 5.00 | 8.00 | 12.00 | 15.00 | |
| Plate, 4½", rnd. | 3.00 | 6.00 | 7.00 | 8.00 | |
| Plate, 6", rnd. | 6.00 | 12.00 | 15.00 | 18.00 | |
| Plate, 6", sq. | 6.00 | 12.00 | 15.00 | 18.00 | |
| Plate, 7", rnd. | 8.00 | 14.00 | 18.00 | 20.00 | |
| Plate, 7", sq. | 8.00 | 14.00 | 18.00 | 20.00 | |
| Plate, 8", rnd. | 10.00 | 17.00 | 22.00 | 27.00 | |
| Plate, 8", sq. | 10.00 | 17.00 | 22.00 | 27.00 | |
| Plate, 9", rnd. | 15.00 | 22.00 | 24.00 | 28.00 | |
| Plate, 10½", rnd. | 25.00 | 45.00 | 55.00 | 62.00 | |
| Plate, 10½", sq. | 25.00 | 45.00 | 55.00 | 62.00 | |
| Plate, 12", rnd. | 30.00 | 50.00 | 60.00 | 65.00 | |
| Plate, 12", 2 hand. rnd. muffin | 30.00 | 50.00 | 60.00 | 65.00 | |
| Plate, 12", 2 hand., rnd. sand. | 30.00 | 50.00 | 60.00 | 65.00 | |
| Plate, 13", 2 hand., sq. sand. | 35.00 | 40.00 | 45.00 | 50.00 | |
| Plate, 13", 2 hand. muffin, sq. | 35.00 | 40.00 | 45.00 | 50.00 | |
| Platter, 14", oval | 25.00 | 35.00 | 40.00 | 45.00 | |
| Salt & pepper, pr. | 45.00 | 67.00 | 89.00 | 99.00 | |
| Saucer, sq. | 4.00 | 8.00 | 10.00 | 10.00 | |
| Saucer, rnd. | 4.00 | 8.00 | 10.00 | 10.00 | |
| Stem, #3380, 1 oz., cordial | 50.00 | 90.00 | 95.00 | 100.00 | 275.00 |
| Stem, #3380, 2½ oz., wine | 15.00 | 35.00 | 25.00 | 40.00 | 50.00 |
| Stem, #3380, 3 oz., cocktail | 13.00 | 32.00 | 22.00 | 38.00 | 47.00 |
| Stem, #3380, 4 oz., oyster/cocktail | 8.00 | 13.00 | 15.00 | 17.00 | 20.00 |
| Stem, #3380, 4 oz., claret | 15.00 | 35.00 | 25.00 | 40.00 | 50.00 |
| Stem, #3380, 5 oz., parfait | 10.00 | 15.00 | 15.00 | 17.00 | 35.00 |

# OLD COLONY, Empress Blank #1401; Carcassone Blank #3390; and Old Dominion Blank #3380, A.H. Heisey & CO., 1930 - 1939 (continued)

| | Crystal | Flam. | Sahara | Moon. | Mari. |
|---|---|---|---|---|---|
| Stem, #3380, 6 oz., champagne | 8.00 | 13.00 | 15.00 | 17.00 | 20.00 |
| Stem, #3380, 6 oz., sherbet | 6.00 | 11.00 | 13.00 | 15.00 | 18.00 |
| Stem, #3380, 10 oz., short soda | 7.00 | 18.00 | 15.00 | 22.00 | 27.00 |
| Stem, #3380, 10 oz., tall soda | 10.00 | 21.00 | 18.00 | 25.00 | 30.00 |
| Stem, #3390, 1 oz., cordial | 20.00 | 100.00 | 85.00 | 125.00 | |
| Stem, #3390, 2½ oz., wine | 10.00 | 18.00 | 25.00 | 30.00 | |
| Stem, #3390, 3 oz., cocktail | 7.00 | 15.00 | 20.00 | 25.00 | |
| Stem, #3390, 3 oz., oyster/cocktail | 7.00 | 15.00 | 20.00 | 25.00 | |
| Stem, #3390, 4 oz., claret | 12.00 | 22.50 | 27.50 | 32.50 | |
| Stem, #3390, 6 oz., champagne | 10.00 | 20.00 | 25.00 | 30.00 | |
| Stem, #3390, 6 oz., sherbet | 10.00 | 20.00 | 25.00 | 30.00 | |
| Stem, #3390, 11 oz., low water | 8.00 | 20.00 | 25.00 | 30.00 | |
| Stem, #3390, 11 oz., tall water | 10.00 | 22.00 | 27.00 | 32.00 | |
| Sugar, dolp. ft. | 16.00 | 29.00 | 40.00 | 44.00 | |
| Sugar, indiv. | 12.00 | 24.00 | 27.00 | 30.00 | |
| Tray, 10", celery | 14.00 | 20.00 | 25.00 | 30.00 | |
| Tray, 12", ctr. hand. sand. | 35.00 | 50.00 | 60.00 | 70.00 | |
| Tray, 12", 12", ctr. hand. sq. | 35.00 | 50.00 | 60.00 | 70.00 | |
| Tray, 13", celery | 17.00 | 20.00 | 26.00 | 30.00 | |
| Tray, 13", 2 hand. hors d'oeuvre | 30.00 | 35.00 | 42.00 | 50.00 | |
| Tumbler, dolp. ft. | 70.00 | 90.00 | 125.00 | 135.00 | |
| Tumbler, #3380, 1 oz., ftd. bar | 20.00 | 30.00 | 35.00 | 40.00 | 45.00 |
| Tumbler, #3380, 2 oz., ftd. bar | 12.00 | 20.00 | 20.00 | 25.00 | 30.00 |
| Tumbler, #3380, 5 oz., ftd. bar | 7.00 | 12.00 | 12.00 | 17.00 | 22.00 |
| Tumbler, #3380, 8 oz., ftd. soda | 10.00 | 21.00 | 18.00 | 25.00 | 30.00 |
| Tumbler, #3380, 10 oz., ftd. soda | 12.00 | 23.00 | 20.00 | 25.00 | 30.00 |
| Tumbler, #3380, 12 oz., ftd. tea | 13.00 | 25.00 | 22.00 | 27.00 | 32.00 |
| Tumbler, #3390, 5 oz. ftd. juice | 7.00 | 15.00 | 20.00 | 25.00 | |
| Tumbler, #3390, 8 oz., ftd. soda | 10.00 | 22.00 | 25.00 | 30.00 | |
| Tumbler, #3390, 12 oz., ftd., tea | 12.00 | 24.00 | 27.00 | 30.00 | |
| Vase, 9", ftd. | 60.00 | 95.00 | 100.00 | 135.00 | |

# OLD SANDWICH, Blank #1404, A. H. Heisey & Co.

Colors: Crystal, "Flamingo" pink, "Sahara" yellow, "Moongleam" green, cobalt

| | Crystal | Flam. | Sahara | Moon. | Cobalt |
|---|---|---|---|---|---|
| Ash tray, individual ................... | 5.00 | 30.00 | 20.00 | 35.00 | 40.00 |
| Beer mug, 12 oz. ...................... | 25.00 | 190.00 | 200.00 | 250.00 | 275.00 |
| Beer mug, 14 oz. ...................... | 27.00 | 200.00 | 225.00 | 275.00 | 300.00 |
| Beer mug, 18 oz. ...................... | 29.00 | 225.00 | 250.00 | 300.00 | 325.00 |
| Bottle, catsup w/#3 stopper (like lg. cruet) .. | 30.00 | 55.00 | 65.00 | 75.00 | |
| Bowl, finger ......................... | 9.00 | 12.00 | 15.00 | 18.00 | |
| Bowl, ftd. popped corn, cupped ........... | 30.00 | 45.00 | 55.00 | 65.00 | |
| Bowl, 11", rnd. ftd., floral .............. | 25.00 | 40.00 | 50.00 | 60.00 | |
| Bowl, 12", oval, ftd., floral ............. | 27.00 | 50.00 | 60.00 | 70.00 | |
| Candlestick, 6" ....................... | 28.00 | 50.00 | 60.00 | 70.00 | 200.00 |
| Cigarette holder ...................... | 25.00 | 30.00 | 35.00 | 40.00 | |
| Comport, 6" .......................... | 30.00 | 70.00 | 75.00 | 80.00 | |
| Creamer, oval ........................ | 7.00 | 20.00 | 22.00 | 25.00 | |
| Creamer, 12 oz. ...................... | 30.00 | 160.00 | 165.00 | 170.00 | |
| Creamer, 14 oz. ...................... | 32.00 | 170.00 | 175.00 | 180.00 | |
| Creamer, 18 oz. ...................... | 35.00 | 180.00 | 185.00 | 190.00 | |
| Cup .................................. | 8.00 | 12.00 | 14.00 | 16.00 | |
| Decanter, 1 pint w/#98 stopper .......... | 65.00 | 160.00 | 170.00 | 180.00 | 325.00 |
| Floral block #22 ...................... | 10.00 | 20.00 | 25.00 | 30.00 | |
| Oil bottle 2½ oz., #85 stopper ........... | 60.00 | 70.00 | 75.00 | 80.00 | |
| Parfait, 4½ oz. ....................... | 10.00 | 15.00 | 20.00 | 25.00 | |
| Pilsner, 8 oz. ........................ | 12.00 | 25.00 | 30.00 | 35.00 | |
| Pilsner, 10 oz. ....................... | 15.00 | 28.00 | 32.00 | 38.00 | |
| Pitcher, ½ gallon, ice................... | 65.00 | 120.00 | 125.00 | 130.00 | |
| Pitcher, ½ gallon, reg. ................. | 60.00 | 119.00 | 124.00 | 129.00 | |
| Plate, 6", square, grnd. bottom ........... | 4.00 | 8.00 | 10.00 | 13.00 | |
| Plate, 7", square ..................... | 5.00 | 10.00 | 13.00 | 15.00 | |
| Plate, 8", square ..................... | 7.00 | 12.00 | 15.00 | 17.00 | |
| Salt & pepper, pr...................... | 30.00 | 40.00 | 50.00 | 60.00 | |
| Saucer ............................... | 7.00 | 10.00 | 12.00 | 14.00 | |
| Stem, 2½ oz., wine..................... | 12.00 | 20.00 | 25.00 | 30.00 | |
| Stem, 3 oz., cocktail .................. | 9.00 | 14.00 | 16.00 | 19.00 | |
| Stem, 4 oz., claret .................... | 10.00 | 15.00 | 17.00 | 20.00 | 90.00 |
| Stem, 4 oz., oyster cocktail ............. | 4.00 | 9.00 | 10.00 | 12.00 | |
| Stem, 4 oz., sherbet ................... | 5.00 | 10.00 | 12.00 | 15.00 | |
| Stem, 5 oz., saucer champagne ........... | 7.00 | 22.00 | 25.00 | 28.00 | |
| Stem, 10 oz., low ft.................... | 9.00 | 22.00 | 26.00 | 30.00 | |
| Sugar, oval .......................... | 7.00 | 20.00 | 22.00 | 25.00 | |
| Sundae, 6 oz. ........................ | 4.00 | 10.00 | 15.00 | 20.00 | |
| Tumbler, 1½ oz., bar, grnd. bottom ........ | 10.00 | 25.00 | 30.00 | 35.00 | |
| Tumbler, 5 oz., juice .................. | 4.00 | 12.00 | 15.00 | 20.00 | |
| Tumbler, 6½ oz., toddy ................. | 7.00 | 14.00 | 16.00 | 19.00 | |
| Tumbler, 8 oz., grnd. bottom, cupped & straight rim....................... | 7.00 | 15.00 | 20.00 | 25.00 | |
| Tumbler, 10 oz. ...................... | 9.00 | 15.00 | 20.00 | 25.00 | |
| Tumbler, 10 oz., low ft. ............... | 9.00 | 15.00 | 20.00 | 25.00 | |
| Tumbler, 12 oz., ftd. iced tea ........... | 10.00 | 17.00 | 22.00 | 27.00 | |
| Tumbler, 12 oz., iced tea ............... | 10.00 | 17.00 | 22.00 | 27.00 | |

# ORCHID, (Etching 1507) ON WAVERLY BLANK #1519, A. H. Heisey & Co., 1940 - 1957

Color: Crystal

Heisey Orchid was (and is) their most popular etching. It becomes a little difficult for writers (and collectors) to learn when the company put that popular etching on various blanks. There are umpteen lines of glass with orchid etch. For this book I have chosen to deal with what I feel are the MAIN blanks or stems to be encountered. Should another TYPE stem or blank be mentioned in the listing, I'll name it in CAPITAL LETTERS at the end of the listing. For instance, many Orchid items are to be found on QUEEN ANNE blanks or #5022 GRACEFUL stems rather than the WAVERLY blank and the TYROLEAN stem with which this listing mainly deals.

| | Crystal | | Crystal |
|---|---|---|---|
| Bell, dinner, #5025, TYROLEAN | 90.00 | Cup | 35.00 |
| Bowl, finger, #3309 | 20.00 | Ice bucket, 2 hand. | 130.00 |
| Bowl, 5½", ftd. mint | 22.00 | Mayonnaise, 5½", 1 hand. | 35.00 |
| Bowl, 6", oval lemon w/cover | 75.00 | Mayonnaise, 5½", ftd. | 35.00 |
| Bowl, 6½", ftd. honey; cheese | 25.00 | Mayonnaise, 5½", 1 hand. div. | 37.50 |
| Bowl, 6½", ftd. jelly | 25.00 | Mayonnaise, 6½", 1 hand. | 40.00 |
| Bowl, 6½", 2 pt. oval dressings | 37.50 | Mayonnaise, 6½", 1 hand., div. | 42.50 |
| Bowl, 7", salad | 40.00 | Oil, 3 oz., ftd. | 127.50 |
| Bowl, 7", 3 pt., rnd. relish | 37.50 | Pitcher, 73 oz. | 165.00 |
| Bowl, 7", ftd. honey; cheese | 35.00 | Pitcher, martini | 400.00 |
| Bowl, 7", ftd. jelly | 50.00 | Plate, 7", mayonnaise | 15.00 |
| Bowl, 7", ftd. oval nut | 30.00 | Plate, 7", salad | 15.50 |
| Bowl, 8", 2 pt. oval dressings | 42.50 | Plate, 8", salad | 22.00 |
| Bowl, 8", 4 pt., rnd. relish | 45.00 | Plate, 10½", dinner | 65.00 |
| Bowl, 9½", crimped floral | 47.50 | Plate, 11", demi-torte | 45.00 |
| Bowl, 9", 4 pt., rnd. relish | 45.00 | Plate, 11", sandwich | 40.00 |
| Bowl, 9", ft. fruit or salad | 50.00 | Plate, 12", ftd. salver | 100.00 |
| Bowl, 9", salad | 50.00 | Plate, 13½", ftd. cake or salver | 175.00 |
| Bowl, 10", gardenia | 60.00 | Plate, 14", torte, rolled edge | 45.00 |
| Bowl, 10½", ftd. floral | 62.50 | Plate, 14", torte | 45.00 |
| Bowl, 11", shallow, rolled edge | 65.00 | Plate, 14", cheese 'n cracker | 52.50 |
| Bowl, 11", 3 ftd. floral, seahorse ft. | 95.00 | Plate, 14", sandwich | 75.00 |
| Bowl, 11", 3 pt., oblong relish | 65.00 | Salt & pepper, pr. | 50.00 |
| Bowl, 11", 4 ftd., oval | 60.00 | Salt & pepper, ft., pr. | 55.00 |
| Bowl, 11", flared | 55.00 | Saucer | 8.00 |
| Bowl, 11", floral | 55.00 | Stem, #5022, GRACEFUL, 1 oz., cordial | 100.00 |
| Bowl, 11", ftd. floral | 65.00 | Stem, #5022, 2 oz., sherry | 75.00 |
| Bowl, 12", crimped floral | 60.00 | Stem, #5022, 4 oz., oyster cocktail | 27.50 |
| Bowl, 13", floral | 65.00 | Stem, #5022, 4 oz., cocktail | 40.00 |
| Bowl, 13", crimped floral | 60.00 | Stem, #5022, 6 oz., saucer champagne | 27.00 |
| Bowl, 13", gardenia | 65.00 | Stem, #5022, 6 oz., sherbet | 22.00 |
| Butter w/cover, 6" | 135.00 | Stem, #5025, TYROLEAN, 3 oz., wine | 60.00 |
| Candleholder, 6", deep (epergne) | 35.00 | Stem, #5025, 4½ oz., claret | 45.00 |
| Candlestick, 2-lite | 50.00 | Stem, #5025, 10 oz., low water goblet | 32.50 |
| Candlestick, 3-lite | 65.00 | Stem, #5025, 10 oz., water goblet | 35.00 |
| Candlestick, 4½", 1-lite, plume | 75.00 | Sugar, indiv. | 20.00 |
| Candy box w/cover, 6", low ft. | 110.00 | Sugar, ftd. | 27.50 |
| Candy w/cover, 5", high ft. | 155.00 | Toast w/dome | 100.00 |
| Cheese (comport) & cracker (11½", plate) | 65.00 | Tray, 12", celery | 45.00 |
| Chocolate w/cover, 5" | 120.00 | Tray, 13", celery | 47.50 |
| Cigarette holder w/cover | 90.00 | Trinket box w/cover, oval, lion finial | 200.00 |
| Comport, 6", low ft. | 40.00 | Tumbler, #5025, TYROLEAN, 5 oz. fruit | 30.00 |
| Comport, 6½", low ft. | 42.00 | Tumbler, #5025, 12 oz., iced tea | 30.00 |
| Comport, 7", ftd. oval | 75.00 | Vase, 4 oz., ftd. violet | 52.50 |
| Creamer, indiv. | 20.00 | Vase, 7", ftd., fan | 65.00 |
| Creamer, ftd. | 27.50 | Vase, 7", ftd. | 60.00 |
| | | Vase, 10", sq. ftd. bud | 65.00 |

## "PEACOCK REVERSE", Line #412, Paden City Glass Company, 1930's

Colors: Cobalt blue, red, yellow

    I have seen this pattern reputed to be made by every major glass company at antique shows. The pieces usually have a very stiff price at these type shows due to it's look of "quality".
    The blank, (line #412) is generally called "crow's foot".

| | Red, Blue |
|---|---|
| Bowl, 4 7/8", sq. | 20.00 |
| Bowl, 8¾", sq. | 47.50 |
| Bowl, 8¾", sq. w/handles | 52.50 |
| Candlestick, 5¾", sq. base | 35.00 |
| Candy dish, 6½", sq. | 47.50 |
| Creamer, 2¾", flat | 45.00 |
| Plate, 5¾", sherbet | 15.00 |
| Sherbet, 4 5/8" h., 3 3/8", diam. | 30.00 |
| Sherbet, 4 7/8" h., 3 5/8", diam. | 30.00 |
| Sugar, 2¾", flat | 45.00 |
| Tumbler, 4", 10 oz., flat | 40.00 |

## "PEACOCK & WILD ROSE", Line #300, Paden City Glass Co., 1930's

Colors: Pink, green, cobalt blue

    This was a popular line for Paden City. It's probable there are other pieces to be found with this particular etching.

| | Pink, Green |
|---|---|
| Bowl, 8½", flat | 22.50 |
| Bowl, 8½", fruit, oval, ftd. | 32.50 |
| Bowl, 8¾", ftd. | 25.00 |
| Bowl, 9½", ctr. hand. | 30.00 |
| Bowl, 9½", ftd. | 27.50 |
| Bowl, 10½", ctr. hand. | 32.50 |
| Bowl, 10½", ftd. | 37.50 |
| Bowl, 10½", fruit | 35.00 |
| Bowl, 11", console | 30.00 |
| Bowl, 14", console | 37.50 |
| Candlestick, 5" | 18.00 |
| Candy dish w/cover, 7" | 57.50 |
| Comport, 6¼" | 20.00 |
| Ice bucket, 6" | 45.00 |
| Ice tub, 4¾" | 40.00 |
| Plate, cake, low ft. | 27.50 |
| Relish, 3 pt. | 20.00 |
| Vase, 10" | 57.50 |

# PLANTATION, Blank #1567, A. H. Heisey & Co.

Color: Crystal; rare in amber

| | Crystal | | Crystal |
|---|---|---|---|
| Ash tray, 3½" | 15.00 | Mayonnaise, 4½", rolled ft. | 18.00 |
| Bowl, 9 quart Dr. Johnson punch | 90.00 | Mayonnaise, 5¼", w/liner | 20.00 |
| Bowl, 5", nappy | 12.00 | Oil bottle, 3 oz., w/#125 stopper | 42.00 |
| Bowl, 5½", nappy | 13.00 | Pitcher, ½ gallon, ice lip, blown | 85.00 |
| Bowl, 6½", 2 hand. jelly | 16.00 | Plate, coupe (rare) | 125.00 |
| Bowl, 6½", flared jelly | 18.00 | Plate, 7", salad | 9.00 |
| Bowl, 6½", ftd. honey, cupped | 22.00 | Plate, 8", salad | 11.00 |
| Bowl, 8", 4 part, rnd. relish | 23.00 | Plate, 10½", demi-torte | 18.00 |
| Bowl, 8½", 2 part dressing | 16.00 | Plate, 13", ftd. cake salver | 65.00 |
| Bowl, 9", salad | 22.00 | Plate, 14", sandwich | 22.00 |
| Bowl, 9½", crimped, fruit or flower | 22.00 | Plate, 18", buffet | 24.00 |
| Bowl, 9½", gardenia | 20.00 | Plate, 18", punch bowl liner | 24.00 |
| Bowl, 11", 3 part relish | 19.00 | Salt & pepper, pr. | 24.00 |
| Bowl, 11½", ftd. gardenia | 24.00 | Saucer | 3.00 |
| Bowl, 12", crimped, fruit or flower | 26.00 | Stem, 1 oz., cordial | 60.00 |
| Bowl, 13", celery | 17.00 | Stem, 3 oz., wine, blown | 24.00 |
| Bowl, 13", 2 part celery | 24.00 | Stem, 3½ oz., cocktail, pressed | 18.00 |
| Bowl, 13", 5 part oval relish | 30.00 | Stem, 4 oz., fruit/oyster cocktail | 14.00 |
| Bowl, 13", gardenia | 28.00 | Stem, 4½ oz., claret, blown | 18.00 |
| Butter, ¼ lb., oblong w/cover | 45.00 | Stem, 4½ oz., claret pressed | 16.00 |
| Butter, 5", rnd. (or cov. candy) | 55.00 | Stem, 4½ oz., oyster cocktail, blown | 17.00 |
| Candelabrum w/two #1503 bobeche & ten "A" prisms | 29.00 | Stem, 6½ oz., sherbet/saucer champagne, blown | 14.00 |
| Candle block, hurricane type | 75.00 | Stem, 10 oz., pressed | 15.00 |
| Candle block, 1-lite | 60.00 | Stem, 10 oz., blown | 16.00 |
| Candle holder, 5", ftd. epergne | 10.00 | Sugar, ftd. | 14.00 |
| Candlestick, 1-lite | 55.00 | Syrup bottle w/drip, cut top | 40.00 |
| Candlestick, 2-lite | 27.00 | Tray, 8½", condiment/sugar & creamer | 18.00 |
| Candlestick, 3-lite | 29.00 | Tumbler, 5 oz., ftd. juice, pressed | 20.00 |
| Candy box w/cover, 7" | 75.00 | Tumbler, 5 oz., ftd. juice, blown | 24.00 |
| Candy w/cover, 5", tall, ftd. | 110.00 | Tumbler, 10 oz., pressed | 26.00 |
| Cheese w/cover, 5", ftd. | 30.00 | Tumbler, 12 oz., ftd. iced tea, pressed | 25.00 |
| Coaster, 4" | 12.00 | Tumbler, 12 oz., ftd. iced tea, blown | 27.00 |
| Comport, 5" | 18.00 | Vase, 5", ftd., flared | 24.00 |
| Comport, 5", w/cover, deep | 40.00 | Vase, 9", ftd., flared | 28.00 |
| Creamer, ftd. | 14.00 | | |
| Cup | 9.00 | | |
| Cup, punch | 12.00 | | |
| Marmalade w/cover | 30.00 | | |

# PLEAT & PANEL, Blank #1170, A. H. Heisey & Co.

Colors: Crystal, "Flamingo" pink, "Moongleam" green

|  | Crystal | Flam. | Moon. |
|---|---|---|---|
| Bowl, 4", chow chow | 5.00 | 8.00 | 10.00 |
| Bowl, 4½", nappy | 5.00 | 8.00 | 9.00 |
| Bowl, 5", 2 hand. bouillon | 6.00 | 10.00 | 12.00 |
| Bowl, 5", 2 hand. jelly | 6.00 | 10.00 | 12.00 |
| Bowl, 5", lemon w/cover | 10.00 | 14.00 | 16.00 |
| Bowl, 6½", grapefruit/cereal | 5.00 | 10.00 | 12.00 |
| Bowl, 8", nappy | 10.00 | 15.00 | 17.00 |
| Bowl, 9", oval vegetable | 11.00 | 17.00 | 19.00 |
| Cheese & cracker set, 10½", tray w/compote | 20.00 | 30.00 | 35.00 |
| Compotier w/cover, 5", hi. ftd. | 25.00 | 45.00 | 55.00 |
| Creamer, hotel | 5.00 | 10.00 | 15.00 |
| Cup | 5.00 | 10.00 | 15.00 |
| Marmalade, 4¾" | 7.00 | 12.00 | 17.00 |
| Oil bottle, 3 oz., w/pressed stopper | 17.00 | 30.00 | 35.00 |
| Pitcher, 3 pint, ice lip | 30.00 | 50.00 | 65.00 |
| Pitcher, 3 pint | 29.00 | 49.00 | 64.00 |
| Plate, 6" | 3.00 | 6.00 | 8.00 |
| Plate, 6¾", bouillon underliner | 3.00 | 6.00 | 8.00 |
| Plate, 7", bread | 4.00 | 7.00 | 9.00 |
| Plate, 8", luncheon | 5.00 | 10.00 | 12.00 |
| Plate, 10¾", dinner | 10.00 | 20.00 | 25.00 |
| Plate, 14", sandwich | 15.00 | 25.00 | 30.00 |
| Platter, 12", oval | 17.00 | 30.00 | 35.00 |
| Saucer | 3.00 | 5.00 | 6.00 |
| Sherbet, 5 oz., footed | 4.00 | 7.00 | 8.00 |
| Stem, 5 oz., saucer champagne | 5.00 | 10.00 | 12.00 |
| Stem, 7½ oz., low foot | 9.00 | 15.00 | 20.00 |
| Stem, 8 oz. | 12.00 | 20.00 | 25.00 |
| Sugar w/lid, hotel | 7.00 | 17.00 | 22.00 |
| Tray, 10", compartmented spice | 15.00 | 25.00 | 30.00 |
| Tumbler, 8 oz., ground bottom | 8.00 | 12.00 | 15.00 |
| Tumbler, 12 oz., tea, ground bottom | 9.00 | 14.00 | 17.00 |
| Vase, 8" | 25.00 | 40.00 | 45.00 |

# PORTIA, Cambridge Glass Company, 1932 · Early 1950's

Colors: Crystal, yellow, heather bloom

If you'll remember your Latin "portare" or your French "porter" meaning "to carry", you'll be able to remember that Portia is the Cambridge etching having the basket (a device for carrying things) filled with cascading flowers.

|  | Crystal |
|---|---|
| Basket, 6", ftd. 2 hand. (upturned sides) | 15.00 |
| Basket, 7", 1 hand. | 65.00 |
| Bowl, 3½", cranberry | 12.00 |
| Bowl, 3½", sq. cranberry | 12.00 |
| Bowl, 5¼", 2 hand. bonbon | 12.50 |
| Bowl, 6½", 3 pt. relish | 14.00 |
| Bowl, 6", 2 pt. relish | 15.00 |
| Bowl, 6", ftd., 2 hand. bonbon | 15.00 |
| Bowl, 6", grapefruit or oyster | 12.00 |
| Bowl, 7", 2 pt. relish | 15.50 |
| Bowl, 7", ftd. bonbon, tab handles | 18.00 |
| Bowl, 7", pickle or relish | 17.50 |
| Bowl, 9", 3 pt. celery & relish, tab hand. | 20.00 |
| Bowl, 9½", ftd. pickle (like corn bowl) | 20.00 |
| Bowl, 10", flared, 4 ftd. | 25.00 |
| Bowl, 11", 2 pt., 2 hand. "figure 8" relish | 27.50 |
| Bowl, 11", 2 hand. | 22.50 |
| Bowl, 12", 3 pt. celery & relish, tab hand. | 27.50 |
| Bowl, 12", 5 pt. celery & relish | 30.00 |
| Bowl, 12", flared, 4 ftd. | 27.50 |
| Bowl, 12", oval, 4 ftd., "ears" handles | 30.00 |
| Bowl, finger w/liner #3124 | 20.00 |
| Bowl, seafood (fruit cocktail w/liner) | 15.00 |
| Candlestick, 5" | 17.50 |
| Candlestick, 6", 2-lite, "fleur de lis" | 25.00 |
| Candlestick, 6", 3-lite | 30.00 |
| Candy box w/cover, rnd. | 40.00 |
| Cigarette holder, urn shape | 37.50 |
| Cocktail icer, 2 pt. | 27.50 |
| Cocktail shaker w/stopper | 45.00 |
| Cocktail shaker, 80 oz., handled ball w/chrome top | 57.50 |
| Cologne, 2 oz., handled ball w/stopper | 27.50 |
| Comport, 5½" | 25.00 |
| Comport, 5 3/8", blown | 32.50 |
| Creamer, handled ball | 15.00 |
| Creamer, indiv. | 10.00 |
| Cup, ftd. sq. | 18.00 |
| Decanter, 29 oz. ftd. sherry w/stopper | 85.00 |
| Fruit/oyster cocktail, #3130, 4½ oz., ped. ft. | 15.00 |
| Hurricane lamp, candlestick base | 90.00 |
| Hurricane lamp, keyhole base w/prisms | 75.00 |
| Ice bucket w/chrome handle | 52.50 |
| Ivy ball, 5¼" | 25.00 |

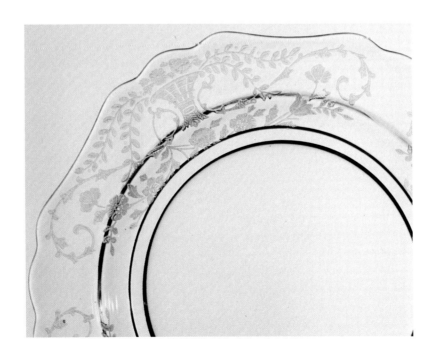

|  | Crystal |
|---|---|
| Mayonnaise, div. bowl w/liner & 2 ladles | 30.00 |
| Mayonnaise w/liner & ladle | 25.00 |
| Oil, 6 oz., loop hand. w/stopper | 37.50 |
| Oil, 6 oz., handled ball w/stopper | 40.00 |
| Oyster cocktail, 4½ oz., low stem | 15.00 |
| Pitcher, ball | 87.50 |
| Plate, 6", 2 hand. | 15.00 |
| Plate, 6½", bread/butter | 6.50 |
| Plate, 8", salad | 12.50 |
| Plate, 8", ftd. 2 hand. | 15.00 |
| Plate, 8", ftd. bonbon, tab handles | 17.50 |
| Plate, 8½", sq. | 15.00 |
| Plate, 10½", dinner | 25.00 |
| Plate, 13", 4 ftd. torte | 27.50 |
| Plate, 13½", 2 hand. cake | 27.50 |
| Plate, 14", torte | 30.00 |
| Puff box, 3½", ball shape w/lid | 30.00 |
| Salt & pepper, pr. | 22.50 |
| Saucer, sq. or rnd. | 3.00 |
| Set: 3 pc. Frappe (bowl, 2 plain inserts) | 20.00 |
| Sherry, 2 oz. | 12.50 |
| Stem, #3121, 1 oz., cordial | 37.50 |
| Stem, #3121, 1 oz., low ftd. brandy | 27.50 |
| Stem, #3121, 2½ oz., wine | 20.00 |
| Stem, #3121, 3 oz., cocktail | 20.00 |
| Stem, #3121, 4½ oz. claret | 22.50 |
| Stem, #3121, 4½ oz. oyster cocktail | 13.00 |
| Stem, #3121, 5 oz., parfait | 17.50 |
| Stem, #3121, 6 oz., low sherbet | 13.00 |
| Stem, #3121, 6 oz., tall sherbet | 15.00 |
| Stem, #3121, 10 oz. goblet | 20.00 |
| Stem, #3124, 3 oz., cocktail | 15.00 |
| Stem, #3124, 3 oz., wine | 17.50 |
| Stem, #3124, 4½ oz., claret | 18.00 |
| Stem, #3124, 7 oz., low sherbet | 13.00 |
| Stem, #3124, 7 oz., tall sherbet | 15.00 |
| Stem, #3124, 10 oz. goblet | 18.00 |
| Stem, #3126, 1 oz., cordial | 32.50 |
| Stem, #3126, 1 oz., low ft. brandy | 25.50 |
| Stem, #3126, 2½ oz., wine | 20.00 |
| Stem, #3126, 3 oz., cocktail | 17.50 |
| Stem, #3126, 4½ oz., claret | 22.50 |
| Stem, #3216, 4½ oz., low ft. oyster cocktail | 12.50 |
| Stem, #3126, 7 oz., low sherbet | 13.00 |
| Stem, #3126, 7 oz., tall sherbet | 15.00 |
| Stem, #3126, 9 oz. goblet | 18.00 |
| Stem, #3130, 1 oz., cordial | 32.50 |
| Stem, #3130, 2½ oz., wine | 20.00 |
| Stem, #3130, 3 oz., cocktail | 17.50 |

|  | Crystal |
|---|---|
| Stem, #3130, 4½ oz., claret | 22.50 |
| Stem, #3130, 7 oz., low sherbet | 13.00 |
| Stem, #3130, 7 oz., sherbet | 15.00 |
| Stem, #3130, 9 oz., goblet | 18.00 |
| Stem, 4 oz., cocktail, plain stem | 12.00 |
| Sugar, ftd. hand. ball | 11.50 |
| Sugar, indiv. | 10.00 |
| Tray, 11", celery | 22.50 |
| Tumbler, #3121, 2½ oz. bar | 16.00 |
| Tumbler, #3121, 5 oz., ftd. juice | 15.00 |
| Tumbler, #3121, 10 oz., ftd. water | 15.00 |
| Tumbler, #3121, 12 oz., ftd. tea | 16.00 |
| Tumbler, #3124, 3 oz. | 12.50 |
| Tumbler, #3124, 5 oz., juice | 12.50 |
| Tumbler, #3124, 10 oz., water | 15.00 |
| Tumbler, #3124, 12 oz., tea | 15.00 |
| Tumbler, #3126, 2½ oz. | 14.50 |
| Tumbler, #3126, 5 oz., juice | 12.50 |
| Tumbler, #3126, 10 oz., water | 15.00 |
| Tumbler, #3126, 12 oz., tea | 15.00 |
| Tumbler, #3130, 5 oz., juice | 12.50 |
| Tumbler, #3130, 10 oz., water | 14.00 |
| Tumbler, #3130, 12 oz., tea | 15.00 |
| Tumbler, 13 oz., "roly-poly" | 15.00 |
| Vase, 5", globe | 25.00 |
| Vase, 6", ftd. | 27.50 |
| Vase, 8", ftd. | 30.00 |
| Vase, 9", keyhole ft. | 37.50 |
| Vase, 10", bud | 25.00 |
| Vase, 11", flower | 35.00 |
| Vase, 11", pedestal ft. | 32.50 |
| Vase, 12", keyhole ft. | 40.00 |
| Vase, 13", flower | 45.00 |

Note: See Pages 150-153 for stem identification.

# PROVINCIAL, Blank #1506, A. H. Heisey & Co.

Colors: Crystal, "Limelight" green

|  | Crystal | Green |
|---|---|---|
| Ash tray, 3", square .............................. | 12.00 | |
| Bonbon dish, 7", 2 hand., upturned sides ............ | 10.00 | 30.00 |
| Bowl, 5 quart punch .............................. | 60.00 | |
| Bowl, individual nut/jelly ......................... | 20.00 | |
| Bowl, 4½", nappy ............................... | 10.00 | 25.00 |
| Bowl, 5", 2 hand. nut/jelly ....................... | 12.00 | |
| Bowl, 5½", nappy ............................... | 12.00 | 30.00 |
| Bowl, 5½", round, hand. nappy .................... | 15.00 | 45.00 |
| Bowl, 5½", tri-corner, hand. nappy ................ | 17.00 | 47.00 |
| Bowl, 10", 4 part relish ......................... | 30.00 | 150.00 |
| Bowl, 12", floral ............................... | 30.00 | |
| Bowl, 13", gardenia ............................. | 30.00 | |
| Box, 5½", footed candy w/cover ................... | 75.00 | 200.00 |
| Butter dish w/cover ............................. | 50.00 | |
| Candle, 1-lite, block ............................ | 15.00 | |
| Candle, 3-lite .................................. | 35.00 | |
| Candle, 3-lite, #4233, 5", vase ................... | 45.00 | |
| Cigarette lighter ............................... | 25.00 | |
| Coaster, 4" .................................... | 5.00 | |
| Creamer, footed ................................ | 15.00 | 60.00 |
| Creamer & sugar w/tray, individual ................ | 30.00 | |
| Cup, punch .................................... | 10.00 | |
| Mayonnaise, 7", (plate, ladle, bowl) ............... | 25.00 | 70.00 |
| Oil bottle, 4 oz., #1 stopper ..................... | 30.00 | |
| Plate, 5", footed cheese ......................... | 10.00 | |
| Plate, 7", 2 hand. snack ......................... | 12.00 | |
| Plate, 7", bread ................................ | 10.00 | |
| Plate, 8", luncheon ............................. | 15.00 | 35.00 |
| Plate, 14", torte ............................... | 20.00 | |
| Plate, 18", buffet .............................. | 25.00 | 135.00 |
| Salt & pepper, pr. .............................. | 15.00 | |
| Stem, 3½ oz., oyster cocktail .................... | 7.00 | |
| Stem, 3½ oz., wine ............................. | 15.00 | |
| Stem, 5 oz., sherbet/champagne .................. | 7.00 | |
| Stem, 10 oz. ................................... | 15.00 | |
| Sugar, footed .................................. | 15.00 | 60.00 |
| Tray, 13", oval celery ........................... | 20.00 | |
| Tumbler, 5 oz., footed juice ...................... | 10.00 | 30.00 |
| Tumbler, 8 oz., ................................ | 12.00 | |
| Tumbler, 9 oz., footed .......................... | 14.00 | 35.00 |
| Tumbler, 12 oz., footed, iced tea ................. | 15.00 | 40.00 |
| Tumbler, 13", flat ice tea ....................... | 15.00 | |
| Vase, 3½", violet .............................. | 15.00 | 60.00 |
| Vase, 4", pansy ................................ | 15.00 | |
| Vase, 6", sweet pea ............................ | 18.00 | |

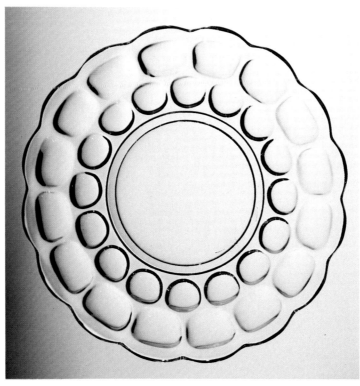

# RADIANCE, New Martinsville Glass Co., 1936 - 1939

Colors: Red, cobalt, ice blue, amber, crystal

The first three colors are considered the most desirable to own in this pattern. Crystal pieces, unless decorated with good platinum or gold (i.e., unmottled), command about HALF the prices listed for "other colors".

| | Red | Ice Blue Amber |
|---|---|---|
| Bowl, 5", nut, 2 hand. | 10.00 | 6.50 |
| Bowl, 6", bonbon | 9.50 | 6.00 |
| Bowl, 6", bonbon, ftd. | 10.00 | 6.50 |
| Bowl, 6", bonbon w/cover | 20.00 | 14.00 |
| Bowl, 7", relish, 2 pt. | 12.50 | 7.50 |
| Bowl, 7", pickle | 9.50 | 6.50 |
| Bowl, 8", relish, 3 pt. | 15.00 | 9.00 |
| Bowl, 10", celery | 12.50 | 7.50 |
| Bowl, 10", crimped | 17.50 | 11.50 |
| Bowl, 10", flared | 20.00 | 10.00 |
| Bowl, 12", crimped | 23.50 | 13.50 |
| Bowl, 12", flared | 22.50 | 12.50 |
| Bowl, punch | 77.50 | 37.50 |
| Butter dish | 317.50 | 147.50 |
| Candlestick, 8" | 15.00 | 9.00 |
| Candlestick, 2-lite | 19.00 | 11.00 |
| Cheese/cracker, (11" plate) set | 30.00 | 15.00 |
| Comport, 5" | 12.00 | 8.50 |
| Comport, 6" | 13.00 | 8.00 |
| Condiment set, 4 pc. w/tray | 125.00 | 87.50 |
| Creamer | 10.00 | 7.00 |
| Cruet, indiv. | 30.00 | 22.50 |
| Cup | 8.50 | 5.00 |
| Cup, punch | 7.00 | 4.00 |
| Decanter w/stopper, hand. | 85.00 | 52.50 |
| Ladle for punch bowl | 75.00 | 40.00 |
| Lamp, 12" | 70.00 | 37.50 |
| Mayonnaise, 3 pc., set | 25.00 | 12.00 |
| Pitcher, 64 oz. (cobalt: $225.00) | 152.50 | 107.50 |
| Plate, 8", luncheon | 7.00 | 5.00 |
| Plate, 14", punch bowl liner | 30.00 | 16.50 |
| Salt & pepper, pr. | 32.50 | 22.50 |
| Saucer | 3.00 | 2.50 |
| Sugar | 11.00 | 7.00 |
| Tray, oval | 20.00 | 15.00 |
| Tumbler, 9 oz. (cobalt: $25.00) | 15.00 | 9.00 |
| Vase, 10", flared | 32.50 | 21.50 |
| Vase, 12", crimped | 47.50 | 37.50 |

# RIDGELEIGH, Blank #1469, A. H. Heisey & Co.

Color: Crystal, "Sahara," "Zircon," rare

|  | Crystal |
|---|---|
| Ash tray, round | 4.00 |
| Ash tray, square | 3.00 |
| Ash tray, 4", round | 10.00 |
| Ash tray, 6", square | 15.00 |
| Ash trays, bridge set (heart, diamond, spade, club) | 25.00 |
| Basket bonbon | 9.00 |
| Bottle, rock & rye w/#104 stopper | 65.00 |
| Bottle, 4 oz., cologne | 40.00 |
| Bottle, 5 oz., bitters w/tube | 45.00 |
| Bowl, indiv. nut | 7.00 |
| Bowl, oval indiv. jelly | 12.00 |
| Bowl, indiv. nut, 2 part | 9.00 |
| Bowl, 4½", nappy, bell or cupped | 5.00 |
| Bowl, 4½", nappy, scalloped | 5.00 |
| Bowl, 5", lemon w/cover | 15.00 |
| Bowl, 5", nappy, straight | 6.00 |
| Bowl, 5", nappy, square | 6.00 |
| Bowl, 6", 2 hand. divided jelly | 12.00 |
| Bowl, 6", 2 hand. jelly | 12.00 |
| Bowl, 7", 2 part oval relish | 12.00 |
| Bowl, 8", center piece | 20.00 |
| Bowl, 8", nappy, square | 25.00 |
| Bowl, 9", nappy, square | 25.00 |
| Bowl, 9", salad | 27.00 |
| Bowl, 10", flared fruit | 29.00 |
| Bowl, 10", floral | 29.00 |
| Bowl, 11", center piece | 30.00 |
| Bowl, 11", punch | 50.00 |
| Bowl, 11½", floral | 27.50 |
| Bowl, 12", oval floral | 32.00 |
| Bowl, 12", flared fruit | 32.00 |
| Bowl, 13", cone floral | 32.00 |
| Bowl, 14", oblong floral | 40.00 |
| Bowl, 14", oblong swan hand. floral | 50.00 |
| Box, 8", floral | 20.00 |
| Candle block, 3" | 15.00 |
| Candle vase, 6" | 15.00 |
| Candlestick, 2", 1-lite | 10.00 |
| Candlestick, 2-lite, bobeche & "A" prisms | 17.50 |
| Candlestick, 7", w/bobeche & "A" prisms | 60.00 |

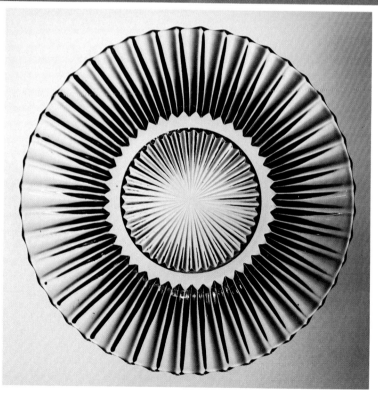

# RIDGELEIGH, Blank #1469, A. H. Heisey & Co. (continued)

| | Crystal |
|---|---|
| Cheese, 6", 2 hand. | 7.00 |
| Cigarette box w/cover, oval | 25.00 |
| Cigarette box w/cover, 6" | 10.00 |
| Cigarette holder, oval w/2 comp. ash trays | 35.00 |
| Cigarette holder, round | 6.00 |
| Cigarette holder, square | 6.00 |
| Cigarette holder w/cover | 15.00 |
| Coaster or cocktail rest | 3.00 |
| Cocktail shaker, 1 quart w/#1 strainer & #86 stopper | 75.00 |
| Comport, 6", low ft., flared | 15.00 |
| Comport, 6", low ft. w/cover | 25.00 |
| Creamer | 15.00 |
| Creamer, indiv. | 10.00 |
| Cup | 10.00 |
| Cup, beverage | 12.00 |
| Cup, punch | 10.00 |
| Decanter, 1 pint w/#95 stopper | 55.00 |
| Ice tub, 2 hand. | 30.00 |
| Marmalade w/cover | 30.00 |
| Mayonnaise | 25.00 |
| Mustard w/cover | 25.00 |
| Oil bottle, 3 oz., w/#103 stopper | 35.00 |
| Pitcher, ½ gallon | 50.00 |
| Pitcher, ½ gallon, ice lip | 55.00 |
| Plate, oval hors d'oeuvres | 20.00 |
| Plate, 2 hand. ice tub liner | 15.00 |
| Plate, 6", round | 5.00 |
| Plate, 6", scalloped | 5.00 |
| Plate, 6", square | 5.00 |
| Plate, 7", square | 6.00 |
| Plate, 8", round | 7.00 |
| Plate, 8", square | 7.00 |
| Plate, 13½", sandwich | 20.00 |
| Plate, 13½", ftd. torte | 20.00 |
| Plate, 14", salver | 45.00 |
| Salt & pepper, pr. | 20.00 |
| Salt dip, indiv. | 12.00 |
| Saucer | 3.00 |
| Soda, 12 oz., cupped or flared | 20.00 |
| Stem, cocktail, pressed | 15.00 |
| Stem, claret, pressed | 20.00 |
| Stem, oyster cocktail, pressed | 10.00 |
| Stem, sherbet, pressed | 7.00 |
| Stem, saucer champagne, pressed | 10.00 |
| Stem, wine, pressed | 20.00 |

# RIDGELEIGH, Blank #1469, A. H. Heisey & Co. (continued)

|  | **Crystal** |
|---|---|
| Stem, 1 oz., cordial, blown | 80.00 |
| Stem, 2 oz., sherry, blown | 45.00 |
| Stem, 2½ oz., wine, blown | 40.00 |
| Stem, 3½ oz., cocktail, blown | 25.00 |
| Stem, 4 oz., claret, blown | 25.00 |
| Stem, 4 oz., oyster cocktail, blown | 15.00 |
| Stem, 5 oz., saucer champagne, blown | 17.00 |
| Stem, 5 oz., sherbet, blown | 12.00 |
| Stem, 8 oz., luncheon, low stem | 12.00 |
| Stem, 8 oz., tall stem | 15.00 |
| Sugar | 15.00 |
| Sugar, indiv. | 10.00 |
| Tray, for indiv. sugar & creamer | 10.00 |
| Tray, 10½", oblong | 20.00 |
| Tray, 11", 3 part, relish | 25.00 |
| Tray, 12", celery & olive, divided | 22.00 |
| Tray, 12", celery | 20.00 |
| Tumbler, 2½ oz., bar, pressed | 15.00 |
| Tumbler, 5 oz., juice, blown | 15.00 |
| Tumbler, 5 oz., soda, ftd., pressed | 12.00 |
| Tumbler, 8 oz., (#1469¾), pressed | 14.00 |
| Tumbler, 8 oz., old fashioned, pressed | 15.00 |
| Tumbler, 8 oz., soda, blown | 15.00 |
| Tumbler, 10 oz., #1469¾, pressed | 12.00 |
| Tumbler, 12 oz., ftd. soda, pressed | 17.00 |
| Tumbler, 12 oz., soda, (#1469¾) pressed | 18.00 |
| Tumbler, 13 oz., iced tea, blown | 15.00 |
| Vase, #1 indiv., cuspidor shape | 22.00 |
| Vase, #2 indiv., cupped top | 20.00 |
| Vase, #3 indiv., flared rim | 22.00 |
| Vase, #4 indiv., fan out top | 24.00 |
| Vase, #5 indiv., scalloped top | 22.00 |
| Vase, 3½" | 20.00 |
| Vase, 6", (also flared) | 15.00 |
| Vase, 8" | 17.00 |
| Vase, 8", triangular #1469½ | 17.00 |

# ROSE, Etching #515, On Waverly Blank #1519, A. H. Heisey & Co., 1949 - 1957

Color: Crystal

Rose, one of the loveliest of Heisey patterns, is very collectible today. Notice that the stems are thorny rose bud designs! Some items of this pattern were taken over and manufactured by Imperial Glass Company after Heisey ceased operation in 1957. These were mostly stemware.

| | Crystal | | Crystal |
|---|---|---|---|
| Bell, dinner #5072 | 95.00 | Comport, 7", oval, ftd. | 100.00 |
| Bottle, 8 oz., French dressing, blown | | Creamer, ftd. | 32.50 |
| #5031 | 85.00 | Creamer, indiv. | 25.00 |
| Bowl, finger #3309 | 25.00 | Cup | 50.00 |
| Bowl, 5½", ftd. mint | 25.00 | Decanter, 1 pt., #4036½ | 100.00 |
| Bowl, 5¾", ftd. mint #1951 | 27.50 | Epergnette, deep | 100.00 |
| Bowl, 6", ftd. mint QUEEN ANNE | 35.00 | Hurricane lamp 2/12" globe #5080 | 125.00 |
| Bowl, 6", jelly, 2 hand., ftd. QUEEN | | Hurricane lamp w/12" globe, | |
| ANNE | 35.00 | PLANTATION | 200.00 |
| Bowl, 6", oval lemon w/cover | 77.50 | Ice bucket, dolp. ft., QUEEN ANNE | 150.00 |
| Bowl, 6½", 2 pt. oval dressing | 35.00 | Ice tub, 2 hand. | 150.00 |
| Bowl, 6½", ftd. honey/cheese | 20.00 | Mayonnaise, 5½", 1 hand. | 50.00 |
| Bowl, 6½", ftd. jelly | 25.00 | Mayonnaise, 5½", div., 1 hand. | 50.00 |
| Bowl, 6½", lemon w/cover QUEEN | | Mayonnaise, 5½", ftd. | 55.00 |
| ANNE | 85.00 | Oil, 3 oz., ftd. | 145.00 |
| Bowl, 7", salad | 40.00 | Pitcher, 73 oz., #4164 | 225.00 |
| Bowl, 7", ftd. honey | 25.00 | Plate, 7", salad | 20.00 |
| Bowl, 7", ftd. jelly | 30.00 | Plate, 7", mayonnaise | 20.00 |
| Bowl, 7", lily, QUEEN ANNE | 37.50 | Plate, 8", salad | 30.00 |
| Bowl, 7", salad dressings, QUEEN ANNE | 40.00 | Plate, 10½", dinner | 75.00 |
| Bowl, 9", ftd. fruit or salad | 50.00 | Plate, 11", sandwich | 75.00 |
| Bowl, 9", salad | 47.50 | Plate, 11", demi-torte | 65.00 |
| Bowl, 9½", crimped floral | 62.50 | Plate, 12", ftd. salver | 150.00 |
| Bowl, 9", 4 pt. rnd. relish | 65.00 | Plate, 13½", ftd. cake | 225.00 |
| Bowl, 10", gardenia | 85.00 | Plate, 14", torte | 90.00 |
| Bowl, 10", crimped floral | 87.50 | Plate, 14", sandwich | 90.00 |
| Bowl, 11", 3 pt. relish | 77.50 | Plate, 14", ctr. hand. sandwich | 150.00 |
| Bowl, 11", 3 ft., floral | 75.00 | Salt & pepper, ftd., pr. | 65.00 |
| Bowl, 11", floral | 65.00 | Saucer | 10.00 |
| Bowl, 11", oval, 4 ft. | 72.50 | Stem, #5072, 1 oz., cordial | 135.00 |
| Bowl, 12", crimped floral | 75.00 | Stem, #5072, 3 oz., wine | 100.00 |
| Bowl, 13", crimped floral | 80.00 | Stem, #5072, 3½ oz., oyster cocktail, | |
| Bowl, 13", floral | 80.00 | ftd. | 27.50 |
| Bowl, 13", gardenia | 75.00 | Stem, #5072, 4 oz., claret | 90.00 |
| Butter w/cover, 6" | 150.00 | Stem, #5072, 4 oz., cocktail | 40.00 |
| Butter w/cover, ¼ lb., CABOCHON | 175.00 | Stem, #5072, 6 oz., sherbet | 25.00 |
| Candlestick, 1-lite, #112 | 35.00 | Stem, #5072, 6 oz., saucer champagne | 35.00 |
| Candlestick, 3-lite, #142 CASCADE | 77.50 | Stem, #5072, 9 oz., water | 42.50 |
| Candlestick, 3-lite | 80.00 | Sugar, indiv | 25.00 |
| Candlestick, 5", 2-lite, #134 TRIDENT | 45.00 | Sugar, ftd. | 30.00 |
| Candlestick, 6" | 40.00 | Tumbler, #5072, ftd. juice | 42.50 |
| Candy w/cover, 5", high ft. | 140.00 | Tumbler, #5072, 12 oz., ftd. tea | 45.00 |
| Candy w/cover, 6¼", #1951 | | Tray, indiv. creamer/sugar, QUEEN | |
| CABOCHON | 95.00 | ANNE | 25.00 |
| Cheese (compote) 5½", & cracker | | Tray, 12", celery | 45.00 |
| (11" plate) | 75.00 | Tray, 13", celery | 47.50 |
| Chocolate w/cover, 5" | 140.00 | Vase, 3½", ftd. violet | 52.50 |
| Cigarette holder, #4035 | 75.00 | Vase, 4", ftd. violet | 55.00 |
| Cocktail icer w/liner, #3304 | | Vase, 7", ftd. fan | 57.50 |
| UNIVERSAL | 50.00 | Vase, 7", ftd. | 52.50 |
| Cocktail shaker, #4036, & #4225 | | Vase, 8", sq. ftd. urn | 60.00 |
| COBEL | 70.00 | Vase, 10", sq. ftd. urn | 75.00 |
| Comport, 6½", low ft. | 60.00 | | |

# ROSE POINT, Cambridge Glass Company, 1940's - 1950's

Color: Crystal

Cambridge Rose Point shows cascading roses around a cameo containing two or three roses. It's very popular with collectors and there are numerous pieces to be found with this design.

|  | Crystal |
|---|---|
| Ash tray, 2½", sq. | 35.00 |
| Bowl, 3", 4 ftd. nut | 25.00 |
| Bowl, 5¼", 2 hand. bonbon (#3400) | 22.00 |
| Bowl, 6", 2 hand. ftd. basket (#3500) | 19.00 |
| Bowl, 6", 2 hand. ftd. bonbon (#3500) | 22.00 |
| Bowl, 6", 2 pt. relish (#3400) | 25.00 |
| Bowl, 6½", 3 pt. relish (#3500) | 25.00 |
| Bowl, 7", 2 pt. relish (#3900) | 28.00 |
| Bowl, 7", relish (#3900) | 25.00 |
| Bowl, 7", tab hand. ftd. bonbon (#3900) | 30.00 |
| Bowl, 8", 3 pt. relish (#3400) | 32.00 |
| Bowl, 8", 3 pt., 3 hand. relish (#3400) | 40.00 |
| Bowl, 9½", pickle (like corn) | 27.50 |
| Bowl, 9", 3 pt. celery & relish (#3900) | 37.50 |
| Bowl, 10", 4 tab ftd., flared (#3900) | 45.00 |
| Bowl, 11", 4 ftd. shallow, fancy edge (#3400) | 60.00 |
| Bowl, 11", tab handles (#3900) | 50.00 |
| Bowl, 11½", ftd. w/tab hand. (#3900) | 57.50 |
| Bowl, 12", 4 ftd., oval w/"ears" hand. (#3900) | 65.00 |
| Bowl, 12", 3 pt. celery & relish (#3900) | 37.50 |
| Bowl, 12", 4 ftd. fancy rim oblong (#3400) | 67.50 |
| Bowl, 12", 4 ftd. flared (#3400) | 60.00 |
| Bowl, 12", 4 tab ftd., flared (#3900) | 60.00 |
| Bowl, 12", 5 pt. celery & relish (#3900) | 42.50 |
| Butter w/cover, 5" | 150.00 |
| Candlestick, 5" | 22.50 |
| Candlestick, 5", 1-lite keyhole base | 25.00 |
| Candlestick, 5", raised drip | 27.50 |
| Candlestick, 6", 2-lite keyhole | 30.00 |
| Candlestick, 6", 2-lite, "fleur de lis" | 35.00 |
| Candlestick, 6", 3-lite | 40.00 |
| Candlestick, 6", 3 tiered lite | 75.00 |
| Candy box w/cover, 5 3/8", #1066 stem | 60.00 |
| Candy box w/cover, 8", 3 pt. | 55.00 |
| Candy box w/cover, rnd. | 95.00 |
| Cheese (comport) & cracker (13" plate) | 67.50 |
| Cigarette box w/cover | 50.00 |
| Cocktail icer, 2 pc. | 35.00 |
| Cocktail shaker, 32 oz. w/stopper | 95.00 |
| Comport, 5" | 22.50 |
| Comport, 5½", scalloped edge | 25.00 |
| Comport, 5 3/8", blown, #3500 stem | 40.00 |
| Comport, 5 3/8", blown, #3121 stem | 47.50 |
| Comport, 5 3/8", blown w/#1066 stem | 47.50 |
| Creamer | 25.00 |
| Creamer, indiv. #3500 pie crust edge | 17.50 |
| Creamer, indiv. #3900 scalloped edge | 17.50 |
| Cup | 25.00 |
| Decanter, 28 oz. w/stopper | 195.00 |
| Epergne (candle w/vases) | 125.00 |
| Hurricane lamp w/prisms | 150.00 |
| Hurricane lamp, candlestick base | 150.00 |
| Hurricane lamp, keyhole base w/prisms | 175.00 |
| Ice bucket w/chrome hand. | 110.00 |
| Mayonnaise, (sherbet type w/ladle) | 35.00 |
| Mayonnaise, div. w/liner & 2 ladles | 65.00 |
| Mayonnaise w/liner & ladle | 40.00 |

# ROSE POINT, Cambridge Glass Company, 1940's · 1950's (continued)

|  | Crystal |
|---|---|
| Oil, 6 oz., loop hand. w/stopper | 100.00 |
| Pitcher, 20 oz. | 145.00 |
| Pitcher, 32 oz. | 140.00 |
| Pitcher, 32 oz. martini (slender) w/metal insert | 450.00 |
| Pitcher, 76 oz. | 145.00 |
| Pitcher, 80 oz., Dalton | 225.00 |
| Pitcher, 80 oz. ball | 145.00 |
| Pitcher, nite set, 2 pc. w/tumbler insert top | 195.00 |
| Plate, 6", 2 hand. | 12.00 |
| Plate, 6½", bread/butter | 10.00 |
| Plate, 8", 2 hand. ftd. | 15.00 |
| Plate, 8", salad | 15.00 |
| Plate, 8", tab hand. ftd. bonbon | 20.00 |
| Plate, 10½", dinner | 75.00 |
| Plate, 12", 4 ftd. service | 42.50 |
| Plate, 13½", tab hand. cake | 50.00 |
| Plate, 13", 4 ftd. torte | 42.50 |
| Plate, 14", service | 42.50 |
| Plate, 14", torte | 42.50 |
| Salt & pepper w/chrome tops, pr., ftd. | 50.00 |
| Salt & pepper w/chrome tops, pr., flat | 37.50 |
| Saucer | 5.50 |
| Set: 3 pc. indiv. cream, sug. & tray | 50.00 |
| Set: 3 pc. reg. cream, sug. & tray | 65.00 |
| Stem, #3121, 1 oz., cordial | 60.00 |
| Stem, #3121, 3 oz., cocktail | 30.00 |
| Stem, #3121, 3½ oz., wine | 40.00 |
| Stem, #3121, 4½ oz., claret | 40.00 |
| Stem, #3121, 4½ oz., low oyster cocktail | 36.00 |
| Stem, #3121, 5 oz., low ft. juice | 25.00 |
| Stem, #3121, 5 oz., low ft. parfait | 47.50 |
| Stem, #3121, 6 oz., low sherbet | 20.00 |
| Stem, #3121, 6 oz., tall sherbet | 25.00 |
| Stem, #3121, 10 oz., water | 28.00 |
| Stem, #3500, 1 oz., cordial | 50.00 |
| Stem, #3500, 2½ oz., wine | 32.00 |
| Stem, #3500, 3 oz., cocktail | 30.00 |
| Stem, #3500, 4½ oz., claret | 29.00 |
| Stem, #3500, 4½ oz., low oyster cocktail | 28.00 |
| Stem, #3500, 5 oz., low ft. juice | 22.50 |
| Stem, #3500, 5 oz., low ft. parfait | 40.00 |
| Stem, #3500, 7 oz., low ft. sherbet | 15.00 |
| Stem, #3500, 7 oz., tall sherbet | 20.00 |
| Stem, #7801, 4 oz. cocktail, plain stem | 22.00 |
| Stem, #7966, 2 oz., sherry, plain ft. | 42.50 |
| Sugar | 25.00 |
| Sugar, indiv. #3500 pie crust edge | 17.50 |
| Sugar, indiv. #3900, scalloped edge | 17.50 |
| Tumbler, #3121, 10 oz., low ft. water | 22.50 |
| Tumbler, #3121, 12 oz., tea | 28.00 |
| Tumbler, #3500, 10 oz., low ft. water | 22.00 |
| Tumbler, #3500, 12 oz., low ft. tea | 22.00 |
| Tumbler, #3900, 5 oz. | 39.50 |
| Tumbler, #3900, 13 oz. | 40.00 |
| Vase, 5", globe | 40.00 |
| Vase, 6", high ftd. flower | 45.00 |
| Vase, 8", high ftd. flower | 55.00 |
| Vase, 9", keyhole base flower | 60.00 |
| Vase, 10", bud | 55.00 |
| Vase, 10", cornucopia | 95.00 |
| Vase, 11", ftd. flower | 65.00 |
| Vase, 11", ped. ftd. flower | 75.00 |
| Vase, 12", keyhole base flower | 85.00 |
| Vase, 13", ftd. flower | 95.00 |

Note: See Pages 150-153 for stem identification.

# SATURN, Blank #1485, A.H. Heisey & Co.

Colors: Crystal, "Zircon" or "Limelight" green

"Zircon" was the color name in 1937 through 1939. This color was remade in 1955 and called "Limelight."

| | Crystal | Zircon/ Limelight |
|---|---|---|
| Ash tray | 15.00 | |
| Bitters bottle w/short tube, blown | 30.00 | |
| Bowl, baked apple | 5.00 | 40.00 |
| Bowl, finger | 4.00 | |
| Bowl, rose, lg. | 30.00 | |
| Bowl, 4½", nappy | 4.00 | |
| Bowl, 5", nappy | 6.00 | |
| Bowl, 5", whipped cream | 10.00 | 45.00 |
| Bowl, 7", pickle | 10.00 | |
| Bowl, 9", 3 part relish | 15.00 | |
| Bowl, 10", celery | 13.00 | |
| Bowl, 11", salad | 25.00 | |
| Bowl, 12", fruit, flared rim | 27.00 | |
| Bowl, 13", floral, rolled edge | 30.00 | |
| Bowl, 13", floral | 30.00 | |
| Candelabrum w/"e" ball drops, 2-lite | 100.00 | 275.00 |
| Candle block, 2-lite | 90.00 | 250.00 |
| Candlestick, 3", ftd., 1-lite | 12.50 | 65.00 |
| Comport, 7" | 30.00 | 120.00 |
| Creamer | 15.00 | 80.00 |
| Cup | 9.00 | 40.00 |
| Hostess Set, 8 pc. (low bowl w/ftd. ctr. bowl, 3 toothpick holders & clips) | 45.00 | |
| Pitcher, 70 oz., w/ice lip, blown | 50.00 | 150.00 |
| Marmalade w/cover | 30.00 | |
| Mayonnaise | 15.00 | 50.00 |
| Mustard w/cover & paddle | 30.00 | 220.00 |
| Oil bottle, 2 oz., w/#1 stopper | 40.00 | 200.00 |
| Parfait, 5 oz. | 9.00 | 42.00 |
| Plate, 6" | 3.00 | 15.00 |
| Plate, 7", bread | 5.00 | 25.00 |
| Plate, 8", luncheon | 7.00 | 35.00 |
| Plate, 13", torte | 15.00 | |
| Plate, 15", torte | 20.00 | |
| Salt & pepper, pr. | 25.00 | |
| Saucer | 3.00 | 15.00 |
| Stem, 3 oz., cocktail | 6.00 | 40.00 |
| Stem, 4 oz., fruit cocktail | 5.00 | 35.00 |
| Stem, 4½ oz., sherbet | 5.00 | 35.00 |
| Stem, 5 oz., sherbet | 5.00 | 35.00 |
| Stem, 6 oz., saucer champagne | 7.00 | 45.00 |
| Stem, 10 oz. | 10.00 | 65.00 |
| Sugar | 15.00 | 80.00 |
| Sugar shaker | 30.00 | |
| Sugar w/cover, no handles | 20.00 | |
| Tray, tid bit, 2 sides turned as fan | 15.00 | 65.00 |
| Tumbler, 5 oz., juice | 4.00 | 55.00 |
| Tumbler, 7 oz. old fashioned | 6.00 | |
| Tumbler, 8 oz., old fashioned | 7.00 | |
| Tumbler, 9 oz., luncheon | 8.00 | |
| Tumbler, 10 oz. | 10.00 | |
| Tumbler, 12 oz., soda | 12.00 | 40.00 |
| Vase, violet | 20.00 | 55.00 |
| Vase, 8½", flared | 25.00 | 150.00 |
| Vase, 8½", straight | 25.00 | 150.00 |

# TROJAN, Fostoria Glass Company, 1929 - 1944

Colors: "Rose" pink, "Topaz" yellow officially; some green seen

Pink Trojan is quite scarce; therefore it is the yellow that is the more collectible. Difficult items to locate include footed oils and the combination bowl, which is a bowl having candle holders on each end serving as handles. Pitchers and unclouded shakers are prized items, also.

| | Rose, Topaz | | Rose, Topaz |
|---|---|---|---|
| Ash tray, lg. | 27.50 | Oyster, cocktail, ftd. | 21.50 |
| Ash tray, sm. | 22.50 | Parfait | 25.00 |
| Bowl, baker, 9" | 37.50 | Pitcher | 250.00 |
| Bowl, bonbon | 12.00 | Plate, canape | 10.00 |
| Bowl, bouillon, ftd. | 15.00 | Plate, 6", bread/butter | 5.00 |
| Bowl, cream soup, ftd. | 15.00 | Plate, 6¼", finger bowl liner | 6.50 |
| Bowl, finger w/6¼" liner | 22.00 | Plate, 7½", salad | 7.50 |
| Bowl, lemon | 10.00 | Plate, 7½", cream soup liner | 5.00 |
| Bowl, mint | 10.00 | Plate, 8¾", luncheon | 10.00 |
| Bowl, 5", fruit | 14.00 | Plate, 9½", sm. dinner | 14.00 |
| Bowl, 6", cereal | 17.50 | Plate, 10", cake, handled | 20.00 |
| Bowl, 7", soup | 20.00 | Plate, 10", grill | 25.00 |
| Bowl, lg. dessert, handled | 18.00 | Plate, 10¼", dinner | 27.50 |
| Bowl, 10" | 25.00 | Plate, 13", chop | 30.00 |
| Bowl, combination w/candleholder handles | 100.00 | Platter, 12" | 30.00 |
| Bowl, 12" centerpiece, sev. types | 32.50 | Platter, 15" | 42.50 |
| Candlestick, 2" | 11.00 | Relish, 8½" | 12.00 |
| Candlestick, 3" | 12.50 | Relish, 3 pt. | 20.00 |
| Candlestick, 5" | 17.50 | Sauce boat | 32.50 |
| Candy w/cover, ½ lb. | 75.00 | Sauce plate | 12.50 |
| Celery, 11½" | 20.00 | Saucer, after dinner | 7.50 |
| Cheese & cracker, set | 37.50 | Saucer | 4.50 |
| Comport, 6" | 23.00 | Shaker, ftd., pr. | 67.50 |
| Comport, 7" | 22.50 | Sherbet, high, 6" | 17.50 |
| Creamer, ftd. | 15.00 | Sherbet, low, 4¼" | 15.00 |
| Creamer, tea | 17.50 | Sugar, ftd. | 17.50 |
| Cup, after dinner | 27.50 | Sugar cover | 50.00 |
| Cup, ftd. | 15.00 | Sugar pail | 70.00 |
| Goblet, claret, 6" | 30.00 | Sugar, tea | 17.50 |
| Goblet, cocktail, 5¼" | 24.00 | Sweetmeat | 11.00 |
| Goblet, cordial, 4" | 47.50 | Tray, 11", ctr. handled | 27.50 |
| Goblet, water, 8¼" | 26.00 | Tray, service | 26.00 |
| Goblet, wine, 5½" | 37.50 | Tray, service & lemon | 30.00 |
| Grapefruit | 40.00 | Tumbler, 2½ oz., ftd. | 24.00 |
| Grapefruit liner | 35.00 | Tumbler, 5 oz., ftd., 4½" | 20.00 |
| Ice bucket | 60.00 | Tumbler, 9 oz., ftd., 5¼" | 15.00 |
| Ice dish | 25.00 | Tumbler, 12 oz., ftd., 6" | 20.00 |
| Ice dish liner (tomato, crab, fruit) | 5.00 | Vase, 8" | 60.00 |
| Mayonnaise w/liner | 27.50 | Whipped cream bowl | 10.00 |
| Oil, ftd. | 195.00 | Whipped cream pail | 70.00 |

## TWIST, Blank #1252, A. H. Heisey & Co.

Colors: Crystal, ''Flamingo'' pink, ''Moongleam'' green, ''Marigold'' amber-yellow, some ''Sahara'', a florescent yellow and some ''Alexandrite'', (rare)

| | Crystal | Pink | Green | Marig. Sahara |
|---|---|---|---|---|
| Baker, 9", oval | 10.00 | 15.00 | 20.00 | 45.00 |
| Bonbon | 5.00 | 10.00 | 15.00 | 20.00 |
| Bonbon, 6", 2 hand. | 5.00 | 10.00 | 15.00 | 20.00 |
| Bottle, French dressing | 20.00 | 35.00 | 45.00 | 90.00 |
| Bowl, cream soup/bouillon | 15.00 | 25.00 | 30.00 | 50.00 |
| Bowl, ftd. almond/indiv. sugar | 10.00 | 20.00 | 25.00 | 55.00 |
| Bowl, indiv. nut | 5.00 | 20.00 | 25.00 | 45.00 |
| Bowl, 4", nappy | 5.00 | 12.00 | 15.00 | 17.00 |
| Bowl, 6", 2 hand. | 7.00 | 15.00 | 17.00 | 20.00 |
| Bowl, 6", 2 hand. jelly | 7.00 | 15.00 | 17.00 | 20.00 |
| Bowl, 6", 2 hand. mint | 7.00 | 15.00 | 17.00 | 20.00 |
| Bowl, 8", low ftd. | 20.00 | 30.00 | 35.00 | 65.00 |
| Bowl, 8", nappy, grnd. bottom | 12.00 | 18.00 | 25.00 | 40.00 |
| Bowl, 8", nasturtium, rnd. | 20.00 | 28.00 | 35.00 | 60.00 |
| Bowl, 8", nasturtium, oval | 20.00 | 28.00 | 35.00 | 60.00 |
| Bowl, 9", floral | 22.00 | 30.00 | 37.00 | 62.00 |
| Bowl, 9", floral, rolled edge | 22.00 | 30.00 | 37.00 | 62.00 |
| Bowl, 12", floral, oval, 4 feet | 25.00 | 32.00 | 40.00 | 65.00 |
| Bowl, 12", floral, rnd., 4 feet | 25.00 | 32.00 | 40.00 | 65.00 |
| Candlestick, 2", 1-lite | 7.50 | 10.00 | 12.50 | 20.00 |
| Cheese dish, 6", 2 hand. | 5.00 | 10.00 | 15.00 | 20.00 |
| Comport, 7", tall | 25.00 | 45.00 | 60.00 | 120.00 |
| Creamer, hotel oval | 15.00 | 30.00 | 35.00 | 40.00 |
| Creamer, individual (unusual) | 10.00 | 20.00 | 25.00 | 55.00 |
| Creamer, zig-zag handles, ftd. | 20.00 | 25.00 | 30.00 | 50.00 |
| Cup, zig-zag handles | 10.00 | 20.00 | 25.00 | 30.00 |
| Grapefruit, ftd. | 10.00 | 15.00 | 20.00 | 30.00 |
| Ice tub | 25.00 | 40.00 | 50.00 | 60.00 |
| Pitcher, 3 pint | 35.00 | 65.00 | 110.00 | --- |
| Mayonnaise | 15.00 | 20.00 | 25.00 | 40.00 |
| Mayonnaise #1252½ | 15.00 | 20.00 | 25.00 | 40.00 |
| Mustard w/cover | 20.00 | 35.00 | 45.00 | 75.00 |
| Oil bottle, 2½ oz., w/#78 stopper | 20.00 | 45.00 | 65.00 | 85.00 |
| Oil bottle, 4 oz., w/#78 stopper | 25.00 | 50.00 | 70.00 | 95.00 |
| Plate, cream soup liner | 5.00 | 7.00 | 10.00 | 15.00 |
| Plate, 8", Kraft cheese | 15.00 | 25.00 | 35.00 | 55.00 |
| Plate, 8", grnd. bottom | 7.00 | 12.00 | 15.00 | 20.00 |
| Plate, 10", utility, 3 ft. | 20.00 | 30.00 | 40.00 | --- |
| Plate, 12", 2 hand. sandwich | 20.00 | 30.00 | 40.00 | 50.00 |
| Plate, 12", muffin, 2 hand., turned sides | 20.00 | 35.00 | 45.00 | 60.00 |
| Plate, 13", 3 part relish | 10.00 | 15.00 | 20.00 | 35.00 |
| Platter, 12" | 15.00 | 30.00 | 40.00 | 60.00 |
| Salt & pepper | 20.00 | 30.00 | 40.00 | 50.00 |
| Saucer | 3.00 | 5.00 | 7.00 | 10.00 |
| Stem, 2½ oz., wine | 15.00 | 20.00 | 25.00 | 30.00 |
| Stem, 3 oz., oyster cocktail | 5.00 | 10.00 | 15.00 | 20.00 |
| Stem, 3 oz., cocktail | 5.00 | 10.00 | 15.00 | 20.00 |
| Stem, 5 oz., saucer champagne | 7.00 | 12.00 | 17.00 | 22.00 |
| Stem, 5 oz., sherbet | 5.00 | 10.00 | 15.00 | 20.00 |
| Stem, 9 oz., luncheon (1 block in stem) | 12.00 | 15.00 | 25.00 | 35.00 |
| Sugar, ftd. | 20.00 | 25.00 | 30.00 | 50.00 |
| Sugar, hotel oval | 15.00 | 30.00 | 35.00 | 40.00 |
| Sugar, individual (unusual) | 15.00 | 25.00 | 30.00 | 55.00 |
| Sugar w/cover, zig-zag handles | 15.00 | 22.00 | 32.00 | 52.00 |
| Tray, 7", pickle, grnd. bottom | 7.00 | 15.00 | 20.00 | 25.00 |
| Tray, 10", celery | 10.00 | 20.00 | 25.00 | 30.00 |
| Tray, 13", celery | 12.00 | 22.00 | 27.00 | 32.00 |
| Tumbler, 5 oz., fruit | 4.00 | 12.00 | 18.00 | 24.00 |
| Tumbler, 6 oz., ftd. soda | 5.00 | 13.00 | 19.00 | 25.00 |
| Tumbler, 8 oz., flat, grnd. bottom | 7.00 | 15.00 | 20.00 | 30.00 |
| Tumbler, 8 oz., soda, straight & flared | 7.00 | 15.00 | 20.00 | 30.00 |
| Tumbler, 9 oz., ftd. soda | 8.00 | 16.00 | 21.00 | 31.00 |
| Tumbler, 12 oz., iced tea | 11.00 | 20.00 | 25.00 | 40.00 |
| Tumbler, 12 oz., ftd. iced tea | 12.00 | 22.00 | 27.00 | 42.00 |

# VERSAILLES, Fostoria Glass Company, 1928 · 1944

Colors: Blue, yellow, pink, green

Versailles is one of the patterns most highly prized by the modern day collector. The company gave the center handled server and the candy dish a fleur de lis "handle" to further connect the glass with its namesake.

As is true of June, the pitcher and footed oils are choice pieces to own.

Notice that only the bowls of the stemware are colored. The stems are crystal, something often done by glass makers.

The whipped cream pail will have a nickel plated handle; but the salad dressing bottle comes with a sterling top.

| | Pink, Green | Blue | Yellow | | Pink, Green | Blue | Yellow |
|---|---|---|---|---|---|---|---|
| Ash tray | 24.00 | 30.00 | 27.50 | Ice dish liner (tomato, crab, fruit) | 5.00 | 10.00 | 7.50 |
| Bottle, salad dressing w/sterling top | 200.00 | 300.00 | 250.00 | Mayonnaise w/liner | 35.00 | 50.00 | 40.00 |
| Bowl, baker, 9" | 30.00 | 45.00 | 40.00 | Oil, ftd. | 200.00 | 300.00 | 250.00 |
| Bowl, bonbon | 10.00 | 14.00 | 12.00 | Oyster cocktail | 20.00 | 27.50 | 22.00 |
| Bowl, bouillon, ftd. | 16.00 | 22.00 | 18.00 | Parfait | 25.00 | 30.00 | 27.50 |
| Bowl, cream soup, ftd. | 16.00 | 24.00 | 20.00 | Pitcher | 250.00 | 400.00 | 300.00 |
| Bowl, finger w/liner | 20.00 | 27.50 | 25.00 | Plate, 6", bread/butter | 4.00 | 5.00 | 4.00 |
| Bowl, lemon | 10.00 | 14.00 | 12.00 | Plate, 7½", salad | 6.00 | 8.00 | 7.00 |
| Bowl, mint | 12.00 | 16.00 | 14.00 | Plate, 7½", cream soup liner | 4.00 | 6.00 | 5.00 |
| Bowl, 5", fruit | 14.00 | 17.50 | 15.00 | Plate, 8¾", luncheon | 8.00 | 10.00 | 9.00 |
| Bowl, 6", cereal | 20.00 | 24.00 | 22.00 | Plate, 9½", sm. dinner | 12.00 | 16.00 | 14.00 |
| Bowl, 7", soup | 24.00 | 30.00 | 27.50 | Plate, 10", grill | 20.00 | 30.00 | 25.00 |
| Bowl, lg. dessert, 2 hand. | 26.00 | 30.00 | 28.00 | Plate, 10", cake, 2 hand. | 26.00 | 34.00 | 30.00 |
| Bowl, 10" | 30.00 | 34.00 | 32.00 | Plate, 10¼", dinner | 32.00 | 40.00 | 35.00 |
| Bowl, 11", centerpiece | 30.00 | 35.00 | 32.50 | Plate, 13", chop | 30.00 | 35.00 | 32.50 |
| Bowl, 12", ctr. piece, sev. type | 30.00 | 35.00 | 32.50 | Platter, 12" | 30.00 | 40.00 | 35.00 |
| Bowl, 13", oval centerpiece | 35.00 | 45.00 | 40.00 | Platter, 15" | 45.00 | 60.00 | 47.50 |
| Candlestick, 2" | 13.00 | 17.00 | 15.00 | Relish, 8½" | 30.00 | 40.00 | 35.00 |
| Candlestick, 3" | 16.00 | 20.00 | 17.50 | Sauce boat | 35.00 | 45.00 | 40.00 |
| Candlestick, 5" | 20.00 | 25.00 | 22.00 | Sauce plate | 10.00 | 15.00 | 12.50 |
| Candy w/cover, 3 pt. | 55.00 | 75.00 | 65.00 | Saucer, after dinner | 4.00 | 6.00 | 5.00 |
| Candy w/cover, ½ lb. | 50.00 | 70.00 | 55.00 | Saucer | 4.00 | 6.00 | 5.00 |
| Celery, 11½" | 30.00 | 40.00 | 50.00 | Shaker, ftd., pr. | 75.00 | 110.00 | 85.00 |
| Cheese & cracker, set | 40.00 | 55.00 | 45.00 | Sherbet, high, 6" | 20.00 | 24.00 | 22.00 |
| Comport, 6" | 22.00 | 30.00 | 26.00 | Sherbet, low, 4¼" | 20.00 | 24.00 | 22.00 |
| Comport, 7" | 25.00 | 35.00 | 30.00 | Sugar, ftd. | 15.00 | 20.00 | 15.00 |
| Comport, 8" | 30.00 | 40.00 | 35.00 | Sugar cover | 60.00 | 100.00 | 80.00 |
| Creamer, ftd. | 15.00 | 20.00 | 15.00 | Sugar pail | 70.00 | 90.00 | 80.00 |
| Creamer, tea | 17.50 | 22.50 | 20.00 | Sugar, tea | 17.50 | 20.00 | 17.50 |
| Cup, after dinner | 17.50 | 40.00 | 30.00 | Sweetmeat | 10.00 | 14.00 | 12.00 |
| Cup, ftd. | 16.00 | 20.00 | 18.00 | Tray, 11" ctr. hand. | 20.00 | 30.00 | 25.00 |
| Decanter | 150.00 | 200.00 | 150.00 | Tray, service | 30.00 | 40.00 | 35.00 |
| Goblet, cordial, 4" | 45.00 | 65.00 | 50.00 | Tray, service & lemon | 32.50 | 42.50 | 37.50 |
| Goblet, claret, 6" | 40.00 | 65.00 | 45.00 | Tumbler, 2½ oz., ftd. | 27.50 | 35.00 | 32.50 |
| Goblet, cocktail, 5¼" | 25.00 | 32.50 | 28.00 | Tumbler, 5 oz., ftd., 4½" | 20.00 | 24.00 | 22.00 |
| Goblet, water, 8¼" | 27.50 | 32.50 | 30.00 | Tumbler, 9 oz., ftd., 5¼" | 20.00 | 25.00 | 21.50 |
| Goblet, wine, 5½" | 35.00 | 50.00 | 42.00 | Tumbler, 12 oz., ftd., 6" | 22.50 | 27.50 | 25.00 |
| Grapefruit | 37.50 | 50.00 | 40.00 | Vase, 8" | 75.00 | 125.00 | 100.00 |
| Grapefruit liner | 25.00 | 35.00 | 30.00 | Vase, 8½", fan, ftd. | 40.00 | 65.00 | 50.00 |
| Ice bucket | 62.50 | 80.00 | 75.00 | Whipped cream bowl | 10.00 | 14.00 | 12.00 |
| Ice dish | 20.00 | 30.00 | 25.00 | Whipped cream pail | 70.00 | 90.00 | 80.00 |

# VESPER, Fostoria Glass Company, 1926 - 1934

Colors: Amber, green, some blue

|  | Green | Amber | Blue |
|---|---|---|---|
| Ash tray | 20.00 | 25.00 | |
| Bowl, finger | 15.00 | 17.50 | |
| Bowl, ftd. bouillon | 12.00 | 15.00 | |
| Bowl, cream soup | 12.50 | 14.00 | |
| Bowl, 5½", fruit | 8.00 | 10.00 | |
| Bowl, 6½", cereal | 12.00 | 15.00 | |
| Bowl, 7¾", soup, shallow | 15.00 | 17.50 | 20.00 |
| Bowl, 8", soup, deep | 15.00 | 17.50 | |
| Bowl, 8" | 20.00 | 22.50 | |
| Bowl, 9" | 25.00 | 27.50 | |
| Bowl, 11", console | 22.50 | 25.00 | |
| Bowl, 13", console | 22.50 | 25.00 | |
| Candlestick, 2" | 12.50 | 12.50 | |
| Candlestick, 4" | 15.00 | 15.00 | 25.00 |
| Candlestick, 9" | 15.00 | 17.50 | 45.00 |
| Candy jar w/cover | 50.00 | 55.00 | 95.00 |
| Candy jar, ftd. w/cover | 85.00 | 100.00 | |
| Cheese, ftd. | 18.00 | 20.00 | |
| Comport, 6" | 22.50 | 25.00 | 30.00 |
| Comport, 7" | 25.00 | 28.00 | 34.00 |
| Comport, 8" | 35.00 | 40.00 | 50.00 |
| Creamer, ftd. | 14.00 | 16.00 | |
| Creamer, fat, ftd. | 18.00 | 20.00 | 20.00 |
| Cup | 12.00 | 14.00 | |
| Cup, after dinner | 18.00 | 20.00 | 30.00 |
| Dish, celery | 15.00 | 17.50 | |
| Finger bowl liner, 6" | 4.50 | 5.50 | |
| Grapefruit | 35.00 | 35.00 | |
| Grapefruit liner | 25.00 | 30.00 | |
| Ice bucket | 50.00 | 55.00 | |
| Oyster cocktail | 16.00 | 18.00 | |
| Pitcher, ftd. | 250.00 | 275.00 | |
| Plate, 6", bread/butter | 4.50 | 5.00 | |
| Plate, 7½", salad | 6.00 | 6.50 | |
| Plate, 8½", luncheon | 7.50 | 8.50 | |
| Plate, 9½", sm. dinner | 10.00 | 11.00 | |
| Plate, 10½", dinner | 20.00 | 25.00 | |
| Plate, 11", ctr. hand. | 22.50 | 25.00 | |
| Plate, 13", chop | 32.00 | 37.50 | |
| Plate, 15", server | 35.00 | 40.00 | |
| Plate w/indent for cheese | 18.00 | 20.00 | |
| Platter, 10½" | 20.00 | 22.50 | |
| Platter, 12" | 25.00 | 30.00 | |
| Platter, 15" | 35.00 | 40.00 | |
| Salt & pepper, pr., 2 styles | 55.00 | 60.00 | |
| Sauce boat w/liner | 55.00 | 65.00 | |
| Saucer, after dinner | 7.50 | 9.00 | 10.00 |
| Saucer | 4.00 | 4.50 | |
| Stem, sherbet | 15.00 | 16.00 | |
| Stem, water | 22.50 | 25.00 | |
| Stem, low sherbet | 14.00 | 15.00 | |
| Stem, parfait | 25.00 | 27.50 | |
| Stem, 2½ oz., ftd. | 20.00 | 22.50 | |
| Stem, 2¾ oz., wine | 22.50 | 25.00 | |
| Stem, 3 oz. cocktail | 22.50 | 25.00 | |
| Sugar, fat ftd. | 18.00 | 20.00 | 20.00 |
| Sugar, ftd. | 14.00 | 16.00 | |
| Tumbler, 5 oz., ftd. | 14.00 | 15.00 | |
| Tumbler, 9 oz., ftd. | 15.00 | 16.00 | |
| Tumbler, 12 oz., ftd. | 18.00 | 20.00 | |
| Urn, sm. | 35.00 | 40.00 | |
| Urn, lg. | 55.00 | 60.00 | 80.00 |
| Vase, 8" | 60.00 | 65.00 | |

# WAVERLY, Blank #1519, A. H. Heisey & Co.

Color: Crystal; rare in amber

|  | Crystal |
|---|---|
| Bowl, 6", oval lemon w/cover | 25.00 |
| Bowl, 6½", 2 hand. ice | 45.00 |
| Bowl, 7", 3 part relish, oblong | 25.00 |
| Bowl, 7", salad | 20.00 |
| Bowl, 9", 4 part relish, round | 22.00 |
| Bowl, 9", fruit | 30.00 |
| Bowl, 9", vegetable | 30.00 |
| Bowl, 10", crimped edge | 15.00 |
| Bowl, 10", gardenia | 15.00 |
| Bowl, 11", seahorse foot, floral | 55.00 |
| Bowl, 12", crimped edge | 35.00 |
| Bowl, 13", gardenia | 17.00 |
| Box, 5", chocolate w/cover | 30.00 |
| Box, 5", tall, ft. w/cover, seahorse hand. | 60.00 |
| Box, 6", candy w/bow tie knob | 25.00 |
| Box, trinket, lion cover (rare) | 900.00 |
| Butter dish w/cover, 6", square | 50.00 |
| Candleholder, 1 lite, block (rare | 80.00 |
| Candleholder, 2 lite | 20.00 |
| Candleholder, 2 lite, "flame" center | 50.00 |
| Candleholder, 3 lite | 50.00 |
| Candle epergnette, 6", deep | 10.00 |
| Candle epergnette, 6½" | 7.00 |
| Candle epergnette, 5" | 5.00 |
| Cheese dish, 5½", ft. | 6.00 |
| Cigarette holder | 30.00 |
| Comport, 6", low ft. | 6.00 |
| Comport, 6½", jelly | 8.00 |
| Comport, 7", low ft., oval | 28.00 |
| Creamer, ft. | 15.00 |
| Creamer & sugar, individual w/tray | 25.00 |
| Cruet, 3 oz., ft. w/#122 stopper | 40.00 |
| Cup | 10.00 |
| Honey dish, 6½", ft. | 6.00 |
| Mayonnaise w/liner & ladle, 5½" | 25.00 |
| Plate, 7", salad | 4.00 |
| Plate, 8", luncheon | 6.00 |
| Plate, 10½", server | 10.00 |
| Plate, 11", sandwich | 12.00 |
| Plate, 13½", ft. cake salver | 40.00 |
| Plate, 14", center handle sandwich | 35.00 |
| Plate, 14", sandwich | 20.00 |
| Salt & pepper, pr. | 25.00 |
| Saucer | 3.00 |
| Stem, 1 oz., cordial | 90.00 |
| Stem, 3 oz., wine, blown | 50.00 |
| Stem, 3½ oz., cocktail | 30.00 |
| Stem, 5½ oz., sherbet/champagne | 15.00 |
| Stem, 10 oz., blown | 20.00 |
| Sugar, ft. | 15.00 |
| Tray, 12", celery | 13.00 |
| Tumbler, 5 oz., ft. juice, blown | 15.00 |
| Tumbler, 13 oz., ft. tea, blown | 20.00 |
| Vase, 3½", violet | 20.00 |
| Vase, 7", ft. | 22.00 |
| Vase, 7", ft., fan shape | 25.00 |

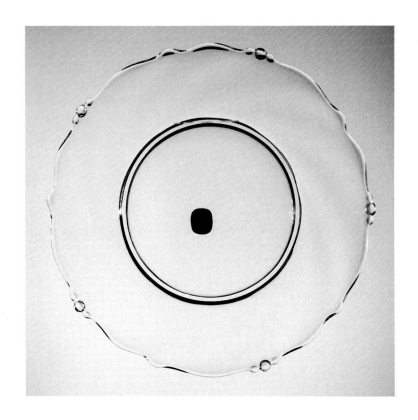

143

# WILDFLOWER, Cambridge Glass Company, 1940's · 1950's

Colors: Crystal, mainly; some few pieces in color

I remember Wildflower via the seven point flowers found in this etching. Granted, there's a big, round flower in the center of the design; but it's those two seven pointers that leap out at me when I see this pattern.

As in Portia and some other crystal Cambridge patterns, there are some pieces of this in color; collectors are mainly interested in the crystal, however, where one can accumulate vast settings.

|  | Crystal |  | Crystal |
|---|---|---|---|
| Basket, 6", 2 hand. ftd. | 17.50 | Plate, 8", salad | 10.00 |
| Bowl, 5¼", 2 hand., bonbon | 13.50 | Plate, 10½", dinner | 35.00 |
| Bowl, 6", 2 hand. ftd. bonbon | 16.50 | Plate, 12", 4 ftd. service | 30.00 |
| Bowl, 6", 2 pt. relish | 15.00 | Plate, 13", 4 ftd. torte | 32.50 |
| Bowl, 6½", 3 pt. relish | 15.00 | Plate, 13½", 2 hand. cake | 32.50 |
| Bowl, 7", relish | 17.50 | Plate, 14", torte | 35.00 |
| Bowl, 7", 2 hand. bonbon | 18.00 | Salt & pepper, pr. | 25.00 |
| Bowl, 7", 2 pt. relish | 17.50 | Saucer | 3.50 |
| Bowl, 8", 3 hand. 3 pt. relish | 22.50 | Set: 2 pc. Mayonnaise (ft. sherb. | |
| Bowl, 9", 3 pt. celery & relish | 25.00 | w/ladle) | 22.50 |
| Bowl, 9½", ftd. pickle (corn) | 22.00 | Set: 3 pc. Mayonnaise (bowl, liner, | |
| Bowl, 10", 4 ft. flared | 30.00 | ladle) | 25.00 |
| Bowl, 11", 2 hand. | 27.50 | Set: 4 pc. Mayonnaise (div. bowl, | |
| Bowl, 11½", ftd. w/tab hand. | 32.50 | liner, 2 ladles) | 30.00 |
| Bowl, 12", 3 pt. celery & relish | 27.50 | Stem, #3121, 1 oz., cordial | 37.50 |
| Bowl, 12", 4 ft. flared | 27.50 | Stem, #3121, 3 oz., cocktail | 20.00 |
| Bowl, 12", 4 ft. oval, "ears" hand. | 40.00 | Stem, #3121, 3½ oz. wine | 22.50 |
| Bowl, 12", 5 pt. celery & relish | 35.00 | Stem, #3121, 4½ oz. claret | 20.00 |
| Candlestick, 3-lite, ea. | 30.00 | Stem, #3121, 4½ oz. low oyster | |
| Candlestick, 5" | 22.50 | cocktail | 15.00 |
| Candlestick, 6", 2-lite "fleur de lis" | 27.50 | Stem, #3121, 5 oz. low parfait | 22.50 |
| Candy box w/cover, 8", 3 hand. | | Stem, #3121, 6 oz. low sherbet | 15.00 |
| 3 pt. | 50.00 | Stem, #3121, 6 oz. tall sherbet | 17.50 |
| Candy box w/cover, rnd. | 47.50 | Stem, #3121, 10 oz., water | 20.00 |
| Cocktail icer, 2 pc. | 25.00 | Sugar | 12.50 |
| Comport, 5½" | 27.50 | Sugar, indiv. | 10.00 |
| Comport, 5 3/8", blown | 37.50 | Tumbler, #3121, 5 oz., juice | 12.50 |
| Creamer | 12.50 | Tumbler, #3121, 10 oz., water | 15.00 |
| Creamer, indiv. | 10.00 | Tumbler, #3121, 12 oz., tea | 17.50 |
| Cup | 16.50 | Tumbler, 13 oz. | 17.50 |
| Hurricane lamp, candlestick base | 80.00 | Vase, 5", globe | 25.00 |
| Hurricane lamp, keyhole base & | | Vase, 6", ftd. flower | 27.50 |
| prisms | 100.00 | Vase, 8", ftd. flower | 30.00 |
| Ice bucket w/chrome hand. | 52.50 | Vase, 9", keyhole ft. | 37.50 |
| Oil, 6 oz. w/stopper | 37.50 | Vase, 10", bud | 25.00 |
| Pitcher, ball | 87.50 | Vase, 11", ftd. flower | 37.50 |
| Plate, 6", 2 hand. | 12.50 | Vase, 11", ped. ft. | 42.50 |
| Plate, 6½", bread/butter | 6.50 | Vase, 12", keyhole ft. | 47.50 |
| Plate, 8", 2 hand. bonbon | 17.50 | Vase, 13", ftd. flower | 57.50 |
| Plate, 8", 2 hand. ftd. | 20.00 | | |

Note: See Pages 150-153 for stem identification.

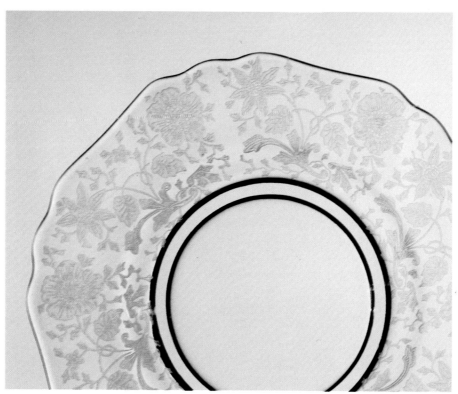

# YEOMAN, **Blank** #3184, A. H. Heisey & Co.

Colors: Crystal, "Flamingo" pink, "Sahara" yellow, "Moongleam" green, "Hawthorne" orchid/pink, "Marigold" deep amber/yellow; some cobalt

Empress etched pieces of Yeoman will bring 10 to 15 percent more than the comparable prices listed below.

| | Crystal | Pink | Sahara | Green | Hawth. | Marigold |
|---|---|---|---|---|---|---|
| Ash tray, 4", hand. (bow tie) . . . . . . | 10.00 | 17.00 | 19.00 | 22.00 | 25.00 | 27.00 |
| Bowl, 2 hand. creme soup . . . . . . . . | 10.00 | 15.00 | 20.00 | 23.00 | 27.00 | 30.00 |
| Bowl, finger. . . . . . . . . . . . . . . . . | 5.00 | 10.00 | 14.00 | 18.00 | 22.00 | 26.00 |
| Bowl, ftd., banana split . . . . . . . . . | 7.00 | 20.00 | 25.00 | 30.00 | 35.00 | 40.00 |
| Bowl, ftd., 2 hand. bouillon . . . . . . . | 10.00 | 20.00 | 25.00 | 30.00 | 35.00 | 40.00 |
| Bowl, 4½", nappy . . . . . . . . . . . . . | 4.00 | 7.00 | 10.00 | 12.00 | 14.00 | 15.00 |
| Bowl, 5", low ftd. jelly . . . . . . . . . . | 12.00 | 20.00 | 25.00 | 27.00 | 30.00 | 37.00 |
| Bowl, 5", oval lemon . . . . . . . . . . . | 6.00 | 10.00 | 14.00 | 17.00 | 19.00 | 23.00 |
| Bowl, 5", rnd. lemon . . . . . . . . . . . | 6.00 | 10.00 | 14.00 | 17.00 | 19.00 | 23.00 |
| Bowl, 5", rnd. lemon w/cover . . . . . | 11.00 | 15.00 | 20.00 | 25.00 | 30.00 | 35.00 |
| Bowl, 6", oval preserve. . . . . . . . . . | 7.00 | 12.00 | 17.00 | 22.00 | 27.00 | 30.00 |
| Bowl, 6", vegetable. . . . . . . . . . . . | 5.00 | 10.00 | 14.00 | 16.00 | 19.00 | 24.00 |
| Bowl, 6½", hand. bonbon . . . . . . . . | 5.00 | 10.00 | 14.00 | 16.00 | 19.00 | 24.00 |
| Bowl, 8", rectangular pickle/olive . . | 12.00 | 15.00 | 20.00 | 25.00 | 30.00 | 35.00 |
| Bowl, 8½", berry, 2-hand. . . . . . . . | 14.00 | 19.00 | 24.00 | 29.00 | 34.00 | 40.00 |
| Bowl, 9", 2 hand. veg. w/cover . . . . | 25.00 | 35.00 | 45.00 | 55.00 | 75.00 | 100.00 |
| Bowl, 9", oval fruit . . . . . . . . . . . . | 20.00 | 25.00 | 35.00 | 45.00 | 50.00 | 55.00 |
| Bowl, 9", baker . . . . . . . . . . . . . . | 20.00 | 25.00 | 35.00 | 45.00 | 50.00 | 55.00 |
| Bowl, 12", low floral . . . . . . . . . . . | 15.00 | 25.00 | 35.00 | 45.00 | 50.00 | 55.00 |
| Cigarette box, (ash tray cover) . . . . . | 25.00 | 35.00 | 45.00 | 55.00 | 65.00 | 75.00 |
| Cologne bottle w/stopper. . . . . . . . | 40.00 | 75.00 | 80.00 | 85.00 | 90.00 | 120.00 |
| Comport, 5", high ftd., shallow . . . . | 15.00 | 25.00 | 35.00 | 45.00 | 55.00 | 65.00 |
| Comport, 6", low ftd., deep . . . . . . . | 20.00 | 30.00 | 34.00 | 38.00 | 42.00 | 48.00 |
| Creamer . . . . . . . . . . . . . . . . . . | 10.00 | 15.00 | 17.00 | 19.00 | 22.00 | 28.00 |
| Cruet, 2 oz. oil . . . . . . . . . . . . . . | 20.00 | 35.00 | 40.00 | 45.00 | 50.00 | 55.00 |
| Cruet, 4 oz. oil . . . . . . . . . . . . . . | 25.00 | 37.50 | 42.50 | 47.50 | 52.50 | 60.00 |
| Cup . . . . . . . . . . . . . . . . . . . . . | 5.00 | 15.00 | 20.00 | 25.00 | 30.00 | 40.00 |
| Cup, after dinner . . . . . . . . . . . . . | 7.00 | 20.00 | 25.00 | 30.00 | 35.00 | 40.00 |
| Egg cup. . . . . . . . . . . . . . . . . . . | 15.00 | 22.00 | 30.00 | 37.00 | 40.00 | 50.00 |
| Grapefruit, ftd. . . . . . . . . . . . . . . | 10.00 | 17.00 | 24.00 | 31.00 | 38.00 | 45.00 |
| Gravy (or dressing) boat w/underplate . . . . . . . . . . . . . . . . | 13.00 | 18.00 | 23.00 | 28.00 | 33.00 | 40.00 |
| Marmalade jar w/cover. . . . . . . . . . | 25.00 | 35.00 | 40.00 | 45.00 | 50.00 | 65.00 |
| Parfait, 5 oz. . . . . . . . . . . . . . . . . | 10.00 | 15.00 | 20.00 | 25.00 | 30.00 | 35.00 |
| Pitcher, quart . . . . . . . . . . . . . . . | 35.00 | 45.00 | 55.00 | 65.00 | 100.00 | 130.00 |
| Plate, 2 hand. cheese . . . . . . . . . . | 5.00 | 10.00 | 13.00 | 15.00 | 17.00 | 25.00 |
| Plate, creme soup underplate. . . . . . | 5.00 | 7.00 | 9.00 | 12.00 | 14.00 | 16.00 |
| Plate, finger bowl underliner . . . . . . | 3.00 | 5.00 | 7.00 | 9.00 | 11.00 | 13.00 |
| Plate, 4½", coaster. . . . . . . . . . . . | 3.00 | 5.00 | 10.00 | 12.00 | | |
| Plate, 6" . . . . . . . . . . . . . . . . . . | 3.00 | 6.00 | 8.00 | 10.00 | 13.00 | 15.00 |
| Plate, 6", bouillon underplate . . . . . | 3.00 | 6.00 | 8.00 | 10.00 | 13.00 | 15.00 |

## YEOMAN, Blank #3184, A. H. Heisey & Co. (continued)

| | Crystal | Pink | Sahara | Green | Hawth. | Marigold |
|---|---|---|---|---|---|---|
| Plate, 6½", grapefruit bowl ....... | 7.00 | 12.00 | 15.00 | 18.00 | 25.00 | 30.00 |
| Plate, 7" ................... | 5.00 | 8.00 | 10.00 | 13.00 | 15.00 | 20.00 |
| Plate, 8", oyster cocktail ......... | 9.00 | | | | | |
| Plate, 8", soup ................ | 9.00 | | | | | |
| Plate, 9", oyster cocktail ......... | 10.00 | | | | | |
| Plate, 10½" ................... | 12.00 | | | | | |
| Plate, 10½", ctr. hand. oval, divided | 15.00 | 25.00 | | 30.00 | | |
| Plate, 11", 4 pt relish ........... | 20.00 | 26.00 | | 30.00 | | |
| Plate, 14" ................... | 20.00 | | | | | |
| Platter, 12", oval .............. | 10.00 | 17.00 | 19.00 | 26.00 | 32.00 | |
| Salt, individual tub, (Cobalt $20.00) | 5.00 | 7.00 | | 12.00 | | |
| Salver, 10", low ftd. ........... | 15.00 | 25.00 | | 40.00 | | |
| Salver, 12", low ftd. ........... | 10.00 | 20.00 | | 30.00 | | |
| Saucer ...................... | 3.00 | 5.00 | 7.00 | 7.00 | 10.00 | 10.00 |
| Saucer, after dinner ........... | 3.00 | 5.00 | 7.00 | 8.00 | 10.00 | 10.00 |
| Stem, 2¾ oz., ftd. oyster cocktail .. | 3.00 | 5.00 | 7.00 | 8.00 | 12.00 | |
| Stem, 3 oz., cocktail ........... | 7.00 | 12.00 | 17.00 | 20.00 | | |
| Stem, 3½ oz., sherbet........... | 5.00 | 8.00 | 10.00 | 12.00 | | |
| Stem, 4 oz., fruit cocktail ........ | 3.00 | 5.00 | 7.00 | 9.00 | | |
| Stem, 4½ oz., sherbet........... | 3.00 | 5.00 | 7.00 | 9.00 | | |
| Stem, 5 oz., soda ............. | 4.00 | 6.00 | 8.00 | 10.00 | | |
| Stem, 5 oz., sherbet ........... | 3.00 | 5.00 | 7.00 | 9.00 | | |
| Stem, 6 oz., champagne ......... | 6.00 | 11.00 | 16.00 | 18.00 | | |
| Stem, 8 oz. .................. | 5.00 | 10.00 | 15.00 | 17.00 | | |
| Stem, 10 oz., goblet ........... | 7.00 | 12.00 | 17.00 | 19.00 | | |
| Stem, 12 oz., tea.............. | 8.00 | 14.00 | 19.00 | 22.00 | | |
| Sugar w/cover ............... | 12.00 | 22.00 | 25.00 | 27.00 | 30.00 | 35.00 |
| Sugar shaker, ftd. ............. | 30.00 | 65.00 | | 60.00 | | |
| Syrup, 7 oz., saucer ftd. .......... | 25.00 | 55.00 | | | | |
| Tray, 7" x 10", rectangular ....... | 26.00 | 30.00 | 38.00 | 35.00 | | |
| Tray, 9", celery ............... | 10.00 | 14.00 | 16.00 | 15.00 | | |
| Tray, 11", ctr. hand., 3 pt. ........ | 15.00 | 18.00 | 22.00 | | | |
| Tray, 12", oblong ............. | 16.00 | 19.00 | 24.00 | | | |
| Tray, 13", 3 pt. relish ........... | 20.00 | 26.00 | 30.00 | | | |
| Tray, 13", celery .............. | 20.00 | 26.00 | 30.00 | | | |
| Tray, 13", hors d'oeuvre w/cov. ctr. | 30.00 | 40.00 | 50.00 | 65.00 | | |
| Tray inserts, 3½" x 4½" ........ | 4.00 | 6.00 | 7.00 | 8.00 | | |
| Tumbler, 2½ oz., whiskey........ | 3.00 | 5.00 | 7.00 | 9.00 | | |
| Tumbler, 4½ oz., soda .......... | 4.00 | 6.00 | 10.00 | 15.00 | | |
| Tumbler, 8 oz................. | 4.00 | 12.00 | 17.00 | 20.00 | | |
| Tumbler, 10 oz., cupped rim ...... | 5.00 | 15.00 | 20.00 | 22.00 | | |
| Tumbler, 10 oz., straight side ..... | 5.00 | 15.00 | 20.00 | 22.00 | | |
| Tumbler, 12 oz., tea ........... | 5.00 | 16.00 | 22.00 | 24.00 | | |
| Tumbler cover, (unusual) ........ | 25.00 | | | | | |

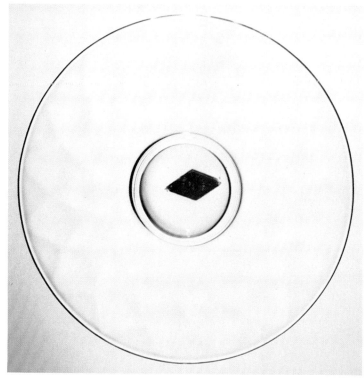

149

# CAMBRIDGE STEMS

1066
11 oz. Goblet

3025
10 oz. Goblet

1402
Brandy Inhaler (Tall)

3035
3 oz. Cocktail

3077
6 oz. Tall Sherbet

# CAMBRIDGE STEMS

3104
1 oz. Cordial

3115
3½ oz. Cocktail

3106
9 oz. Goblet Tall Bowl

3120
6 oz. Tall Sherbet

3121
10 oz. Goblet

# CAMBRIDGE STEMS

3122
9 oz. Goblet

3124
3 oz. Wine

3126
7 oz. Tall Sherbet

3130
6 oz. Tall Sherbet

3135
6 oz. Tall Sherbet

152

# CAMBRIDGE STEMS

3400
9 oz. Lunch Goblet

3500
10 oz. Goblet

3600
2½ oz. Wine

3625
4½ oz. Claret

3775
4½ oz. Claret

3779
1 oz. Cordial

## CAMBRIDGE'S RARITIES

| | |
|---|---:|
| Candy, crystal, CHANTILLY | 100.00 |
| Pitcher, emerald green, GLORIA | 250.00 |
| Pitcher, yellow, PORTIA | 500.00 |
| Pitcher, Heatherbloom, PORTIA | 500.00 |
| Pitcher, Moonlight blue, CLEO | 125.00 |
| Pitcher, alpine crystal, CAPRICE | 125.00 |
| Pitcher, small crystal, ROSEPOINT | 145.00 |
| Pitcher, pink tankard, APPLEBLOSSOM | 125.00 |
| Pitcher, amber Daulton, GLORIA | 350.00 |
| Pitcher, pink ball juice, DIANE | 375.00 |
| Tumbler, crystal old fashioned, ROSEPOINT | 75.00 |

## HEISEY'S RARITIES

| | |
|---|---:|
| Bowl, fern, "Zircon" color, dolphin handle | 100.00 |
| Butter, ¼ lb., "Dawn" color | 110.00 |
| Candle block, Lariat blank (1540), one pair known to date | --- |
| Candy, amber color, Waverly blank (1519) | 350.00 |
| Creamer & sugar, "Vaseline" color | 425.00 |
| Creamer & sugar, "Hawthorne w/Moongleam handles" | 400.00 |
| Creamer & sugar, crystal, cut and signed by Krall | 1,000.00 |
| Goblet, "Alexandrite" color, Creole blank | 135.00 |
| Mug, cobalt | 300.00 |
| Pitcher, "Moongleam" color, Ipswich blank | 400.00 |
| Pitcher, "Flamingo" color, Optic Tooth blank #4206 | 125.00 |
| Plate, black, Lariat blank (1540) | 1,200.00 |
| Relish, "Zircon" color, Whirlpool blank (1506) | 150.00 |
| Vase, "Flamingo" color, Optic Tooth blank (4206) | 80.00 |

# HEISEY'S "ALEXANDRITE" Color (Rare)

| | |
|---|---:|
| Cream & sugar, pr. | 400.00 |
| Creole goblet | 135.00 |
| Creole wine | 140.00 |
| Cup & saucer, set | 110.00 |
| Jelly (or mint) w/dolphin feet | 85.00 |
| Mayonnaise w/dolp. ft. & ladle | 185.00 |
| Plate, 8" (Empress 1401) | 60.00 |
| Salt & pepper, pr. | 100.00 |

# HEISEY'S COBALT and TANGERINE Colors (Rare)

**Tangerine**

| | |
|---|---|
| Champagne, Duquesne blank (3389) . . . . . . . . . . . . . . . . . . . . . . . . . . . | 175.00 |
| Goblet, Duquesne blank (3389) . . . . . . . . . . . . . . . . . . . . . . . . . . . . . . | 190.00 |
| Juice tumbler, Duquesne blank (3389) . . . . . . . . . . . . . . . . . . . . . . . . | 125.00 |
| Plate, 8", Empress blank (1401 . . . . . . . . . . . . . . . . . . . . . . . . . . . . . | 180.00 |

**Cobalt**

| | |
|---|---|
| Bowl, "Thumbprint & Panel" . . . . . . . . . . . . . . . . . . . . . . . . . . . . . . . . | 125.00 |
| Candlestick, 2-lite, "Thumbprint & Panel" . . . . . . . . . . . . . . . . . . . . . . | 200.00 |
| Cigarette holder, Carcassone blank (3380) . . . . . . . . . . . . . . . . . . . . . | 75.00 |
| Goblet, low, ftd., Carcassone blank (3380) . . . . . . . . . . . . . . . . . . . . . | 95.00 |
| Goblet, high, ftd., Carcassone blank (3380) . . . . . . . . . . . . . . . . . . . . | 90.00 |
| Plate, 8", round, Empress blank (1401) . . . . . . . . . . . . . . . . . . . . . . . . | 50.00 |
| Sherbet, Carcassone blank (3380) . . . . . . . . . . . . . . . . . . . . . . . . . . . . | 80.00 |
| Wine, Spanish stem (3404) . . . . . . . . . . . . . . . . . . . . . . . . . . . . . . . . . | 110.00 |

## HEISEY'S "DAWN" Color (Rare)

Butter, "Town & Country", ¼ lb. . . . . . . . . . . . . . . . . . . . . . . . . . . . . . .   110.00
Candleholders, pr. . . . . . . . . . . . . . . . . . . . . . . . . . . . . . . . . . . . . . . .   100.00
Celery dish, "Lodestar" . . . . . . . . . . . . . . . . . . . . . . . . . . . . . . . . . . .    50.00
Centerbowl, low, "Lodestar" . . . . . . . . . . . . . . . . . . . . . . . . . . . . . . .    75.00
Creamer & sugar, pr. . . . . . . . . . . . . . . . . . . . . . . . . . . . . . . . . . . . . .    80.00
Mayonnaise w/ladle . . . . . . . . . . . . . . . . . . . . . . . . . . . . . . . . . . . . . .    65.00
Nappy, 4½ " . . . . . . . . . . . . . . . . . . . . . . . . . . . . . . . . . . . . . . . . . . . .    35.00
Plate, "Town & Country" . . . . . . . . . . . . . . . . . . . . . . . . . . . . . . . . . .    40.00
Relish, divided, "Lodestar" . . . . . . . . . . . . . . . . . . . . . . . . . . . . . . . . .    60.00
Tumbler, "Town & Country" . . . . . . . . . . . . . . . . . . . . . . . . . . . . . . . .    30.00

## Publications I recommend

## DEPRESSION GLASS DAZE

### THE ORIGINAL NATIONAL DEPRESSION GLASS NEWSPAPER

Depression Glass Daze, the Original, National monthly newspaper dedicated to the buying, selling & collecting of colored glassware of the 20's and 30's. We average 60 pages each month filled with feature articles by top notch columnists, readers "finds", club happenings, show news, a china corner, a current listing of new glass issues to beware of and a multitude of ads!! You can find it in the DAZE! Keep up with what's happening in the dee gee world with a subscription to the DAZE. Buy, sell or trade from the convenience of your easy chair.

Name _____ Street _____

City_____ State_____ Zip_____

☐ 1 year-$14.00    ☐ Check enclosed    ☐ Please bill me
☐ MasterCard    ☐ VISA (Foreign subscribers - please add $1.00 per year)

Exp. date_____ Card No._____

Signature _____

Orders to D.G.D., Box 57GF, Otisville, MI 48463 - Please allow 30 days

## GLASS review

A colorful magazine devoted to keeping glass collectors informed about all kinds of glass - antique to contemporary collectibles. Filled with articles, pictures, price reports, ads, research information and more! 10 "BIG" issues yearly.

Name _____ Street _____

City_____ State_____ Zip_____

☐ New    ☐ 1 year-$12.50    ☐ Single Copy $2.00
☐ Renewal    ☐ 1 Yr. Canada or Foreign $15.00 (U.S. Funds please)

Orders to P.O. Box 542, Marietta, OH 45750

**Heisey Club Membership To:**

| **Heisey Collectors of America** | **National Cambridge Collectors, Inc.** |
|---|---|
| Box 27GF | Box 416GF |
| Newark, OH 43055 | Cambridge, OH 43725 |
| Dues: $12.00 Yearly | Dues: $10.00 Yearly |

Depression glass has long been a popular collectible in this country. Many glass enthusiasts have turned to kitchen glassware of the same period as a natural "go-with". These kitchen containers, gadgets, and utensils can be found in many of the same shades as the tableware that has become so highly collectible. Nostalgic and colorful, Depression kitchen glassware is now the subject of an authoritative identification and value guide.

Hundreds of pieces of glass are featured in full color in this large format, 8½" x 11" hardbound volume. It includes canisters, salt and peppers, reamers, straw holders, containers, pitchers and many other miscellaneous kitchen pieces. This book is filled with information about the glass, including manufacturers, sizes, colors, and current values. It also includes a section of catalog reprints and many catalog illustrations showing how the glass was originally sold.

Gene Florence is one of the country's best known glass authors. He has written several books in the antiques field including two on Depression glass, *The Collector's Encyclopedia of Depression Glass* and *Pocket Guide to Depression Glass*. This new volume on Depression kitchen glassware will be welcomed by Depression glass lovers everywhere.

**Item #1281, 8½" x 11", 128 Pgs., HB** . . . . . . . . . . . . . . . . . . . . . . . . . . . . . . . . . . . . . . . . . **$17.95**

### Additional Books By Gene Florence

*Collector's Encyclopedia of Depression Glass* . . . . . . . . . . . . . . . . . . . . . . . . . . . . . . . . . . . .$17.95
*Kitchen Glassware of the Depression Years* . . . . . . . . . . . . . . . . . . . . . . . . . . . . . . . . . . . . . . $17.95
*Pocket Guide to Depression Glass* . . . . . . . . . . . . . . . . . . . . . . . . . . . . . . . . . . . . . . . . . . . $ 9.95
*Occupied Japan, Volume I* . . . . . . . . . . . . . . . . . . . . . . . . . . . . . . . . . . . . . . . . . . . . . . . . . . $ 9.95
*Occupied Japan, Volume II* . . . . . . . . . . . . . . . . . . . . . . . . . . . . . . . . . . . . . . . . . . . . . . . . .$12.95
*Akro Agate* . . . . . . . . . . . . . . . . . . . . . . . . . . . . . . . . . . . . . . . . . . . . . . . . . . . . . . . . . . . . . .$9.95

Add $1.00 postage for the first book, $.35 for each additional book.

Copies of these books many be ordered from:

Gene Florence
P.O. Box 22186
Lexington, KY 40522

COLLECTOR BOOKS
P.O. Box 3009
Paducah, KY 42001